INDIA'S ECONOMIC CRISIS
The Way Ahead

INDIA'S ECONOMIC CRISIS

The Way Ahead

BIMAL JALAN

DELHI
OXFORD UNIVERSITY PRESS
OXFORD NEW YORK
1991

Oxford University Press, Walton Street, Oxford OX2 6DP

NEW YORK TORONTO
DELHI BOMBAY CALCUTTA MADRAS KARACHI
PETALING JAYA SINGAPORE HONG KONG TOKYO
NAIROBI DAR ES SALAAM
MELBOURNE AUCKLAND

and associates in
BERLIN IBADAN

Computerset by Resodyne, New Delhi 110030
Printed at Rekha Printers Pvt. Ltd., New Delhi 110020
and published by S.K. Mookerjee, Oxford University Press
YMCA Library Building, Jai Singh Road, New Delhi 110001

For
PRATEEK, MADHU, NIDHI
and their generation
who will inherit what we leave behind

Contents

Preface vii

Introduction 1
1. Development Strategy and Performance 21
2. Savings, Exports and Literacy 36
3. The 'End' of Government? 61
4. Towards Balance of Payments Viability 97
5. Policies for Higher Savings 168

Epilogue 216

List of References 227
Index 244

Preface

I started writing this book in 1989 in Washington. I was then serving as India's Executive Director on the Board of the International Monetary Fund. A large number of developing countries, particularly in Latin America and Africa, were facing acute economic difficulties and were approaching the Fund for financial assistance. Several of them had over-borrowed from commercial banks, some were affected by unfavourable external developments, and nearly all were making reappraisals of their economic policies and development strategies. Several leaders with impeccable socialist credentials, such as those in Zambia, Venezuela and Spain, had declared themselves in favour of much less state intervention and a greater reliance on the market. The U.S.S.R., China, Hungary, Poland, Czechoslovakia and Vietnam were also undergoing profound economic changes. In the midst of these developments, the economic situation in India looked relatively calm—on the surface. But economists in government and outside were aware that the underlying economic situation, particularly with regard to the fiscal position and the balance of payments, had worsened considerably and required urgent tackling. My original purpose was to take a close look at India's long-run development strategy and policy in the light of both the recent academic research on development issues and the experience of other developing countries. I felt that India's choice of economic strategies had been unavoidable within the particular historical context in which this choice was made. However, re-thinking was now required on certain basic issues in the light of changes in India's political economy and the accumulated experiences of our past.

The writing of this book was interrupted for a year

because of a new official assignment, and I was able to resume work on it only in New Delhi in December 1990. Meanwhile, India had gone through two changes of government. There had also been several important domestic developments which had an impact on the country's economic situation. The economy, already in a difficult position, was plunged further into a deep financial crisis by the Gulf conflict. In view of these developments, the focus and the content of this book changed somewhat: it seemed that much greater attention needed to be paid to the immediate crisis and to the policies required to overcome this crisis over the medium term.

This book is written from the perspective of an economist involved in administration and policy formulation. My search has been to find some *practical* answers to the problems of macro-economic policy and strategy within the constraints of a multi-party parliamentary democracy of the type which prevails in India. An attempt has been made to take into account the experiences of other countries as well as the results of academic research, but the main focus is on *what is possible* and on *what must be done*. I shall feel amply rewarded if, in some small way, this book contributes to the emergence of a consensus on economic policy priorities for India in the 1990s. The book is about India; however, I hope portions of it will also interest economists in other developing countries and international institutions.

I owe a large intellectual debt to several friends, colleagues and fellow economists; particularly Pranab Bardhan and Kaushik Basu, who read the draft script at short notice and gave me their comments. Anandarup Ray, Vinod Dubey and Oktay Yenal were kind enough to read an earlier draft of some chapters in Washington. Srinivas Madhur, Jagmohan Bajaj and D. Amarnath were generous with their help in several ways. I take responsibility for residual errors.

I am grateful to Hephzie Ohal who typed some of the chapters in Washington; and to Tamal Chatterjee in Delhi, for doing a splendid job of putting together the whole manuscript for press.

The views expressed here are mine, and not those of the government, nor of the Economic Advisory Council with which I am presently associated.

New Delhi
15 May, 1991

BIMAL JALAN

Introduction

The year 1990-1 has been among the cruellest in India's post-Independence economic history. A new government took over in December 1989, at a time when the fiscal deficit was high and the foreign-exchange reserves low (covering only about six weeks of imports). The Budget, introduced in March 1990, made an attempt to reduce the fiscal deficit and begin the process of correction in the balance-of-payments position. For a while the economic situation seemed to show some improvement. The fiscal deficit was, by the end of August 1990, significantly lower than in the previous year, and foreign-exchange reserves were slightly higher (in contrast to a sharp decline in the reserves in the corresponding period of the previous year). However, there was a dramatic reversal of this situation in the next few months. Consequent upon the annexation of Kuwait by Iraq on 2 August 1990, crude oil prices rose sharply. Within a period of six weeks these prices doubled. Even though the Gulf War did not last long, India's fragile economy was badly shaken.

The direct economic impact of the conflict in the Gulf was exacerbated by domestic social and political developments. The implementation of the Mandal Commission report was announced by the government on 7 August 1990. This led to massive student protests and a breakdown of the law-and-order situation in several parts of the country. This event was followed by the conflict in Ayodhya over the Ram Janambhoomi–Babri Masjid. For four weeks or so there was further disruption, conflict and high tension. A direct political consequence was the fall of the government on 7 November 1990. Another minority government took office in mid-November. This series of events, in tandem with the conflict in the Gulf, was sufficient to shake international confidence in India's economic viability. The country found it more and more difficult to borrow internationally, and there was also an adverse impact on the inflow of funds from non-resident Indians.

During the 1980s it had seemed, for a while, that the economy was poised upon a breakthrough. The Economic Survey of the Government of India for 1988-9, in fact, announced that 'the Indian economy is now on a new growth path' (p. 1). The growth rate for the decade was certainly higher, and there was evidence of substantial output growth in several sophisticated industries, such as electronics. The capital markets were buoyant, and industrial growth averaged more than 8 per cent for the period 1985-90. During this period there was also some reassessment of the control system. A number of committees were appointed; these submitted reports on trade policy, public-sector policy and on a 'shift from physical to financial control' (Government of India, 1978, 1979, 1985). Each of these committees recommended a move away from quantitative control to fiscal methods of economic management. Several recommendations made by these committees were implemented, and there was considerable loosening of direct controls, particularly in the field of industrial licensing.

As is evident now, the gains from the policy changes of the 1980s have proved temporary. The growth in industrial production has been overshadowed by a balance-of-payments crisis of unprecedented magnitude. There has been a large accumulation of external debt, and a widening of the current-account deficit which has rendered the economy highly vulnerable to external and internal shocks. Between September and November 1990 foreign-exchange reserves, which were already low, fell by nearly 50 per cent. The effort to reduce the rate of fall in foreign-exchange reserves meant a severe curtailment in the imports of both oil as well as industrial raw materials and components. The domestic prices of petroleum products were increased sharply to compensate for the rise in international prices. Although unavoidable this added to costs and prices in the economy. By the end of 1990, the economic situation became highly precarious. Exchange reserves were at rock bottom, inflation had crossed the double-digit level and was moving higher, and the fiscal deficit was sharply widening. Paradoxically, this severe financial crisis was taking place at a time when the real sectors of the economy seemed to be performing reasonably well. As a result of an excellent monsoon, agricultural production was at its peak. Industrial production was increasing at the rate of over 8 per cent per annum, and exports were doing well. The financial crisis was, however, of such magnitude that gains in the real sector were severely eroded by a crisis of confidence and the shortage of international liquidity.

On 18 January 1991 India's foreign-exchange reserves stood at only Rs 1666 crores. This was barely sufficient to meet even the daily cash requirements of an economy of India's size. But for a loan from the International Monetary Fund (of about Rs 3200 crores),* which was approved in mid-January, there was a strong possibility that India would have been forced to default on its international obligations for the first time in its post-independence history.

This was the dismal economic situation at the beginning of 1991. India had been affected by external shocks before, but the short-term situation had never been as difficult. The only previous parallel was perhaps the situation in 1958—with one difference. Then, the world environment was favourable for development. The first Aid India Consortium was organized in 1959. Both multilateral institutions and bilateral donors came forward with massive external assistance to finance the Second Five Year Plan. The situation is very different in 1991, and there is no equivalent response from the international community.

Underlying this sense of despondence *vis-à-vis* the immediate economic prospects, there is a widespread feeling in the country that something is 'missing' or wrong in the

* One crore is equal to ten million. The average exchange rate of the Rupee in 1990-1 was Rs 17.95 to US $ 1.

way we have organized our economy over the last forty years. True, there has been economic progress. But our achievements seem to have fallen far short of our original expectations. The economy seems to lurch from one crisis to another; poverty is still massive; pervasive social inequalities persist; the quality of public and social services has deteriorated; there are important regional imbalances; the so-called parallel economy seems to be flourishing. The state, on the other hand, faces an acute fiscal crisis and paucity of resources for investment.

The short- as well as the long-term problems are now acute. The domestic capacity to tackle these problems has been eroded by political and economic developments over the past two years. The international environment is also unfavourable. The global political balance has undergone a transformation with the end of the Cold War, the unification of Germany, conflict in the Middle East, and developments in the U.S.S.R. and Eastern Europe. In the light of these changes, some of the basic and interrelated premises of India's development planning and policies require reexamination. The first of these concerns assumptions regarding the nature of the state.

The nature of the state in post-colonial societies has received some attention in political science, particularly within Marxist literature (Debray, 1967; Alavi, 1972; Saul, 1979). The state has become increasingly central in post-colonial social formations and occupies a strategic position *vis-à-vis* the economy. According to Saul (1979), there are three important features of the dominant state. First, the origins of modern states in developing societies lay in the colonial state. The colonial state was equipped with a powerful bureaucratic-military apparatus and mechanisms of government. This overdeveloped apparatus and its institutionalized practices were inherited by the post-colonial societies and their new rulers. The apparatus became a readily available means of regulating and controlling the operations of indigenous social classes.

Second, in the name of promoting economic development, the post-colonial state appropriated a very large part of the economic surplus and deployed it in bureaucratically directed economic activity.

Third, the state arrogated to itself an important ideological function. It symbolized the unity of the social formation by seeming to transcend narrow class and sectional interests, and it thus helped legitimize the *status quo*.

The early development literature, in the forties and fifties, similarly assigned a central role to the post-colonial state. The dominant assumption here, however, was the notion of a benevolent state, which, equipped with sufficient information and knowledge, was expected to act solely in society's interest. The state was here expected to pursue a Benthamite social-welfare function, correcting market failures and launching countries along the road of rapid development.

This vision of the state was fully shared by India's post-independence leadership. Political freedom was, in fact, viewed as an indispensable means to overcome mass poverty and to industrialize the economy through direct state action. Thus, the Second Five Year Plan (1956) was clear that

> the pattern of development and the structure of socio-economic relations should be so planned that they result not only in appreciable increases in national income and employment but also in greater equality in incomes and wealth. Major decisions regarding production, distribution, consumption and investment—and in fact all significant socio-economic relationships—must be made by agencies informed by social purpose (p. 22).

The assumption of a welfare-maximizing state has turned out to be unrealistic. In the recent literature on public choice there has been a lively debate about the real nature of the state, in both developing and industrial societies. Mancur Olson's (1982) thesis regarding 'distributional coalitions' has been particularly influential. Olson argues that these coalitions were overwhelmingly oriented towards struggles over the distribution of income and wealth rather than towards the production of additional output. The 'free-rider' argument, extended to organizations, suggested that a typical lobby in a society is more likely to be a narrow special-interest group, or a distributional coalition. The benefits of any resources spent by the group to *expand* the society's output have to be shared with the rest of society, while the benefits of the same resources spent on *redistributing* a society's output in its favour accrue entirely to the group.

In an interesting analysis of the relationship between economic and political behaviour, Bardhan (1984) has extended Olson's thesis to the case of a large and heterogeneous coalition of three dominant classes (with multiple veto powers) in contemporary India. These classes are industrialists, rich farmers, and educated professionals who have their main economic base in public employment. Bardhan sees the policy package of the Indian state as an expression of the coalition of these disparate groups. The government budget is seen as a gigantic mechanism for dispensing subsidies, overt and covert, to various sectors of the dominant coalition, whether through public employment, rationed credit, fertiliser subsidy, or other sorts of subsidies. The system of interconnected bargains among dominant groups creates vast numbers of conflicts that require arbitration. These conflicts provide the opportunities for political leadership to step in and appropriate a part of the benefits generated. Politics ceases to be autonomous in the sense of providing a process through which coherent policy can be formulated and implemented.

The Olson–Bardhan framework is of relevance in explaining the evolution of state policy in recent years. Since 1985 three successive governments have acknowledged the severity of the economic crisis and attributed it primarily to two factors, namely to the increase in non-Plan public expenditure, particularly on account of subsidies; and to the losses shown by public-sector enterprises. Successive finance ministers have, in their budget speeches, mouthed commitments to control budgetary deficits. Several committees, including cabinet committees, were set up for this purpose. Similar commitments were made for reducing losses in the public sector, and for providing functional autonomy to such enterprises. In reality, however, budgetary deficits have continued to grow, and public-sector losses have continued to increase. In 1990-1 the centre's fiscal deficit reached 8.6 per cent of GDP, which is an all-time high. The government's inability to tackle these problems, despite its firm assurances, is clearly due to the push and pull of various interest groups. There is a coalition of interests among political decision-makers, bureaucrats, trade unions, and industry. All of them stand to gain from excess expenditure by the government and the public sector. Morris (1991) has examined the effects of the 'dysfunctional interface' between state and public enterprise on the performance of the latter. He points out that:

> If we characterize the Indian state as a coalition of various groups—the big capitalists, the small capitalists and the middle classes, and the farmers, then it is well known that such a state has to make major compromises and adjustments, not just in terms of policy, but also in its implementation. Loopholes in laws and contradictions in policy become vehicles to accommodate the sectarian interest of groups, which may not be ideologically justifiable. Such a state incurs enormous costs in administration, not only because of the need to balance between the interests of various groups, but also because it has to give the appearance of doing so in a fair and 'objective' fashion. The bureaucrats, as 'neutral' and informed elements, are therefore placed in a position of great power, and it is to them that falls the immediate role of mediation and adjustment, and of clothing the more sectarian policies and provisions in terms not at discord with the rhetoric and ideology (Morris, 1991, mimeo).

Alternative socio-political theories of state action in India have been advanced by Lipton (in terms of 'urban bias') and Bhagwati and Srinivasan and others in terms of 'rent-seeking' (see Toye 1988; Rubin, 1985). While none of these theories can provide a complete explanation of the behaviour of the state in India, it is necessary to pay greater attention to the political process, as it actually operates, while considering the future direction of development policy. The state cannot be assumed to be a disinterested reconciler of conflicting interests for the benefit of society as a whole. A relevant factor to be taken into account is also the changing perception regarding what the President of India, in his Republic Day Address on 26 January 1991, referred to as 'the evolving patterns of our polity'. The President drew attention to recent changes that have occurred in the pattern of parliamentary democracy in India, observing that 'in a multi-party political system, we may not be able to avoid coalition governments in the interests of the nation' (Address by the President of India, p. 10). The change in the political situation and the underlying assumption about the stability of governments have considerable implications for the formulation of economic policy and strategy in the 1990s.

A basic premise of India's Plans, as well as the early development literature, was that the required administrative response would be forthcoming in abundant measure to meet the tasks assigned to different levels of administration—from the centre to the village level. The administration was expected to work in complete harmony and coordination in order to carry out these various tasks. It must be said to the credit of our early planners that they explicitly recognized the vast administrative requirements of the strategy they visualized. Thus, the Second Plan devoted a whole chapter to spelling out 'Administrative Tasks and Organization'. It clearly stated that 'while the area of agreement on matters of policy is considerable, doubt exists whether, in its range and quality, administrative action will prove equal to the responsibilities assumed by the central and state governments in the Second Five Year Plan.'

This doubt about administrative constraints proved valid. Thus, the Third Five Year Plan (1961) observed that 'the administrative machinery has been strained and, at many points in the structure, the available personnel are not adequate in quality and numbers' (p. 277). It was also lucid in recognizing that the expansion of administrative responsibilities was itself an important cause of inefficiency and delay. 'As large burdens are thrown on the administrative structure, it grows in size; and as its size increases, it becomes slower in its functioning. Delays occur and affect operations at every stage and the expected outputs are further deferred' (p. 277). Over the years, the size of the administration has grown manifold, as the responsibilities assumed by the state have expanded. The Seventh Five Year Plan (1985) pointed out that

> there are too many levels of decision-making, adding to delay but not necessarily to the quality of decision-making . . . Over-centralization in decision-making is manifested by a large number of meetings continuously taking place at the headquarters . . . Co-ordination is one of the major weaknessees in our systems (p. 419).

Despite this experience, little progress has been made to reduce administrative intervention. The economic costs of administrative failure have been examined in several studies of the development experience. An early exposition of the costs associated with administrative delays and indecision is by Little, Scitovsky, and Scott (1970). On the basis of a detailed examination of the experience of several developing countries, this work identifies the principal economic costs as the rise in capital–output ratios, a slowdown in capital formation, and the diversion of scarce administrative manpower and entrepreneurial energies to unproductive tasks. Graft and other forms of malpractice are a further cost. The costs involved are not merely financial: corruption is seen as a cost which often rendered it difficult or impossible for discriminatory policy measures to achieve their aim.

Another lacuna in the old strategy was the absence of a link between priorities and policies. The priorities were clear, but the instruments chosen to achieve these priorities failed to deliver. A command-type planning, based on the Soviet model, proved unsuitable for directing investments in an economy which was largely privately owned and where the judicial and legal framework guaranteed freedom of choice to individuals. The system of direct control and physical allocation, which was essentially derived from provisions introduced during World War II, proved more successful in preventing competition than in directing investments according to clear priorities. There was a dichotomy between physical production targets as set out in the Plan, and the framework of macro-economic policies—particularly tariff and fiscal policies. Studies have shown that several of the so-called priority industries received very low or negative protection, which discouraged their growth, while non-priority industries received very high effective rates of protection (Kelkar and Kumar, 1990). The Plans assigned an important role to the fiscal system for bringing about a better distribution of income; yet, the ratio of direct taxes in national income has actually gone down over the years (Long Term Fiscal Policy, 1985). Agriculture enjoyed a high priority, but agriculture exports were discouraged or banned altogether, which had the effect of reducing farmers' incomes. The Plans encouraged import substitution to reduce import dependence, but industrial and tariff policies encouraged domestic manufacture for the domestic market based on imports of components and raw materials (see Joseph, 1989). Numerous other instances of a similar mismatch between policies and priorities can be cited. A closer harmonization between macro-economic policies and the country's priorities would have yielded better development results.

At this point, it should be stated that I, along with most Indian economists and civil servants at that time, shared the vision and the assumptions of India's Plans and the early development literature regarding the nature of the state, of its supposedly unlimited capacity to intervene in society's interest. Thus, for example, when commenting on the conclusions of the series of studies undertaken by the Organization for Economic Co-operation and Development (Little, Scitovsky and Scott, 1970), I suggested that the fact of administrative failure could either point to the need for less controls or 'in favour of greater regimentation, stiffer controls, enforced through penalties, and radical transformation of property relations' (Jalan, 1975, p. 3). The choice between these two options seemed then to depend more on value judgments about the nature of social organization, rather than harder economic realities. In similar vein, I earlier said:

> as regards the question of development strategy, notwithstanding the claims of project enthusiasts, the choice between alternative development strategies cannot be considered a matter of logical debate among economists, involving as it does the choice of a particular inter-temporal pattern of consumption as well as a particular role for the state in determining the pattern and the pace of development (p. 7).

In retrospect, these points seem valid in principle, but they did not pay adequate attention to the real determinants of state action, nor to the economic consequences of excessive bureaucratic intervention.

Still, though the realities and limitations of state action must be recognized, it would be a mistake to put—as much of the neo-classical economics does—the entire weight of past failure in development upon deficiencies in the macro-economic policies of an interventionist state. This is too simplistic. Take, for example, the relatively poor performances of India in respect of population control and literacy. Are these on account of the excesses of an interventionist state? Several countries with widely different degrees of intervention and records of development have done much better than India. The development literature has long recognized the crucial importance of literacy in promoting growth and increasing productivity. Yet, after nearly forty-five years of independence, nearly half India's population remains illiterate. Inside India, can one explain the performance of Kerala with a 91 per cent literacy rate, and that of Bihar with a 39 per cent literacy rate, in terms of failures of macro-economic policies, or of state control over the allocation of resources?

An important macro-economic failure in India has been in the fiscal field: fiscal deficits in the 1980s have been too high. As a result, public savings available for capital formation have been eroded. This development has little to do with planning deficiencies or a failure in trade and industrialization policies. Several interventionist as well as non-interventionist states have high (or for that matter low) fiscal deficits, depending on factors which have more to do with the political economy than with development strategy. Similarly, India has had balance-of-payments problems in twenty-nine out of thirty-five years since 1956-7, which has been highly disruptive to its development. This is regretable. However, balance-of-payments problems, at one time or another, have characterized all kinds of economies, including industrial countries with very different perceptions on the role of the state.

It seems that, in considering future strategic and policy options, we have to do much more than simply redefine the role of the state, or reformulate macro-economic policies. These are important; but equally vital is the business of attending to other crucial objectives where India's performance has been much less promising than that of other countries—particularly those that have experienced sustained growth despite the marked differences among them in their economic and political systems.

It is interesting to note that, as early as the Third Plan, serious doubts were being raised by several experts about the effectiveness of Indian planning techniques. The Second Plan was rocked by a foreign-exchange crisis of huge dimensions. The Third Plan had got off to a very poor start, and, by the end of its first year, it developed a series of bottlenecks which gravely affected its progress. Nearly thirty years ago A.H. Hanson (1963), a sympathetic observer, in his essay called 'Crisis in Indian Planning', felt compelled to ask this question: 'the men are able, the organization is adequate, the procedures are intelligently devised. Why, then, have the Plans, since 1956, so persistently run into crisis'? (p. 187). Hanson's answer to this question is also interesting:

> for various reasons, Indian planners have never treated the 'objective function' with sufficient respect. Their tendency is to give themselves the fullest benefit of every possible doubt . . . . Too many of their aims are contingent upon the adoption, by various sections of the Indian community, of attitudes they are exceedingly unlikely to adopt, at least to the desired and requisite extent (p. 187).

Today we can no longer afford to give ourselves the benefit of doubt. Economic challenges in the 1990s require a different approach. This approach must build on the successes of the past. At the same time, it must discard old assumptions that have been found wanting. The political, administrative and international scene has changed too substantially for India to ignore that it needs to adapt its economic policies and planning techniques to realities on the ground.

A book such as this cannot hope to deal comprehensively with all the issues of policy and strategy that are relevant to India in the future. The treatment of the subject is necessarily selective and focused on what are considered to be crucial factors for India's development in the near future, including the role of the government. The first chapter traces the intellectual and historical case for the choice of development strategy by India after independence. I point out that the initial choice of the strategy was a response to the prevailing intellectual perception of the initial conditons and the role of the state in development. India's own political and social history also supported the case for an inward-looking strategy of industrialization, with the state in command. At the same time, a fair criticism of India's development strategy is that it was inherently unresponsive to the changing internal and external circumstances after the early 1960s.

The factors and determinants of growth have fascinated development economists. Given the experience of rapidly-growing developing countries, it is possible to identify a few factors which seem crucial for India's development and growth. Chapter 2 identifies three such factors, i.e. high savings, sustained balance-of-payments viability, and a high literacy ratio. India's savings performance was good from 1953-4 to 1967-8. Thereafter there was a drop in the rate of growth of savings and capital formation, which also coincided with a period of decline in the rate of growth of industrial production (upto 1982-3). After this period the savings ratio has remained stagnant, and the higher growth in industrial production has been financed through a greater reliance on foreign savings. The behaviour of public savings in the 1980s was particularly poor. The ratio of public savings to GDP declined to less than 2 per cent of GDP in 1990-1 from 4.5 per cent of GDP in the late 1970s. The sharp decline in public savings lies at the heart of the savings problem within the Indian economy.

With regard to the balance of payments, India's performance has been truly dismal. Except for some brief periods, India has been continuously subject to balance-of-payments problems since 1956-7. Policy-making during this entire period was dominated by concern over the balance of payments. The evolution of the industrial and trade policy, in particular, was heavily influenced by the concerns over the balance-of-payments situation, and this introduced several distortions. An important policy challenge for the 1990s is to find a solution to this persistent balance-of-payments problem. In respect of literacy, too, India's performance was poor in comparison with other developing countries, particularly those that grew fast. As a percentage of GDP, India spent nearly as much as several other countries which have a much higher literacy ratio. However, the bulk of the expenditure was on higher education, not on primary education.

Chapter 3, 'The "End" of Government?', examines the reasons for the recent swing in the development literature, as well as in political opinion favouring less government intervention in the economy. It is pointed out here that government policies need to be adapted to the changing environment, without counter-productively swinging the pendulum too far in the opposite direction. The need to redefine the role of government cannot be converted into an argument for the elimination of the government's role in the economy. In India, the role of government has expanded in response to perceived compulsions. However, over the years, the system has expanded well beyond the administrative capacity to manage it. Techniques of intervention must pay much greater attention to economic forces as they actually operate. These need to work in society's interest, not by exhortation but by the appropriate use of tariff, fiscal and financial policies. Equity considerations must remain important in policy formulation. Without equity and social justice, development means little in a poor society. At the same time, international experience and recent development research suggest that these social goals can be met more effectively by making a greater use of 'capitalist' tools.

At the same time, we desperately need a judicious and productive use of resources that the government controls directly. It is in this area that scarce administrative and managerial resources need to be concentrated. The provision of adequate public and social services should become an important objective, and targets and implementation schedules in these areas need to be worked out in detail. An effective management of the public sector is another priority.

Chapter 4 deals with policies for restoring our balance-of-payments viability. There are clear differences between the aid as well as the fiscal situation prevailing in the country in the late fifties and now. In the earlier period, almost the entire current-account deficit was financed through inflows of concessional assistance, which kept the debt service burden low. In the eighties, the entire *incremental* deficit was financed through non-concessional loans on market-related terms. Another important difference is that in the eighties, as distinct from the earlier years, the fiscal policy was highly expansionary. Published documents show that the emergence of a severe balance-of-payments problem in the second half of the eighties was foreseen by the government. The reasons why the actual evolution of the balance-of-payments policy has been different from what was planned have to be found in the political economy and increasing uncertainty of electoral politics in India after 1983-4.

India's export performance and trade regime have been examined extensively in the literature. By all accounts, India's long-run export performance has been quite poor in comparison to other developing countries, and also in relation to the growth of world trade. India's share in world exports has fallen not only in overall manufacturing and total trade, but also in sectors like textiles where India had an initial advantage. India's trade regime is also world famous for its inward orientation and bias against exports. As a result, export profitability has been substantially lower than domestic profitability. The effective protection rates are high and variable across industries without any apparent economic rationale. While a number of incentives have been provided to compensate for the low profitability of exports, the incentive structure is complex and non-transparent. The trade regime, both in respect of imports and exports, continues to be a veritable jungle of administrative rules, regulations and exemptions.

In considering future policy options, a number of issues arise in the light of the theoretical and empirical findings in the literature on trade policy. On major issues of policy—such as 'outward orientation', import liberalization and the sequencing of reforms—the academic debate still seems inconclusive. For example, while a number of studies have highlighted the favourable effects of 'outward-looking' strategies, these conclusions have been questioned by several writers who have emphasized the importance of initial conditions, historical factors and political environment in determining the outcome of policy. On balance, however, it seems that the incentive structure does have an important effect in determining the pattern and pace of development.

An appropriate response in the Indian situation at the present juncture is to aim at what Fishlow (1985) has aptly called 'export adequate growth', as distinct from 'export led' growth. Policies which tilt the advantage in favour of exports are likely to be more sustainable in view of financing constraints than those which call for a dramatic shift in the strategy of development. There is, however, need for a bold programme of simplification, administrative reform, and a shift to non-discretionary import controls. The objective of policy reform should be to try and eliminate the balance-of-payments crisis in the next two to three years, and thereby make crisis management less of a preoccupation of policy-makers in the 1990s. The chapter ends with a discussion of certain broad directions of fiscal, trade, external borrowing, and foreign-investment policies for the future.

Chapter 5 deals with policies for increasing domestic savings. A satisfactory economic theory of savings behaviour in developing countries is not available. The available empirical evidence shows that beyond policies to maintain monetary and financial stability and the pursuit of a realistic interest-rate policy, there is not a great deal more that the government can do to increase household savings directly. The most direct means by which governments can increase savings is to increase public savings. A number of studies are now available regarding the implications of growing public debt in India, and of its macroeconomic impact. All these studies (e.g. Rangarajan, *et al.*, 1989) have concluded that the emerging debt profile of public debt in India is unsustainable.

The need to restrain the growth of debt and reduce fiscal deficits has been recognized by successive governments. There has also been a fair amount of consensus on the measures necessary for containing the growth of non-Plan expenditure. However, despite pious intentions and declarations, government expenditure and fiscal deficits have continued to grow. In the light of past experience, I suggest that in future the government should adopt 'a policy-based approach' rather than a purely quantitative or marginalist approach to expenditure control. I also argue that there is need for a constitutional amendment to put a limit on revenue deficits of government. In a multi-party parliamentary system, a constitutional provision which is applicable to all governments—present and future—is likely to be more effective.

In the early years of planning, the growth of public investment provided important gains to the economy. Public-sector enterprises contributed to the expansion of infrastructure, to an increase in output in core sectors, and to the induction of high technology. They also acted as a countervailing power to the growth of monopolies in the private sector. The most conspicuous failure of the public sector was, however, in generating profits for re-investment. Government departments have been ill-equipped to manage the vast range of enterprises, serving multiple purposes, in different sectors of the economy. In the light of past experience, I argue that a 'hard' budget constraint on public enterprises should be introduced by legislation. The government should be prohibited by law from financing the losses of public-sector units. There should also be a radical change in the present dispensation with regard to the management of public-sector enterprises. The old assumption that competition is bad and public monopolies good needs to be put on its head. Public-sector enterprises should be reorganized as multi-product conglomerates and made to compete with each other. Certain other crucial changes are also necessary in the management and macroeconomic policies which affect public enterprises.

In view of India's own experience and the findings of theoretical and empirical research, the Epilogue suggests a programme of action which can lay the foundations of sustainable growth in the 1990s.

The development experience of poor countries has spawned considerable academic literature on growth strategies and policies. In recent years neo-classical perception of how societies work and neo-classical theories of growth have been ascendant, so much so that, writing in the hundredth anniversary issue of the *Economic Journal* (January 1991), James Buchanan claims the emergence of a 'scientific consensus' in favour of market economies: 'In 1990 few, who profess to call themselves economists in East or West, will challenge the elementary proposition to the effect that economies that are described by individual (private) ownership of the means of production work better than economies where individual ownership is absent' (p. 16).

This may well be true. There is also no doubt that the development literature of the last few years has enhanced our understanding of the processes of growth. Yet it seems that, on most major issues of policy and strategy, academic opinion is inconclusive: the literature is more marked by its lack of unanimity than by consensus. As we shall see in subsequent chapters, this is true of most important controversies in development economics. This is true, for example, of controversies regarding determinants of growth, import substitution *versus* export promotion strategy, the effects of controls and state intervention, and the role of foreign private investment and privatization. This lack of consensus is a matter of some regret. Many developing countries have been passing through great difficulties in the 1980s, and there seems an urgent need for certain shared perceptions and prescriptions in development policy which are able to command the respect of economists of different political persuasions.

An important reason for the absence of consensus seems to be the tendency to 'over-kill' in the neo-classical literature, its search for a universal paradigm which is valid for all countries at all times. Seemingly straightforward policy prescriptions, such as 'get the prices right' or 'open up the economy', while admirable for their simplicity, miss much of the diversity and complexity that has characterized the development process. Faced with such propositions, it becomes easy to cite any number of examples and any amount of historical evidence in support of the opposite view. At a theoretical plane, for example, it can be shown that under imperfect competition the market equilibrium in general is not Pareto-efficient, and that all relevant information cannot be incorporated in prices. At the empirical level, it can be shown that the thirty-year period of 1950-80 saw higher growth rates and greater improvement in living standards in the developing world than the earlier half-century. This period was characterized by active state intervention in the economy. Albert Hirschman (1987) borrowed Jean Fourastie's felicitous expression—'les trente gloriouses'—to describe this epoch in Latin American history.

The neo-classical literature is right in highlighting the limitations of state power and administrative action. It is also right in pointing out the conflicting pulls and pressures to which state action is subject, and the need to put greater reliance on generalized instruments of macro-economic policy. But it is wrong in overemphasizing the distortionary effects of all forms of intervention and in preaching the virtues of untempered markets, to the exclusion of all else, in societies where a large section of the people do not even participate in markets. What we need now is a synthesis between the neo-classical insights into the working of markets with the legitimate concern of the state to make these markets work in favour of society as a whole. While each society has to work out the best mix of policies for itself, the results of historical experience and scientific research can provide valuable guidance on which policies and what programmes work best within the administrative, economic and political constraints.

1

Development Strategy and Performance

The last few years have been a period of intense debate about Indian economic policy and strategy. There is a fairly widespread view that, in the 1980s, India recognized the limitations of its post-independence economic strategy and adopted a 'new economic policy.'[1] This so-called new economic policy consisted of a gradual process of easing out government controls, of industrial deregulation, and of some import liberalization. While many observers and experts welcomed these changes and directly attributed the apparent faster rate of growth of the Indian economy in the 1980s to these changes, there were some who feared that these changes would create more problems than they solved. There were apprehensions that policy-change might destroy the broad national consensus that characterized the evolution of Indian economic policy in the first thirty-five years after independence.[2] These fears arose because of the growing dependence of the Indian economy on imports, the greater vulnerability of its balance of payments, its greater reliance on debt, and the consequent greater susceptibility to outside pressures of India's economic policy directions. Rising consumerism and the display of conspicuous wealth by the elite exacerbated these fears.

The debate on economic policy in the 1980s also naturally focussed on whether the strategy of development adopted after independence was right, and the effect of this strategy on India's economic development. This strategy, which was greatly influenced by the Soviet planning model, gave a central role to the state in the control and direction of economic activity.[3] Following the Soviet experience, it was believed that the savings rate in the economy, and the growth rate, could be increased if India invested heavily in the capital-goods and heavy-industry sectors at the expense of the consumer-goods sector.[4] Since the investment requirements in these sectors were high, largely beyond the capability of the private sector, and the financial profitability was low, it followed that such investments would have to be undertaken by the state.

The Second Five Year Plan (1956) was quite clear that—'It cannot be emphasized too strongly that unless steps are taken to augment rapidly the output of the means of production and to build up the fuel and energy resources which are so vital to development, the scale and pace of advance in the coming years will be inhibited' (p. 28). As for policies to achieve these objectives, the Plan went on to say that:

> In some cases fiscal or price incentives may have to be relied on; in others, a licensing system may be essential; in still others, fixation of profit margins, allocations of scarce raw materials or other regulatory devices may be necessary . . . If the targets of planned investment are to be achieved, means have to be found to secure that the necessary resources do in fact become available and are not devoted to consumption . . . (p. 42).

The state emerged both as the mobilizer of savings as well as an important investor and owner of capital. Since the state was to be the primary agent of economic change, it followed that private-sector activities had to be strictly regulated and controlled to conform to the objectives of state policy.

In this scheme foreign trade had a relatively small role, partly because of the belief that trade was biased against developing countries and primary producers, and partly because of the intellectual conviction that export prospects were severely limited. India's First Five Year Plan (1951) was practically silent on exports. It only highlighted the limitations to prospects of increasing export earnings since 'the prices obtainable for exports depend on world factors and may, therefore, be subject to large variations' (p. 29). The Second Five Year Plan (1956) attempted a projection of balance of trade but concluded that no significant increase in export earnings in the short run could be expected (pp. 97-9). The intellectual basis for pessimism about exports, which was widely shared by development economists of the time, was broadly the same as that articulated by Nurkse in his 'export lag' thesis. In the famous Wicksell Lectures (1959), Nurkse drew attention to the tendency for the exports of primary producing countries to lag behind the rate of increase in international trade in general, and of the trade between and from industrial countries (see Chapter 4).

The primacy accorded to capital accumulation by the state also meant, in the early years of planning, a relative neglect of public investment in agriculture.[5] This relative neglect of agriculture was supported by the prevailing view that a growing labour force in developing countries could only be absorbed in industry, and that in the early stages of industrialization it was necessary for agriculture to contribute to the building up of modern industry by providing cheap labour. A faster development of the industrial sector was the central objective of planning.

This is a thumbnail and inadequate sketch, but it suffices for our purposes to highlight the main points of contemporary criticisms of India's earlier development strategy. These are: the neglect of exports and trade opportunities, excessive protectionism and import substitution, undue reliance on physical controls, and the inefficiency of the public sector. Much of this criticism is exaggerated, but those who have welcomed the new direction in India's economic policy have welcomed it because, in their view, this policy is expected to correct the deficiencies that were inherent in the earlier strategy.

So far as actual performance is concerned, the main highlights are easy to recapitulate.[6] There is little doubt that the rate of growth of the Indian economy in the post-independence period was substantially higher than that registered by the country in the previous 100 years. It is estimated that the rate of growth of the Indian economy between 1871 and 1946 was barely sufficient to keep pace with the growth of population.[7] The rate of growth during the period 1951-84 was about 3.8 per cent per annum, and 4 per cent upto 1989-90. (The actual number may vary, depending on the treatment of drought years, and also the statistical method used for calculation.[8]) This rate of growth was, however, lower than that of developing countries as a group (5.2 per cent). It was also substantially lower than that registered by China (5.4 per cent) and several other developing countries such as Korea (7.2 per cent), Taiwan (9.1 per cent), Thailand (6.8 per cent), Indonesia (5.5 per cent), and Malaysia (6 per cent).[9] Per capita income growth in India was less than 2 per cent per annum during the four decades after independence. Population grew at 2.15 per cent per annum, as compared with 1.21 per cent per annum in the preceding three decades. This largely offset the benefit of higher growth in the post-independence period.

Despite the central role accorded to industrial development in India's planning, industrial growth was 5.3 per cent per annum from the early 1950s to the early 1980s (Sundrum, 1987). The share of the industrial sector in GDP increased from 15 to 23 per cent over the whole period, but its share of the labour force rose only from 12.6 to 13.8 per cent. The deceleration in the growth rate of industry since the mid-1960s (upto 1980-1) was particularly striking. The annual growth rate of GDP in the manufacturing sector declined from 7.4 per cent before the drought years of the mid-1960s to only 4.3 per cent between 1967-8 and 1980-1.[10] The growth of agricultural output was also slow. The annual growth of income of agriculture between 1950-1 to 1984-5 was 2.12 per cent per annum, and per capita agricultural income hardly increased (Dandekar, 1988).[11] This is comparable to that of China, but much less than that achieved in some other developing countries. The growth rate in agriculture, particularly food output, was barely ahead of population growth.

India's export performance was relatively poor, and the country failed to take advantage of the expansion of world trade in the post-war period. In the 1950s there was a virtual stagnation of exports (Singh, 1964). Exports grew somewhat faster at 3.3 per cent annually in the 1960s, and 7.5 per cent per annum in the 1970s. India's exports were 7.8 per cent of GDP in 1980-1, which was virtually the same as in 1950-1. The share of exports in the GDP of developing countries as a group, on the other hand, increased from 15 per cent of their GDP in 1960, to 22 per cent. The fall in India's share of world trade was even more dramatic—it fell from 2.4 per cent at the time of independence to only 0.4 per cent in the 1980s.

Except for brief periods, India has experienced continuing balance-of-payments problems, which made the task of economic management and planning extremely difficult. Bureaucratic controls proliferated, leading to excessive delays in the approval and implementation of projects, and to an increase in the cost of investment. The capital–output ratio increased significantly. The incremental capital–output ratio increased from 3.89 in the 1950s to 5.46 in the 1960s, and to 6.04 in the 1970s. A part of this increase was due to structural shifts in the investment pattern, but a significant part was also due to lower productivity and higher capital intensity.[12]

Critics of India's performance have drawn attention to the fact that India's record in health, education, and other social indicators has similarly remained far from satisfactory. While there was some improvement, the pace of change was well below India's own requirements and of the record of other countries. According to the Human Development Report 1990 of the United Nations, India ranked low on the human development index (with an index value of only 0.44, as against China's 0.72 and Korea's 0.90). In India, the reduction in the under-five infant mortality rate was 2.3 per cent per annum during 1960-88, as against 5.4 per cent per annum in China and 4.5

per cent per annum in Korea. In 1985, the adult literacy rate in India was only 43 per cent, as against 69 per cent in China. (Korea's literacy rate was already high in 1970, at 88 per cent, and illiteracy is likely to have been eliminated by 1985.) As for poverty levels, according to Planning Commission calculations, there was a reduction in the percentage of people living below the poverty line, from about 50 per cent in 1972-3 to about 37.4 per cent in 1983-4. (Provisional estimates for 1987-8 place this figure at 30 per cent.) The absolute number of the poor in the mid-eighties, however, remained over 270 million. The data on changes in the distribution of income over time are unsatisfactory; however, most analysts suggest that the improvement, if any, was quite small. The asset distribution, too, has not improved much and, in 1982, 55 per cent of landed rural households owned less than 1 hectare of land.[13]

These statistics provide a broad assessment of Indian performance. However, they do not prove much about the superiority, or otherwise, of the old strategy over an alternative strategy. Both Korea and China have done better, but they followed varying strategies. The initial political and social conditions there were also very different from those in India. As pointed out by Chakravarty (1987a) in his analysis of the foundations of India's development strategy, India's choice of strategy was influenced greatly by a perception of the important factors perpetuating structural backwardness. Thus, the basic constraint on development was seen as being an acute deficiency of material capital, and the low capacity to save. Agriculture was believed to be subject to secular diminishing returns. Industrialization was, therefore, seen as essential to absorb surplus labour in agriculture. It was also believed that industrialization, under the prevailing world market conditions and domestic structural constraints, was feasible only if the state took the lead in setting up industries that required large investments. A reliance on the market mechanism was likely to result in excessive consumption by upper-income groups, and in under-investment.

It may be recalled that there was remarkable unanimity

among the pioneers of development economics in the forties and fifties on the proposition that industrialization was synonymous with development, and that industrialization was not feasible in underdeveloped economies without an active role assigned to the state. Thus, on the basis of the time-series data on the national products of different countries, Kuznets (1955) showed that the process of economic development was always accompanied by a shift in the labour force from low-productivity agriculture to high-productivity manufacturing. Such a shift required a higher degree of capital accumulation. Nurkse (1953), in his famous doctrine of the 'vicious circle of poverty', said that poor societies remain poor because they could not save enough in view of their low per capita incomes. Rosenstein-Rodan (1943) argued that the production process in modern industry was subject to indivisibilities and economies of scale. This required large investments in social overhead capital areas such as transport, communications, power, and urban infrastructure. Such investments could only be forthcoming if the state played an active role in mobilizing and investing social resources. Scitovsky (1954) pointed to the limitations of a price-guided system in taking advantage of external economies. The implication was that the market mechanism could be relied on to take care of the production problem in the economy, but investment allocation required state intervention. Gerschenkron (1962) introduced the concept of 'relative backwardness' among countries, and suggested that in relatively backward countries the state itself had to substitute for the market and 'force' industrialization. Reviewing this early literature, Datta Chaudhuri (1990) correctly concludes that:

> the success of Keynesian activism in fighting the Great Depression in the western countries, the success of the Marshall Plan in engineering the quick reconstruction of the war-damaged economies of western Europe, and the achievements of the Soviet industrialization drive in the 1930s had created a virtual intellectual consensus in the world on the power of the 'visible hand'(p. 26).

The early development literature was also sanguine

about the need for the state to exercise its regulatory and fiscal powers to alter colonial patterns of trade. The conclusions of Prebisch (1950) and Singer (1950)—on the secular tendency of the terms of trade turning against countries exporting primary products and importing manufactures—had an important impact on the thinking of planners in developing countries. Prebisch and Singer attributed the tendency of terms of trade of primacy producers to decline to the power of trade unions in advanced countries, and to conditions of under-employment in the periphery. Equally influential was Lewis's paper on the implications for development strategy of 'unlimited supply of labour' (Lewis, 1954). Lewis argued that under conditions of an unlimited supply of labour, the gains from productivity increases in the export sector were likely to accrue to importing countries. Singer, Prebisch and Lewis's works thus provided a powerful case for import substitution and protection.

These perceptions were widely shared by political leaders and Indian intellectuals of the time, and the business of choosing an economic strategy responded to these perceptions. The neglect of economic development by the state in the colonial period had an inevitable consequence. The conviction grew that development was not possible without the guiding hand of the state: the state was required to take on the role of planner, saver, investor, and manager in order to quicken the pace of development. The trade regime in India was, for about a century, free, but this did not result in growth or prosperity. There was practically no industry or diversification of trade, and the country was heavily dependent on imports of manufactures. It is striking that as late as 1830 India's share of world manufacturing output was 17.6 per cent, as against the U.K.'s share of 9.5 per cent and the United States's share of 2.4 per cent. By 1900, however, India's share had dwindled to 1.7 per cent, as against the U.K.'s share of 18.5 per cent and the United States's share of 23.6 per cent (Kennedy, 1989, p. 149).[14]

The colonial experience was sufficent to reinforce the belief that the free-trade regime was biased against India and other developing countries and could not be relied upon to generate growth and improve living standards. The call for Swadeshi therefore became an important element in the political struggle against colonial rule. It was inevitable that, after independence, the building of an indigenous manufacturing base should become an important objective of economic policy. This strategy was also an aspect of the struggle for economic and political independence from the U.K. and other Western powers. The apparent success of the Soviet Union in building up a strong manufacturing base, and its emergence as a superpower within a relatively short period of time, strengthened belief in the efficacy of the state as the primary agent of accumulation.

The post-independence period in India was characterized by several external and domestic shocks, such as war, drought, oil-price increases and political upheaval. In defence of the earlier Indian strategy, it can be argued that while the growth rate was slower, India was able to maintain a stable and democratic political system with a mixed economy against very difficult odds. This was an unique achievement in the developing world. The country was able to achieve self-sufficiency in food. It was also able to develop a diversified industrial structure. And it was able to raise its savings rate, from 10 per cent of GDP in 1950-1 to 21 per cent in the mid-1980s.[15]

The debate on what could have been, if a different path were chosen, can go on endlessly without shedding much light on the desirable course of policy in the future.[16] Fortunately, it is not necessary to settle this debate in order to consider what India should now do. The choices made in the early stages of development depended on the opportunities and the knowledge available then. Sen (1983) has put the point succinctly:

> Development economics was born at a time when government involvement in deliberately fostering economic growth in general, and industrialization in particular, was very rare, and when the typical rates of capital accumula-

> tion were quite low. That situation has changed in many respects, and, while that may suggest the need to emphasize different issues, it does not in any way invalidate the wisdom of the strategies then suggested (p. 732).

Nor can it be argued with any degree of confidence that if an alternative strategy were chosen, the aggregate and long-term results would have been more favourable throughout the post-independence period. Perhaps the growth rate would have been higher for a while, but the economy could have become more dependent and unable to cope with the weight of adverse external developments—as indeed has happened in the eighties, when there was some shift in the strategy.

It thus seems that the initial choice of India's economic strategy is understandable within the particular economic and political context in which this choice was made.[17] This said, it is now necessary to recognize the drawbacks and weaknesses of the strategy as it has evolved over the past forty years.

By the 1960s it had become clear that the domestic and international context was rapidly changing, and the economy was facing a new set of internal and external challenges which could not be visualized at the beginning of the Planning era. In fact the failure on the external front had already become evident by 1958, when the Plan and the economy had to be rescued through a massive international aid effort. Internally, the aftermath of increased defence expenditures resulting from the 1962 war with China, and from the two wars with Pakistan, led to the emergence of a fiscal problem and to a slowdown in the rate of growth of public investment—which was supposed to be the engine of industrial growth. The devastating droughts of 1965-7 and India's dependence on food imports from the United States underlined the weakness of the agricultural strategy. It is a fair criticism of India's development strategy that the country's economic policy was unresponsive to changing internal and external circumstances. India failed to adapt sufficiently rapidly to changing circumstances wherein the industrial economy became more complex; nor was it responsive enough as the international environment changed from the relatively stable period of the 1950s and early 1960s to an environment characterized by rapid change.

It was also clear that a command-type planning, as developed in the Soviet Union, could not work effectively in an economy which was substantially privately run and where producers and consumers had freedom of choice when making economic decisions. The legal and judicial framework was also such that the power of the state to enforce economic decisions was severely hamstrung. The instruments of planning relied heavily on administrative and physical control. The state took on too much in too many areas, and in too great detail. This vast playground, like Hamlet's Denmark, was growing to seed and becoming impossible to manage or administer. Limitations in administrative resources and capability became important constraints to development. The 'quality' of state intervention was also extremely poor. Recent research on competitiveness and relative industrial performance in different countries has demonstrated that Indian methods of intervention were much less efficient than, say, those by Korea, Japan and Taiwan (Lall, 1990).

Another conspicuous failure, particularly in the eighties, has been the inability of the fiscal system to generate sufficient real resources for investment and capital formation. An important assumption in the choice of strategy was the primary role assigned to the public sector for increasing savings in the economy. It was assumed that the propensity to save out of incomes in the public sector would be higher than that in the private sector. Experience has belied this expectation. While revenues have generally increased in line with plan targets, public savings have tended to decline, leading to an insufficiency of resources for public investment.

Indian Plans have failed to develop a viable strategy for the management of balance of payments. Ever since 1956-7, except for a few years, the balance-of-payments problem has merely varied in its intensity. The Plans over-emphasized the import substitution of finished products, and insufficient attention was paid to interlinkages among various sectors, and to the impact of the tariff regime in encouraging an import-intensive input structure. There was an under-estimation of the economy's import requirements of industrial raw materials, e.g. metals and chemicals, petroleum products, fertilizers and sophisticated capital goods. Unrealistic assumptions about the impact of the import-substitution strategy on the economy's import requirements led to a relative neglect of exports. This resulted in growing current-account deficits, which have become extremely difficult to finance in recent years.

In the 1990s India has to find solutions to these economic problems. It is imperative to take stock, learn from the experience of the last forty years, and take strong corrective action in areas where the country's performance has been less than adequate. In considering policy priorities for the 1990s, it is also relevant to examine the experience of countries which have experienced sustained high growth, and the factors which account for this sort of performance. The next chapter attempts this in order to derive economic lessons for India.

Notes

1. There is no official Indian resolution or statement or even formal acceptance that there was such a thing as a 'New Economic Policy'. In fact, most official documents carefully avoid the use of such terms. However, it is generally agreed that since the beginning of 1985, in particular, there have been significant changes in policy with regard to taxation, industrial licensing, imports, technology, and investment priorities. These changes, taken together, are considered significant enough by several writers to mark a new departure in India's approach to economic policy.

2. Interestingly, there is a clear divide among Indian economists who have commented on new economic policies. By and large, and allowing for some differences in emphasis, several eminent economists who helped shape past policies and held important official positions favour a change in direction. It is accepted that controls and state intervention have become excessive and unwieldy, and there is need for greater reliance on fiscal and financial policies rather than direct controls. See for example, Patel (1987), Singh (1986), Dhar (1989), and Chelliah (1989). On the other hand, several well-known academic economists are inclined to take a less favourable view of policies, particularly those relating to liberalization of state controls. See Raj (1986), Dandekar (1988), Kurien (1987 and 1989), Patnaik (1987), and Sau (1988). Recent developments in the political economy of India have also attracted the attention of researchers abroad, including political scientists. See, for example, Rubin (1985), Kochanek (1985), Harriss (1987), Rudolph and Rudolph (1987), Toye (1988), and Kohli (1989).
3. See Chakravarty (1987a), p. 13. Chakravarty cites a paper by Mahalanobis, the architect of Indian planning, to show that Mahalanobis (1960) himself saw the similarity between his work and that of Feldman, the Russian economist. Raj (1986, p. 18) has argued that the intellectual basis for the Indian approach was not just the Soviet model, but lay in the simple facts and logic of the earlier historical experience.
4. An early contribution to development economics by Galenson and Leibenstein (1955) showed that the greater the capital intensity of new production, the greater would be the share of profits in the ensuing income streams, and therefore the higher the reinvestment out of profits in the next period.
5. In the Second and Third Plans, as originally envisaged, the outlays on agriculture were 11.3 per cent and 14 per cent respectively.
6. Various aspects of India's development experience have been studied by a number of authors, including Rao (1983), Raj (1984), and Dandekar (1988). A highly comprehensive and authoritative recent study of India's economic performance in a long-term perspective is by Sundrum (1987). I have drawn heavily from his work for my analysis of India's post-independence performance.

7. See Heston and Summers (1980), and Mukherjee (1969). Per capita income growth in India was 0.7 per cent per annum during 1871-1911, and virtually nil during 1911-46. For the latter period, some experts, including Daniel Thorner and Angus Maddison, have argued that per capita income may have actually declined by 5 to 15 per cent. For alternative estimates see Heston (1983).
8. Breaking the period 1951-84 into 1951 to 1965 (coinciding roughly with the Nehru era) and 1968 to 1984 (omitting the two severe years of drought in 1965-7), Bhagwati (1987) has estimated that the trend growth rate was 3.88 per cent in the former period and 3.75 per cent in the latter. The decadal growth rates of the 1950s (3.59 per cent), 1960s (3.13 per cent) and 1970s (3.62 per cent) are similar. Sundrum's (1987) estimate for the period 1950-83 is 3.6 per cent, which is quite close.
9. Data on growth rates, including sectoral growth rates in India, are from Sundrum (1987).
10. The study of deceleration in growth rate after the mid-1960s has been a subject of some fascination among Indian economists. Several alternative explanations for this observed trend have been offered. For a detailed analysis, see Ahluwalia (1985). See also Mitra (1977) and Nayyar (1978) for a different perspective.
11. According to Maddison's estimate, the growth rate of agriculture in the half century before independence was only 0.63 per cent. Cited in Sundrum (1987, p. 118).
12. The estimates of capital–output ratios over time and their decomposition have been a matter of controversy among Indian economists. Raj (1984), for example, has argued that the increase in the capital–output ratio in India in the 1970s was not unusual, and occurred in several other countries. Also, the increase was predominantly due to shifts in the investment pattern. The later statistical work of Sundrum (1987), however, establishes that both structural shifts and an increase in sectoral capital–output ratios took place.
13. The Planning Commission estimates of the poverty ratio have been criticized as being too optimistic because of data problems, and also the fact that 1983 was the year of record grain output. See, for example, Kurien (1989) and Bhagwati (1988a). Sundrum (1987) has analysed the available data on distribution of income in detail. For a recent review of the

research on poverty in India, and some interesting results, see Ghosh (1989) and Gaiha (1989).

14. The estimates of shares of manufacturing output among the world's leading powers in Paul Kennedy's highly acclaimed book are based on Bairoch (1975 and 1982).
15. The data on savings after 1980-1 are not comparable with the earlier data because of the introduction of a new series of national income statistics.
16. Bhagwati (1988a) has, for example, suggested that a more export-oriented strategy would have resulted in faster growth, greater labour absorption, and better income distribution. Kenneth Arrow, in a public lecture in Calcutta in 1986, stated that an emphasis on agriculture rather than on heavy industry would have been a more efficient use of the country's scarce resource, capital, and would have meant less injustice to its abundant workforce. Cited in Adiseshiah (1988).
17. For a theoretical discussion of the alternative approaches to development strategy in a historical perspective, see Bardhan (1988). Bardhan compares three approaches, which he terms 'neo-classical', 'Marxist' and 'structuralist-institutionalist', to five broadly defined problems: theory of household behaviour, resource allocation, income distribution and growth, trade and development, and economic policy and the state.

2

Savings, Exports and Literacy

According to data compiled by the World Bank, and published annually in the World Development Report, there were nineteen countries which achieved rates of growth of 6 per cent per annum or more during the period 1965-89.[1] This group of countries, which sustained high growth rates over a long period, is quite heterogeneous, comprising countries in different geographical areas and with different political and economic systems. The group includes low-income countries (e.g. China and Lesotho), oil-exporting countries (e.g. Oman and Saudi Arabia), highly indebted countries (e.g. Brazil and Ecuador), countries which are export-oriented (e.g. Korea and Taiwan), and countries with low export shares (e.g. Egypt and Cameroon). Notwithstanding these and other differences, a striking fact about these high-growth countries is the increase in the rate of domestic savings that occurred during the period.

Experience of High-Growth Countries

The average savings rates (as per cent of GDP) increased along with the growth of income. This is what the conventional growth theory, as well as some of the more recent theoretical work on the savings–growth relationship, would lead us to expect.[2] However, it is even more remarkable that the marginal savings rate also showed a sharp increase *during* the period. For the group as a whole, the marginal savings rate increased from 25.7 per cent of GNP during 1965-70 to 36.8 per cent during 1985-9 (see Table 2.1). A large majority of countries, taken individually, also showed a significant increase in the marginal savings rate.

At the other end, there were only a few countries (India, Colombia and Chile) which showed a significant increase in the savings rate for quite a long period, but which did not register a corresponding increase in the growth rate.[3] It may be noted that a high and rising marginal rate of savings and investment (as distinguished from the initial level of savings and investment) seems to be associated with sustained high growth. A cross-section analysis of the experience of developing countries by Sundrum (1990) in the 1960s and 1970s also showed that the relationship between the growth of income and the *growth* of investment was stronger than between the growth of income and the *level* of investment.

We cannot be sure of which came first, savings or growth. The economic literature on the 'causal' link between savings and growth remains inconclusive.[4] Nevertheless, the association between the two is too strong to be ignored. On the basis of the experience so far, it is fair to suggest that a sustained increase in growth rate is not feasible without an increase in the savings rate unless foreign capital is available in abundance. The evidence also suggests that if foreign commercial borrowings are used as a substitute for domestic savings, the debt trap and the subsequent decline in the growth rate are unavoidable.

A second striking feature about the high-growth countries is that all of them managed to avoid prolonged balance-of-payments problems during the period of high growth. Their reserve position at the end of 1988 was generally good, except in the case of heavily indebted countries, and one or two other countries with special problems (these countries suffered a decline in reserves in the 1980s, along with the decline in their growth rates). The export performance was also generally good, with the group as a whole showing quantum rates of growth of 10 per cent per annum during 1965-80, and 7 per cent in the period 1980-8 (Tables 2.2 and 2.3). In most of these countries, including those with less impressive export performances, the rate of growth of imports was lower or broadly of the same magnitude as that of exports. This is significant. Export orientation may be good for growth, but what is even more important is the *balance* between the growth of imports and exports. Except in very special circumstances, such as unlimited availability of foreign savings or a sharp favourable swing in the terms of trade, a substantially higher rate of growth of imports over that of exports cannot be sustained for long.

Another striking feature of the fast-growing countries is that most of them show a high adult literacy ratio. Table 2.4 shows the growth in primary and secondary school enrolment between 1965 and 1988, and adult literacy ratios for the countries in the group for the years 1970 and 1985. Fast-growing countries like China, Indonesia, Korea, Malaysia, Singapore and Thailand had high adult literacy ratios of 69 per cent or more in 1985 as against the Asian average of 61 per cent. The estimate for India for the same year is 44 per cent, (the figure for 1971 was 34 per cent and for 1991 it is provisionally estimated at 52 per cent, see Table 2.6). Except for Korea, where the literacy ratio was already very high, most of the fast-growing countries, for which earlier data are available, also showed a substantial improvement in the literacy ratio over time. The adult literacy ratio improved from 54 per cent in 1970 to 74 per cent in 1985 in Indonesia, from 60 per cent to 74 per cent in Malaysia, from 74 per cent to 86 per cent in Singapore, and from 79 per cent to 91 per cent in Thailand.

The success in achieving high literacy ratios seems to have played an important role in generating high growth in these countries. The contribution of education has, of course, been long recognized in the literature. Marshall viewed education as 'a national investment' and stressed the need for general education for every man, for

> it makes him more intelligent, more ready, more trustworthy in his work; it raises the tone of his life in working hours; it is thus an important means towards production of material wealth; at the same time, regarded as an end in itself, it is inferior to none of those which the production of material wealth can be made to subserve.[5]

More recently, Theodore Schultz has done pioneering work in the field of economic analysis for education. According to Schultz (1963), the contribution of material capital to growth was twice that of schooling in the United States between 1909 and 1929. However, between 1929 and 1957, the contribution of schooling exceeded that of material capital. Denison (1962) also carried out a study based on historical comparisons and concluded that about 21 per cent of the economic growth in the United States between 1929 and 1957 could be attributed to education.

An important recent study by Psacharopoulos (1984) on the contribution of education to economic growth has revealed that countries with a better-educated population had higher economic growth and more equitable distribution of income.[6] On the basis of historical experience, Psacharopoulos (1988) has argued that movement in primary education has the highest social rate of return, and, unless a population is literate, other investment projects may fail. Haveman and Wolfe (1984) have also identified the many non-market benefits of education.[7] In a recent review of the major themes in economic literature on education and development, Schultz (1988) concludes that

> Studies across persons, households, farms and firms have documented, first generally in the United States and then in many low-income countries, strong empirical regularities between educational attainment of populations and their productivity and performance in both market and non-market [home] production activities. Micro-economic empirical studies have refined and extended this base of evidence, showing that more educated men and women receive more earnings and produce more output than do the less educated in a wide range of activities (p. 544).

We have identified three factors which are associated with consistent high-growth performance, i.e. a high marginal rate of savings, sustained balance-of-payments viability, and a high literacy ratio. A number of theories have been advanced and tested on the main determinants of growth. (See Stern, 1991, and Sundrum, 1990, for a review of the literature on growth theories.) These have improved our understanding of the growth process; however, as pointed out by Stern (1991), a large part of the 'residual' still remains unexplained, and none of the theories is fully able to capture the complexity of the growth process. In the absence of a fully satisfactory theory, we have to rely on 'reasonable' hunches, taking into account the result of theoretical and empirical work. The experience of fast-growing countries does seem to suggest that the three factors given above are crucial for sustained growth.

To a certain extent, these three factors are 'pre-selected'. However, there is sufficient theoretical and empirical basis to believe that if a country is doing well on these three criteria, it is likely to be doing well in respect of growth and development. At the theoretical and empirical level, a number of studies have highlighted the important role of savings, exports, and human capital—either as separate factors or as factors acting together—in promoting growth. For example, Otani and Villanueva (1989) have examined the impact of a number of factors on growth with the help of an aggregate growth model. These factors included domestic savings, export performance, the rate of expenditure on human capital, the cost of capital, and the rate of population growth. Otani and Villanueva conclude that the rate of aggregate domestic savings, export growth and expenditure on human capital, along with cost of capital, played a critical role in development. Applying their model to a sample of fifty-five developing countries for the period 1970-85, they found that the contribution of savings, exports and education was sufficiently high to explain the actual growth rate for the entire group. These results are not conclusive and there is need for further research; however, it is difficult to name a developing country which has done well in respect of savings, balance of payments and literacy, but has nevertheless failed to grow.[8] There were, no doubt, other factors, such as political stability, a favourable international environment, and social mobility, which were equally important in explaining high growth in individual countries. But these other factors are likely to have contributed to the successful implementation of other economic policies to increase the growth rate, rather than being independent factors in development.

India's Experience: Savings

Let us now briefly examine India's record on these three counts, i.e. savings, balance of payments and literacy. India has one of the highest savings rates in the developing world, particularly among low-income countries. Gross savings rates increased rather sharply—from about 10.1 per cent of GDP in 1951-2 to 15.3 per cent in 1966-7 and 21.2 per cent in 1980-1. The growth rate of national income during this entire period was, however, relatively low compared with that in fast-growing countries—about 3.6 per cent per annum. It is also interesting that since, 1980-1, there has been very little increase in the savings rate. According to the new series of national income statistics, the ratio of gross domestic savings remained stagnant in the region of 21 per cent of GDP in the 1980s. (Data after 1980-1 are not strictly comparable with the earlier data.) Yet the growth rate during the 1980s was significantly higher—5.5 per cent per annum. On the face of it, the Indian experience seems to contradict the experience of high-performance countries in respect of the role of domestic savings in the growth process.

A closer analysis of the data on savings, capital formation and growth performance in India, however, indicates that this is not necessarily true. The bulk of the increase in the domestic savings rate prior to 1980-1 occurred during the period 1953-4 to 1966-7. The savings rate during this period increased from 8.8 per cent to 15.3 per cent. Between 1966-7 and 1980-1, in proportionate terms, the increase was only about half as much, and the savings ratio increased from 15.3 per cent to 21 per cent. The marginal savings rate in the two periods was 19 per cent and 24 per cent respectively, which was significantly lower than that for fast-growing countries. The data on gross fixed capital formation are even more telling. The ratio of gross fixed capital formation to GDP increased from 8.4 per cent in 1953-4 to 15.6 per cent in 1966-7, and further to only 19.3 per cent in 1980-1.[10]

Trends in fixed capital formation during the period 1950-1 to 1979-80 were analysed in depth by a technical Working Group on Savings. (K.N. Raj was the Chairman.) This Group submitted its report in 1982. The Working Group (Reserve Bank of India, 1982) came to four interesting conclusions, which are of significance when analysing the growth performance of the Indian economy during this period: (i) the greater part of the increase in the rate of gross capital formation as well as in the gross fixed capital formation took place in the period between the early 1950s and the middle of the 1960s; (ii) in real terms, after allowing for a higher increase in the prices of capital goods relative to all other commodities, the rate of growth of fixed capital formation as a proportion of GDP was only about as high towards the end of the 1970s as it was in the middle of the 1960s, and only about two-thirds higher than in the middle of the the 1950s; (iii) the increase in the rate of capital formation between the middle of the 1950s and the middle of the 1960s was mainly in the public sector. After the middle of the 1960s, there was a sharp fall in the rate of gross fixed capital formation in the public sector; and (iv) the rate of private capital formation in agriculture was fairly stagnant throughout the sixties.

The growth performance of the Indian economy upto 1980-1 has to be examined in the light of these findings. The relevant data are shown in Table 2.5. It seems that the impact of growth in domestic savings and fixed capital formation was reflected in higher growth rates in industry during the period 1953-4 to 1967-8, and a drop in the growth rate of savings was associated with a drop in the rate of manufacturing production thereafter (upto 1981-2).[11] This is not an unexpected result. As mentioned earlier, the increase in the rate of capital formation between the middle of the 1950s and the middle of the 1960s was mainly in the public sector. Both from the demand and the supply sides, the impact of higher rates of capital formation in the public sector was felt in the industrial sector.[12] In line with India's development strategy, the incremental capital formation in the early stages was largely in the infrastructure sectors (including power, railways and communications), and capital goods and basic industries (e.g. machinery and steel). In the earlier period, the relatively high rate of growth in investment in these sectors also helped create demand for industry. In the latter period, the demand-side effects of relatively slow growth in investment/savings were also felt in the industrial sector.[13]

The period after 1981-2 is, however, interesting. The stagnation in the savings rate during this period was associated with a marked increase in the growth rate of manufacturing output and an increase in the growth rate of national income to 5.5 per cent per annum. These growth rates are much higher than the historical trend. There are two main developments which explain this outcome. First, there was a decline in the capital–output ratio in the eighties. The capital–output ratio was about 4.1 during this period, as compared with a figure of around 6 in the seventies. A possible explanation for the fall in the capital–output ratio is the shift in the structure of investment in favour of those sectors and uses that generate higher income per unit of capital (Roy and Sen, 1991).

Second, there has been an increase in the contribution of foreign savings in the eighties. The current-account deficit increased from 0.1 per cent of GDP in 1978-9 to 1.6 per cent in 1981-2, and further to 2.4 per cent in 1989-90. As a proportion of gross capital formation, foreign savings increased from 0.5 per cent in 1978-9 to 7.2 per cent in 1981-2 and 10 per cent in 1989-90. Quite a substantial part of foreign borrowings during this period was on commercial terms. According to World Bank Debt data, India's total outstanding foreign debt increased from $ 18.7 billion in 1980 to $ 56.3 billion in 1989, and debt to private creditors increased from about $ 2 billion to $ 21.4 billion during this period.[14] A significant part of the manufacturing growth in new industries during this period was based on imports of components and raw materials. For example, two of the fastest growing sectors have been automobiles, including two-wheelers, and electronics, where real output has more than doubled in seven years. Both these sectors are heavily dependent on imports of technology and components, and have grown behind high protective tariffs. The growth of value added at domestic prices in these sectors has been very high, but it is not clear whether these sectors would also show a similar growth in value added at world prices, and whether their domestic growth rates can be sustained for long. The greater reliance on foreign commercial borrowings for accelerating the growth rate poses several questions for development policy, particularly on the balance-of-payments front.

An interesting aspect of the savings performance of the Indian economy lies in the behaviour of public savings (including the savings of public enterprises). The contribution of public sector (both centre and states) to overall savings increased from 1.2 per cent of GDP in 1953-4 to over 3 per cent of GDP in the mid-1960s, and further to 4.3 per cent of GDP in 1977-8. In the eighties, however, there was a sharp decline in public savings. By 1989-90 the public savings as a proportion of GDP declined to less than 2 per cent of GDP.[15] This is the heart of the savings problem in the Indian economy.

India's Experience: Balance of Payments

Except for relatively brief periods, India has been subject to continuous balance-of-payments problems since 1956-7. (See Chapter 4.) It is no exaggeration to say that Indian economic policy-making during this entire period has been dominated by a concern with balance of payments. Industrial and trade policies, in particular, have been heavily influenced by concern over their actual or likely impact on the difficult payments position. At independence, India had large sterling reserves. In 1950-1 the reserves (excluding gold) amounted to about 158 per cent of merchandise imports. These reserves were, however, drawn down rather sharply in order to meet the investment and import requirements of the First Five Year Plan. By 1957-8 reserves in nominal rupee terms had come down to about one-third of the level prevailing in 1950-1. In that year, India faced a severe balance-of-payments crisis. Tackling this crisis required an international rescue operation, including the formation of the Aid India Consortium, and a drawing from the International Monetary Fund. Tough quantitative restrictions on imports were introduced, along with a rigorous exchange-control regime.

The balance-of-payments position remained highly precarious until 1968-9. There were several drawings from the IMF, and the reserves in that year were at a low level of about 21 per cent of imports. The balance-of-payments problems during this period were further exacerbated by the impact of two severe droughts and two wars. There was a slight improvement in the reserve position between 1968-9 and 1973-4, but the overall situation remained difficult, necessitating the continuation of highly restrictive import and exchange controls.

Then came the first oil shock. The four-fold increase in international crude oil prices between September 1973 and April 1974 raised the petroleum oil bill from Rs 200 crores to Rs 1160 crores, and the current account deteriorated from a small surplus in 1972-3 to a deficit of Rs 960 crores in 1974-5. As a per cent of GDP, the current-account deficit was 1.4 per cent in 1974-5 as compared with 0.4 per cent in the preceding three years. As a per cent of exports of goods and services, the deficit increased to just over 25 per cent, from an average of 8 per cent in 1970-1 to 1972-3. Contrary to most expectations, however, the Indian economy coped remarkably well with these developments, and the period 1976-7 to 1979-80 saw a sharp turnaround in India's balance-of-payments position. Reserves increased from about Rs 600 crores in 1974-5 to Rs 5160 crores in 1979-80. In 1979-80 reserves were 54 per cent of imports.

The improvement in the balance-of-payments during

this period saw the faint beginnings of the process of import and industrial liberalization. The story of how this turnaround was brought about is highly interesting, given India's past history. (For details, see Ahluwalia, 1986.) Briefly, the turnaround was brought about by a remarkable success in controlling inflation and increasing exports. The growth rate of imports was also brought down, leading to a sharp improvement in the trade account. In addition, there was improvement in external flows and private transfers by Indian workers in the Middle East.

Oil prices again doubled in 1979, raising India's oil import bill from Rs 1680 crores to Rs 5260 crores in 1980-1. The current account deteriorated sharply, and India again faced a 'potential' balance-of-payments crisis—'potential' because the reserves in 1980-1 were still at a comfortable level. In order to meet the situation, India entered into an extended arrangement with the IMF, under which it could draw SDR 5 billion over a three-year period. Actual drawings by the end of 1983-4 were SDR 3.9 billion, when the programme was terminated in view of the improvement in the reserve position. The reserves continued to remain at a relatively comfortable level until about April 1988. Thereafter they began to decline again and reached a low of Rs 4800 crores, equivalent to only forty-five days' imports, by mid-1989. Since then, the position has become highly precarious, particularly after the Gulf War of 1990-1. In the latest period, the pressure on balance of payments has been accentuated by substantial increases in debt-service payments on account of repayment to the IMF and commercial creditors. The debt-service ratio, as a percentage of exports of goods and services, increased from 9.1 per cent in 1980 to 26.3 per cent in 1989. In dollar terms, debt-service payments increased from $ 1.3 billion in 1980 to $ 4.9 billion in 1989.

During the 1980s, as mentioned earlier, India borrowed substantial amounts from commercial markets. Another important change which affected the payments situation adversely was the decline in the availability of concessional assistance, particularly from the International Development Association (IDA) in the World Bank Group. As World Bank loans carry commercial terms, this change had important implications for India's balance of payments in the 1990s.

To sum up, except for relatively brief periods India has faced a difficult balance-of-payments situation. During the period 1956-7 and 1975-6, the balance-of-payments deficit was financed largely through concessional flows. In the more recent period the situation has been very different, and import growth has been substantially financed through commercial borrowings. Exports have done well in the last two years, but not well enough to reduce the current-account deficit. (See Chapter 4 for a detailed analysis.)

The balance-of-payments concern is likely, once again, to dominate India's economic policy-making in the 1990s. One important change from the past, which would complicate the task of balance-of-payments management, is the sharp rise in the stock of foreign debt. Another complicating factor is the increasing dependence of important sectors of Indian industry on imports of capital goods and components. The policy challenge for the 1990s is to find a solution to these problems without intensifying the system of bureaucratic controls, further loss of efficiency, and a drop in the growth rate of the economy.

India's Experience: Literacy

The adult literacy ratio in India increased from 34 per cent in 1970 to 44 per cent in 1985. The latest provisional Census for 1991 shows a significant improvement in the literacy rate between 1981-91. Table 2.6 shows the literacy rate in 1991 as compared with earlier census results since independence. The figures for 1991 are, however, not comparable with earlier years, as data for 1991 relate to the literacy rate in the population aged seven years and above. Figures for earlier censuses related to the age group above five years.

India's literacy ratio is one of the lowest in Asia, and compares with an average ratio of 61 per cent for Asia, 80 per cent for Latin America, and 59 per cent for all developing countries in 1985. Although the gross enrolment ratio for India at the primary-school level is 93.6 per cent (1986), the percentage of dropouts from school is very high. According to the census data for 1981, only 47 per cent of the children in the age group 6-11 years attend school, and this proportion falls to 38 per cent in the case of girls (see Table 2.7). An assessment made by the ministry of education shows that nearly 50 per cent of the children drop out before reaching class V, while about 70 per cent who began education in class I drop out before reaching class VIII.[16] The dropout rates for classes I-V have fallen only slightly, from 67 per cent in the early 1960s to 60 per cent in the early 1980s to 50 per cent in more recent years.

Notwithstanding the improved record in the 1980s, the literacy rate in India is still very low. This is despite the fact that India spends nearly as much on education (as per cent of GNP) as Korea. Public spending on education in India was 3 per cent in 1985 (3.6 per cent in the Seventh Plan, see Table 2.8) as compared with 3.4 per cent in Korea and 3 per cent for the Asian region as a whole. An important reason for India's poor performance in respect of literacy is that the proportion of spending on primary education is not only relatively low, but this has also been declining as a proportion of total expenditure in the Five Year Plans. The growth in the number of schools at the elementary level has not even kept pace with the growth of population (see Table 2.9). The share of elementary education in the total expenditure for the education sector as a whole has declined from 56 per cent in the First Plan to 44 per cent in the Seventh Plan, while that of secondary education rose from 13 to 24 per cent, and of university education from 9 to 16 per cent. In contrast to this, a recent study shows that developing countries typically devoted 60 per cent or more of educational expenditure to elementary schooling during the 'drive' to achieve universal literacy (Colletta and Sutton, 1988).

To a certain extent, the new education policy adopted in 1986 sought to remove the distortions.[17] A Technology

Mission on Literacy was launched in May 1988. The thrust of the new policy in the area of primary education was two-fold: (i) universal enrolment and universal retention of children upto fourteen years of age; and (ii) a substantial improvement in the quality of education. Government, local bodies, voluntary agencies and individuals were to be fully involved in this effort. The policy adopted in 1986 was reviewed subsequently by a committee which submitted its final report to the government in December 1990. This committee, while endorsing the approach of the 1986 policy, has suggested that different types of strategies have to be adopted for different categories of 'out of school' children, such as very young children and children who were in the labour market. In order to enhance the capability of the school to attract and retain children, the committee also emphasized the need for a decentralized and participative mode of planning and management, so that firm linkages are established between the school and the community.

These are welcome initiatives. However, the literacy programme continues to be underfunded, and significant organizational weaknesses persist in spreading the reach of the programme. Much more needs to be done by way of increasing expenditure on primary education, if necessary at the expense of higher education. India has the necessary skills, and the expansion of higher education that has already taken place should ensure an adequate supply of primary schoolteachers for an expanded programme of primary education.

From an economic point of view, not much more needs to be said on the policy for education. A programme for eliminating illiteracy by the end of this century must be launched as early as possible.[18] This is a question of priorities in public spending for education, and does not necessarily involve a large increase in the overall budgetary resources allocated to education.

It may be appropriate to end this discussion with a recent observation by Galbraith: 'In our time . . . no literate population is poor, no illiterate population is other than poor. Perhaps poverty and illiteracy have larger causes; nonetheless, this unshakable association should remain always in mind.'[19]

Notes

1. The latest World Development Report, 1990, provides data on GDP growth rates for the periods 1965-80 and 1980-8 separately. For the entire period, taken together and updated to 1989, growth rates were specially computed and are shown in Table 2.1.
2. See Sen (1983) on the relevance of conventional theory to the growth experience of developing countries. Much of the theoretical work on the effects of growth on savings relates to industrial countries. The standard benchmark for analysing long-term effects of saving on capital accumulation and growth is provided by Solow's (1956) famous model. A striking implication of this model and its descendants is that the long-run rate of growth is unaffected by the savings rate. At most, changes in saving behaviour induce temporary deviations from a long-run growth path, which is determined entirely by an *exogenous* process of technological advance. However, empirical work has suggested that growth rates in the industrialized countries are in fact highly correlated with savings rates (see Summers and Carroll, 1989). The empirical findings have led to the construction of a number of alternative models which build on the earlier work of Arrow (1962) and Uzawa (1965), and which regard the long-run growth rate to be *endogenous* and related to the savings rate. Endogenous growth models assume that there are externalities associated with capital accumulation, such as accumulation of human capital, research and development, and new product development and learning. These externalities eliminate the effects of diminishing returns, and raise the rate of growth. Among such models are those developed by Romer (1986 and 1987), Krugman (1987), and Grossman and Helpman (1989). It may also be noted that the so-called Cambridge growth models, associated principally with Joan Robinson and Nicholas Kaldor, also implicitly recog-

nized the possibility of variation in savings-income ratio over time by distinguishing between savings out of profits and savings out of wages. The propensities to save by these two classes were found to be statistically significant (Houthakker, 1965). The Cambridge-type models, which incorporate distribution issues, are likely to be more relevant for understanding the savings behaviour in developing countries.

3. See World Development Report, 1990, Table 9, for data on savings rates in countries which are not covered in Table 2.1 of the text.
4. Nurkse (1953) was an early exponent of the 'vicious circle' hypothesis. According to this view, poor countries were too poor to save sufficiently, resulting in low rates of investment, with an adverse impact on the growth of real output and the level of per capita income. Some others have, however, argued that while a higher savings rate is required for growth, the *availability* of domestic savings is not a constraint because of the possibility of capital flows, and the possibility of substitution of productive investment for unproductive expenditure by upper-income groups. Thus, Arthur Lewis has argued that 'saving is a function of the opportunity to invest' (Lewis, 1978, p. 155). Bauer and Yamey (1957, p. 12) also say that 'it is often nearer the truth to say that capital is created in the process of development than that development is a function of capital accumulation'. My argument does not depend on establishing a 'causal' link between savings and growth. The point is that sustained high growth is 'associated' with a higher savings rate, and that without a rise in the savings ratio over time, sustained growth is unlikely to occur in developing countries. Sundrum (1990) has emphasized the favourable 'demand side' effects of an increase in the investment rate, in addition to the 'supply side' effects of an increase in the savings rate (*ex post*, of course, the two rates must be equal). Interestingly, Sundrum also found a positive relationship between *growth* of investment and *growth* of income in developing countries for the period 1950-80. In fact this relationship was stronger than that between the growth of income and the *level* of investment, as measured by the investment ratio to income (Sundrum, 1990, pp. 175-81).
5. Alfred Marshall, *Principles of Economics* (6th edition, London, 1910), pp. 209, 217. I am grateful to S.N. Raghavan for this reference, and for providing data in Tables 2.7, 2.8 and 2.9.

6. Also see Lewis (1962).
7. Psacharopoulos's (1988) paper contains a survey of the recent literature on the contribution of education and literacy to development.
8. Several authors have emphasized that growth is not synonymous with development. See, for example, Streeten (1981). However, it is equally true that development is hardly possible without growth and an increase in incomes. The acceleration of growth, therefore, must be an integral part of a viable development strategy.
9. In a paper published in 1974, Chakravarty attributed the decline in the savings income ratio after the mid-1960s to the faster rise in the price of agricultural production in relation to that of the non-agricultural sector. There was some evidence that the marginal propensity to save in agricultural households as a whole was lower than that in non-agricultural households. The shift in the terms of trade in favour of the former implied a decline in the savings–income ratio. This paper also contains an interesting discussion of the Lewis model in the Indian context.
10. See *Economic Survey*, 1989-90, Government of India, p.S-8.
11. Bhagwati (1987) has taken the view that the low rate of growth in India is due to low productivity arising from wrong macroeconomic policies and development strategy, rather than insufficiency of savings. He has argued that even after allowing for shifts in relative prices of capital goods and quality changes, the savings/GNP ratio during the period 1950-80 would have increased by more than 70 per cent on a conservative basis, without much impact on growth. This is correct if overall GNP growth rates are taken. However, if growth rates of the manufacturing sector are considered, which is not unreasonable in the Indian case, we see a close association between high growth in the rates of capital formation and high growth rates in manufacturing output during different periods.
12. See Sundrum (1990) for an analysis of factors in growth from both demand and supply sides. Sundrum found that the demand-side effects of investment were important in explaining the role of investment/savings in growth.
13. The stagnation in public investment from the middle of the 1960s, following the severe agricultural drought in 1965-6 and 1966-7, and its impact on demand for products of heavy industry and on investment in railways, electricity and mining,

have received considerable attention in the literature on India's industrial performance. See Ahluwalia (1985), Chapter 5.

14. See Chapter 4 for more details.
15. The data on public-sector savings are from National Account Statistics, published by the Central Statistical Organization. The data include savings of state governments and enterprises. There are several differences in the concept of public-sector savings as used in the national income accounts, and 'public savings' as defined in certain other documents of government and international institutions.
16. The data are from a document, 'Challenges of Education', Ministry of Education, Government of India, 1985.
17. The National Policy on Education (Government of India, 1986b) declared that 'life-long education is a cherished goal of the education process'. In respect of primary education, the enrolment and retention of children upto fourteen years of age is an important goal. By 1990 the policy aimed at providing five years of schooling (or its equivalent through the non-formal streams) to all children upto the age of eleven. This goal has not been achieved.
18. I have argued that literacy is an important 'input' into the development process. Sen (1989) has suggested, and rightly so, that literacy is also important in itself: 'The point is made that mere literacy should not be identified with education. What this overlooks is the denial of freedom that is involved in the incarceration that illiteracy represents, the removal of which has been part of the fiery rhetoric from the beginning of Indian planning.' (p. 380).
19. John K. Galbraith, 'Economics in the Century Ahead', *The Economic Journal*, January 1991, vol.101, p.46.

TABLE 2.1
RATE OF GROWTH AND MARGINAL SAVINGS RATES IN HIGH-GROWTH COUNTRIES

Country	Rate of growth (% per annum)	Marginal savings rate as percentage of GNP		
	1965–89	1965–70	1985–89	1965–89
1. Botswana	12.3	(-) 65.4	73.2	37.2
2. Brazil	6.0	26.8	42.5	27.4
3. Cameroon	6.3	108.7	145.1	24.5
4. China	7.5	32.0	43.1	38.8
5. Congo	6.6	(-) 19.0	449.8	22.9
6. Ecuador	6.0	16.6	(-) 111.7	17.2
7. Egypt	6.6	(-) 51.9	(-) 34.8	3.8
8. Hong Kong	8.4	7.6	37.4	32.5
9. Indonesia	6.7	16.6	18.4	39.0
10. Korea, Rep. of	8.8	28.6	58.0	43.3
11. Lesotho	7.6	(-) 109.6	183.7	(-) 27.0
12. Malaysia	6.6	34.2	29.4	35.6
13. Oman	10.9	–	–	–
14. Paraguay	6.1	13.9	11.1	16.9
15 Saudi Arabia	8.0	–	–	–
16. Singapore	8.5	–	–	–
17. Syria	6.5	4.6	9.3	10.6
18. Thailand	6.9	26.6	21.1	23.0
19. Taiwan	9.2	34.3	34.7	33.5
AVERAGE	7.4	25.7	36.8	32.8

– : Not available.
SOURCE: World Bank.

TABLE 2.2
RATE OF GROWTH OF EXPORTS AND IMPORTS IN HIGH-GROWTH COUNTRIES

Country	*Average annual growth rates (per cent)*			
	Exports		*Imports*	
	1965-80	*1980-88*	*1965-80*	*1980-88*
1. Botswana	–	–	–	–
2. Brazil	9.3	6.0	8.2	(-) 2.9
3. Cameroon	5.2	6.8	5.6	2.5
4. China	5.5	11.9	7.9	13.1
5. Congo	12.5	4.6	1.0	(-) 2.1
6. Ecuador	15.1	5.7	6.8	(-) 2.8
7. Egypt	2.7	6.2	6.0	1.5
8. Hong Kong	9.5	12.3	8.3	10.4
9. Indonesia	9.6	2.9	14.2	(-) 2.1
10. Korea, Rep. of	27.2	14.7	15.2	9.9
11. Lesotho	–	–	–	–
12. Malaysia	4.4	9.4	2.9	0.4
13. Oman	–	–	–	–
14. Paraguay	7.9	15.7	4.6	4.9
15. Saudi Arabia	8.8	(-) 16.3	25.9	(-) 9.3
16. Singapore	4.7	7.3	7.0	4.9
17. Syria	11.4	(-) 0.5	8.5	(-) 8.2
18. Thailand	8.5	11.3	4.1	6.2
19. Taiwan	19.0	13.9	15.1	8.5
AVERAGE	10.1	7.0	8.8	2.2

– : Not available.

SOURCE: *World Development Report*, 1990, World Bank. The growth rates are for merchandise exports and imports, and are calculated from quantum indices of exports and imports.

TABLE 2.3
FOREIGN EXCHANGE RESERVES IN HIGH-GROWTH COUNTRIES

Country	Gross international reserves		
	Millions of US dollars		*In months of import coverage*
	1970	*1988*	*1988*
1. Botswana	–	2,258	17.7
2. Brazil	1,190	1,118	0.4
3. Cameroon	81	163	0.7
4. China	–	23,751	5.0
5. Congo	9	8	0.1
6. Ecuador	76	568	2.1
7. Egypt	165	2,261	1.8
8. Hong Kong	–	–	–
9. Indonesia	160	6,322	3.3
10. Korea, Rep. of	610	12,478	2.6
11. Lesotho	–	56	1.2
12. Malaysia	667	7,491	4.0
13. Oman	13	1,173	6.6
14. Paraguay	18	338	3.0
15. Saudi Arabia	670	22,438	7.9
16 Singapore	1,012	17,073	4.2
17. Syria	57	342	1.6
18. Thailand	911	7,112	3.6
19. Taiwan	627	79,430	16.0
AVERAGE	418	10,554	3.9

– : Not available.
SOURCE: *World Development Report*, 1990, World Bank.

TABLE 2.4
LITERACY IN HIGH-GROWTH COUNTRIES

Country	*School enrolment*				*Adult literacy rate*	
	Primary		*Secondary*			
	1965	*1987*	*1965*	*1987*	*1970*	*1985*
1. Botswana	65	114	3	32	41	71
2. Brazil	108	103	16	39	66	78
3. Cameroon	94	109	5	26	33	–
4. China	89	132	24	43	–	69
5. Congo	114	–	10	–	35	63
6. Ecuador	91	117	17	56	72	83
7. Egypt	75	90	26	69	35	45
8. Hong Kong	103	106	29	74	77	88
9. Indonesia	72	118	12	46	54	74
10. Korea, Rep. of	101	101	35	88	88	–
11. Lesotho	94	113	4	–	62	73
12. Malaysia	90	102	28	59	60	74
13. Oman	–	97	–	38	–	30
14. Paraguay	102	102	13	30	80	88
15. Saudi Arabia	24	71	4	44	9	–
16. Singapore	105	–	45	–	74	86
17. Syria	78	110	28	59	40	60
18. Thailand	78	95	14	28	79	91
19. Taiwan	–	–	–	–	–	–
AVERAGE	78	98	17	46	60	75

– : Not available

SOURCE: *World Development Report*, 1990; for data on school enrolment, Human Development Report, 1990 (United Nations Development Programme), for adult literacy rates.

NOTE : Enrolment ratios are in terms of percentage of the relevant age group. For some countries with universal primary education, the gross enrolment ratios may exceed 100 per cent because some pupils are younger or older than the country's standard primary school age. Literacy rates relate to population group, fifteen years or older.

TABLE 2.5
SAVINGS, CAPITAL FORMATION AND OUTPUT IN INDIA DURING 1953-54 TO 1989-90

Item	*1953-54 to 1966-67*	*1967-68 to 1980-81*	*1981-82 to 1989-90*	*1953-54 to 1989-90*
1. Marginal Savings Rate as percentage of GDP	19.0	24.0	22.0	22.0
2. Growth Rate of Gross Fixed Capital Formation (at 1980-81 prices)	7.4	4.2	5.5	5.7
3. Growth Rate of Gross Fixed Capital Formation as percentage of GDP	4.3	1.6	1.2	2.5
4. Growth Rate of GDP at Factor Cost (at 1980-81 prices)	3.5	3.8	5.5	4.1
5. Growth Rate of Value Added in Agriculture (at 1980-81 prices)	1.5	3.9	3.8	2.9
6. Growth Rate of Agricultural Production (Index No.)	2.1	4.3	3.9	3.4
7. Growth Rate of Value Added in Manufacturing (at 1980-1 prices)	6.3	4.3	7.2	5.7
8. Growth Rate of Industrial Production (Index No.)	7.4	4.5	7.8	6.4

SOURCE: Government of India publications. The growth rate for any given period is the simple average of annual growth rates.

TABLE 2.6
LITERACY RATE IN INDIA : 1951-91

Year	*Persons*	*Males*	*Females*
1951	18.33	27.16	8.86
1961	28.31	40.40	15.34
1971	34.45	45.95	21.97
1981	43.56 (41.42)	56.37 (53.45)	29.75 (28.46)
1991	52.11	63.86	39.42

SOURCE: 'Provisional Population Totals', Census of India, 1991, Government of India.

NOTE : Literacy rates for 1951, 1961 and 1971 relate to the population aged five years and above. The rates for the years 1981 and 1991 relate to the population aged seven years and above. The literacy rates for the population aged five years and above in 1981 have been shown in brackets.

TABLE 2.7
PROPORTION OF CHILDREN ATTENDING SCHOOL: 1981
(PER CENT)

Population	*6-11 years*	*11-14 years*	*6-14 years*
All	47.15	51.96	48.72
Male	54.88	63.81	58.11
Female	38.45	38.67	38.52
Rural	41.27	45.69	42.69
Male	50.57	59.52	53.50
Female	31.28	30.12	30.93
Urban	68.83	72.93	70.26
Male	72.70	78.32	74.66
Female	64.71	66.98	65.52

SOURCE: Y.P. Aggarwal, 'Towards Education for All Children - Intent and Reality', *Journal of Educational Planning and Administration*, 2, (1 & 2), 1988. (Computed from Census of India, 1981.)

NOTE : The percentages given above do not correspond to the enrolments in Classes I to V and VI to VIII.

TABLE 2.8

SHARE OF EDUCATION IN DIFFERENT FIVE YEAR PLAN OUTLAYS / EXPENDITURE

Five Year Plan	*Share (per cent)*
First Plan	7.86
Second Plan	5.83
Third Plan	6.87
Annual Plans (1966-69)	4.86
Fourth Plan	5.04
Fifth Plan	3.27
Sixth Plan	2.70
Seventh Plan	3.55

SOURCE: Five Year Plan Documents; Economic Surveys of Government of India.

TABLE 2.9

TRENDS IN GROWTH OF ELEMENTARY AND SECONDARY EDUCATION (PER CENT PER ANNUM)

	1950-51 to 1960-61	*1960-61 to 1970-71*	*1970-71 to 1980-81*	*1980-81 to 1986-87*
1. Expenditure on Schools				
Nominal	10.7	13.8	14.5	16.9
Elementary	10.2	13.3	14.4	16.6
Secondary	11.6	14.6	14.6	17.4
2. Number of Schools	5.6	3.0	2.2	1.6*
Elementary	5.5	2.8	2.1	1.5*
Secondary	9.0	7.8	3.3	3.6*
3. Number of Teachers	6.3	5.3	3.0	2.4*
Elementary	5.7	4.6	2.7	1.6*
Secondary	8.9	7.8	3.8	4.2*

* : 1980-1 to 1984-5

SOURCE: Selected Educational Statistics (different issues), Department of Education, Ministry of Human Resources Development.

3

The 'End' of Government ?

In an essay on the perceived pendular swings in collective behaviour, Albert Hirschman asked 'whether our societies are in some ways predisposed toward oscillations between periods of intense preoccupation with public issues and almost total concentration on individual improvement and private welfare goals' (Hirschman, 1982, p. 3). A similar question can be asked *vis-à-vis* periodic shifts in the views —of both the general public and experts—on the role of government in development.

In the 1950s and 1960s there was a broad consensus that governments must intervene directly and play an activist role in development. Early development economics showed unquestioning faith in the ability of the state to correct market failures and imperfections, and to effectively direct the process of economic development. In fact even the World Bank, a capitalist institution with a development mission, was reluctant to lend to countries that did not have a government sponsored 'Development Plan.'[1] By the beginning of the 1980s there was a sharp swing away from this opinion, particularly in industrial countries and international financial institutions. Economists were not far behind.

The literature of the recent years is full of neo-classical accounts of the 'public failures' of regulatory interventionist states.[2] Governments are beginning to be seen as the main bottlenecks in development. Getting governments out of the business of development has become an important element in the policy advice given by international institutions, economic experts, and donor agencies. The rise of Thatcherism in the U.K. and Reaganism in the U.S.A. contributed to this changed mood.[3] Another important contributory factor has been the increasing economic difficulties of many developing countries, and the failure of their governments to take timely corrective action. Partly in response to their own experience and partly in response to international pressure, several developing countries are currently questioning the role of government in their economies. Thus, Carlos Andres Perez, President of Venezuela, who has strong socialist credentials, has called for the 'de-ideologization' of politics in the third world, and for less government intervention in the economy. Similarly, the prime minister of Spain, Felipe Gonzalez, who is also the leader of the Socialist Party, has dwelt on the virtues of promoting 'efficiency' through greater use of market forces. An even more striking case is the politico-economic conversion of Zambia's Kenneth Kaunda, a long-standing exponent of the virtues of socialism and central planning in Africa.[4] Leaders of a number of other developing countries, particularly in Africa and Latin America, who are passing through economic difficulties, have similarly committed themselves to reducing the role of government and the public sector in their economies. In China the government had initiated a wide-ranging process of economic reform and shift to a market economy in the mid-eighties. However, after the events of June 1989, there has been a reappraisal and the pace of economic liberalization seems to have slowed down.

Before we examine the issues involved, it is necessary to remind ourselves that, for the first thirty years or so, the gains from planning and state intervention in developing countries were quite remarkable. For a century before 1950 economic growth in developing countries had barely kept pace with population growth. There was very little industrial activity and the bulk of the population was engaged in low-productivity agricultural occupations that were subject to large fluctuations. In contrast, the last forty years have been years of significant progress. World Bank data show that during 1965-80 the growth of national income in the developing world exceeded 6 per cent per annum. Today's highly-indebted developing countries registered an even higher growth rate of 6.6 per cent per annum during this period, and the sub-Saharan region registered a growth rate of 5.6 per cent per annum. Manufacturing production in the developing world increased by 8 per cent per annum.[5] This was unprecedented—in terms of their own history as well as in comparison to rates of growth registered by presently industrialized countries in the early stages of their development. The growth rate was 2 per cent per annum in the U.K. between 1790 and 1820; 2.7 per cent in Germany between 1850 and 1880; about 4 per cent in the United States between 1820 and 1850; and some 4 per cent in Japan between 1876 and 1900 (Pearson Commission, 1969, p. 27).

It cannot be denied that the acceleration of growth rates in the post-1950 period was made possible by structural changes that were brought about through the adoption of new strategies of development conceived and implemented by the governments of these countries.[6] There were substantial gains in productivity, in the savings rate, and in altering the pattern of production. Not that all the policies were right, or that mistakes were not made; it is also clear that policies and strategies need to be adapted to changing technological, trading and institutional arrangements. Yet the pendulum need not swing so far as to prelude productive interventions by government in the economy.

While considering the reasons for the apparent errors and false starts in our thinking about development, Paul Streeten argues that

> Many of the difficulties encountered in the path of development are neither the result of ideological errors, nor attributable to vested interests, but are the offspring of the successful solution of previous problems. Scientific confidence asserts that there is a solution to every problem, but experience teaches us that there is a problem to every solution, and often more than one.

Analysing the current revulsion against governments along these lines, Streeten further observes:

> Those who believe that governmental organizations do not solve problems, but are the problem, have failed to see that it is sometimes the success of government action which undermines itself. It was the spectacular success in the quarter century after World War II of Keynesian demand management and international co-operation (though some would deny that these were responsible for the success) that carried the seeds of the Keynesian counter-revolution (Streeten, 1986, pp. 240 and 242).

The success of interventionist strategies in breaking away from past stagnation, however, also led to an exaggerated belief in the efficacy of state power. The solution to every problem was found in the expansion of government activity in that area, irrespective of cost or result. Soon the expansion of government became an objective in itself, and every priority or failure in the economic field generated a response in the form of a new regulatory law or a new public-sector corporation. The expansion of government was assiduously promoted by coalitions of powerful interests, which benefited directly from the increased economic power of the state. This gave rise to the political economy problems of the sort discussed by Olson and Bardhan. Over time, the scale of government became so large that the quality of intervention, as well as the quality of services provided by the state, deteriorated. Hirschman (1980 and 1982) has pointed out that a similar process took place in several industrialized countries. The wide expansion in government services led to a drop in the average quality of these services. This was an important reason for disenchantment with the welfare state in the West.

The Role of Government in India

In India the role of government (including state government) has expanded in practically all spheres of the economy.[7] In the fifties, since savings and incomes were low, government had to take on the task of mobilizing incremental savings through taxation. The base of entrepreneurship, as in many other developing countries, was small, and concentrated in some regions of the country. Large investments required in the steel and machine-building sectors could only be undertaken directly by government in view of the underdeveloped financial sector. By the end of the 1960s the concentration of economic power in a few business houses became a major political and economic issue; this further strengthened the role of the state in the industrial sphere. Banks were nationalized in order to break the nexus between private industry and finance, and to make available credit to traditionally under-funded sectors, such as agriculture and small-scale industry.

As government's own need for resources for investment increased, it became necessary to curb or control the private sector's demand for resources through the rationing of foreign exchange, credit controls and industrial licensing. Every action to ration and allocate scarce resources according to predetermined priorities required balancing conflicting objectives. As needs and requirements got larger and resources became smaller, the administrative process had to become more complex and embrace more functions in view of the linkages among different sectors.

As the administrative system became more complex and more inefficient, leading to greater scarcity of resources and greater dissatisfaction, government had to step in and provide relief in the form of special employment programmes and anti-poverty programmes. Government thus became not only a provider of services and an allocator of resources, but also a provider of jobs—in large enterprises as well as small.

Each step had a rationale and a logic of its own, and was perhaps unavoidable under the circumstances.[8] In our current assessment of the economic effects of the expansion of the system we must remember that, for quite some time, the results seemed beneficial. The savings ratio increased and industry expanded. India became a producer of capital goods and self-reliant in food. The public distribution system for food was strengthened, which helped in the prevention of famines and making available food at reasonable prices, at least in urban areas. Millions of jobs were created under special employment programmes, and the poverty ratio declined—even though the incidence of absolute poverty remained large and widespread.

In redefining the scope of government in India, it is useful to distinguish among the different types of roles that the government now plays. First, the government has primary responsibility for planning in the country. The planning process involves state governments also, and in a formal sense the Plan is approved by the National Development Council, which includes chief ministers of all state governments. In reality, however, the primary responsibility is that of the centre, which has command over the distribution of Plan resources. The centre also decides on the inter-sectoral priorities of the Plan.

Second, the government owns and manages a large number of public enterprises. The total number of industrial and commercial enterprises was close to 250 in 1990. In addition, the management of the entire transport and telecommunications sector is with government. This includes railways, airlines, roads, posts and telegraph, telephones, and substantial parts of bus transport and shipping. The responsibility for power generation and distribution is also largely that of government (mainly state governments). In all, 18.5 million persons were employed in the public sector in 1989, as against 7.4 million in organized industry in the private sector (i.e. establishments employing 10 or more persons).

Third, government is an important provider of public goods and services in the field of education, health and social welfare.

Fourth, the government has virtual monopoly of banking and financial intermediation. There are a number of small private banks and financial institutions, but their total share in deposits and financial flows is negligible.

Fifth, the government exercises control over private-sector economic activity through the issue of industrial licenses, foreign-exchange permits, and other regulations. It is important to note that the so-called 'new economic policy' in India involved some diminution of government in its last role, but not in any others.

Planning and Policies

Let us briefly examine the relevance of these different roles for the future. India was among the first developing countries to adopt central planning as a developmental tool. The fact that the central planning of development was to be pursued within a democratic and federal form of government gave this added significance. Planning also became synonymous with the country's struggle to achieve self-reliance, economic independence and social justice. Despite some disillusionment with the planning process in recent years, all political parties remain committed to planning as a desirable and necessary tool of social and economic development.

Aside from this political rationale, there is a genuine economic case for planning in India. In a situation where resources are scarce and needs great, it is essential that the allocation of resources, particularly public-sector resources, reflect development objectives and priorities. Since there are also conflicting and competing regional demands for these resources, it is equally important that these resources be allocated through a process of consultation with the states. Whatever its imperfections, planning in India has been instrumental in institutionalizing this process, and in balancing conflicting interests and competing demands.

While planning must remain an important function of government, its content needs to be changed in the light of experience.[9] It is a fair criticism of Indian planning that past Plans have been more concerned with setting production targets than with indicating a set of policies or a programme for achieving these targets. There is an excessive preoccupation with growth targets and inter-sectoral balances, when even the elementary data for making such exercises are not available. (For example, the projections of capital–output ratios, the savings ratio, and demand elasticities have been widely off the mark in previous Plans.) Production and investment targets have been fixed on the basis of inadequate and unreliable data on input–output relationships and arbitrary assumptions about behaviour patterns. While the technical sophistication in building planning models has increased, the data base has become weaker. Plans have also tended to over-promise, and spread resources thinly over a large number of programmes, so that progress in any one area (e.g. literacy) has been very slow.[10]

To achieve better results from planning it is necessary that the Plans should not pretend to undertake detailed investment planning for the whole economy. In a mixed economy, with a large unorganized, non-financial and internal sector, this is simply not feasible; in any case, it is not being effectively done now. As Dandekar observed several years ago in the context of agricultural planning:

> A plan is a plan in the total sense of the term when it is essentially a plan of action on the part of one who makes the plan. In the present context, if a government has prepared the plan, it must be a plan of action by government and other public authorities. The reason why our plan for agricultural development is not a plan in the true sense of the term is that it is not essentially a plan for state action. It is much more or much less than that. In fact, it covers many fields and areas over which the government has little authority to make decisions or initiate actions.[11]

While the Plans have attempted to do too much in planning investments for the economy as a whole, they have done too little planning for the public sector. At present, although sectoral targets are set in each Plan, there is very little long-term investment planning as such, with the result that actual investment decisions are taken on a case-by-case basis from year to year in response to regional and other pressures. This has led to a considerable mismatch of investments in different sectors, to delays in implementation, to the over-commitment of resources, and to the under-funding of projects.

A major lacuna of the planning system, as it has evolved over time, has been the absence of a link between Plan priorities and macro-economic policies to support those priorities. The techniques were derived from the command-type planning developed in the Soviet Union. These techniques have proved unsuitable for directing investments in an economy where a major portion is privately owned, and where the political and judicial systems ensure a comparative freedom of choice to individual consumers and entrepreneurs. The control and regulatory regime, which was essentially derived from provisions introduced during the Second World War, was more successful in preventing competition and promoting inefficient import substitution than in directing investments in 'desired' directions.[12] The growth of black money in the economy (the 'parallel' economy) and smuggling have ensured that the pattern of effective consumer demand and the pattern of income growth in the economy have had very little to do with Plan priorities. An obvious illustration of this is that while India can claim to be fairly self-sufficient in automobiles—a non-priority product in the Plans—it is a large importer of fertilizers and edible oils—both these command a very high priority in the Plan.

Important anomalies in the industrial structure have develolped as a result of the tenuous link between macro-economic policies, particularly tariff and fiscal policies, and the inter-sectoral targets of the Plan. For example, it is now widely accepted that large portions of the metal-based sectors of capital goods, other engineering industries, transport equipment, etc., have been receiving very low or negative protection (see Kelkar and Kumar, 1990). This is despite the fact that the Plans have always given the highest priority to the production of capital goods. Protection rates provided to chemical-based industries, on the other hand, have been high. The consequence is that, over the last fifteen years, chemical-based industries have exhibited good growth whereas the engineering sector has suffered low growth. Another consequence of this kind of anomalous fiscal structure is that labour-using industries, such as the engineering industry, have been discriminated against, whereas capital-using industries, such as petrochemicals, have received high protection rates. As pointed out by Mohan and Aggarwal (1990), this has had regional consequences as well. With the bias against metal-using industries, the eastern region has lost relative to the western region—where the chemical and petrochemical industries have been based.

Given this experience, it is important now to effect certain changes in the scope and technique of planning. For a more successful and growth-oriented sort of planning in the future, Plans should devote much greater attention to government's investment activities, over which they have direct control. The government's direct investment activities generally cover four distinct areas: (a) special employment programmes, which lead to the creation of assets; (b) investment in education and social services, such as health; (c) investment in economic infrastructure, such as roads, railways and power; and (d) commercial and industrial enterprises.

Of these, investments in respect of (a) and (b) are largely within the purview of state governments. It is appropriate that state planning boards should have full responsibility for planning investment in these sectors. It is not necessary for the central government to lay down guidelines for the whole country in these areas, or impose uniform procedures and standards, since these would be insensitive to the diverse requirements of different regions. Financial transfers from the centre to state governments for such programmes can take place within the framework of normal central assistance for state Plans. It may be argued that state governments will not discharge their responsibilities effectively without central government supervision. It is true that the performance of state governments in these areas varies a great deal. However, this is so despite the involvement of the central government in monitoring and implementing these programmes. Past experience does not show that central intervention in these areas necessarily leads to better and more efficient planning. The administrative and manpower resources saved by the Centre on this account may be more effectively deployed in other tasks.

For a proper development of the country, the two central tasks are planning investments in infrastructure, and improving the efficiency of investments in public-sector commercial enterprises. Since, excluding railways, investments in infrastructure are also undertaken by public enterprises, both these tasks boil down to the job of planning for the public sector as a whole.

It is necessary that in future the Plans clearly lay down broad investment priorities in the public sector, including time-tables for implementation. The Annual Plans should be concerned mainly with annual reviews of progress in implementation. The Planning Commission should also assume primary responsibility for monitoring the implementation of projects, particularly infrastructural projects which have large externalities and which affect everything else in the Plan. At present this responsibility is diffused among ministries and public-sector organizations.

As far as the rest of the economy is concerned, the enunciation of a consistent set of macro-economic policies is vital, and this should be the primary focus of planning. To a certain extent, this was attempted in the Sixth Plan (1980-5). In the past few years, however, the approach to macro-economic policies has been much more *ad hoc*. The Plan should clearly lay down the tariff, financial, and fiscal policies which affect investment decisions. It is important that a link be established between the macro-economic policy framework and the country's investment priorities. Past experience shows that tariff and fiscal policies have given signals which are contrary to declared objectives. As a result, structural anomalies have developed in the pattern of industrial investment. Government must adhere to the declared fiscal and tariff policy framework during the course of the Plan. If this course is adopted, there would be much greater transparency and stability in macro-economic policies. It is also likely to make policy-making much less sensitive to private and sectional interests, as policies would have been decided and announced in advance, rather than correspond to the compulsions of a particular case.

No two economies are alike. In a real sense, India is a special case because of its size, its linguistic and regional heterogeneity, and its history. However, in respect of the quality of state intervention for a regulaton of the activities of the private sector, there is much to be learnt from countries like Japan and Korea. These countries have achieved remarkable success in promoting their industrial development, and in increasing their per capita incomes. Other indicators of development, including social indicators, have improved dramatically. Their experience has been studied comprehensively by a number of researchers.[13] While views on the relative role of different factors in their development efforts differ, it is now generally accepted that state intervention was strong and widely spread in Japan and Korea, and in some other Asian countries which have followed similar strategies. However, unlike India, their intervention was strategic, not detailed. It was also more developmental, less 'preventive' or negative. The state was able to promote activities that were desired. The Indian regulatory system, on the other hand, used its licensing and allocative powers to allocate investment and markets, and to curb competition. In both Japan and Korea, competition was actively encouraged, while in India a virtue was made of fragmenting markets and assigning predetermined market shares to non-competing domestic firms. The preoccupation with details, selectivity, and a case-by-case approach is most evident in relation to policies for export promotion. The Indian system concentrated on identifying products and providing specific amounts of assistance on a case-by-case basis, in an environment which generally favoured domestic production for the domestic market. The Japanese or the Korean system, on the other hand, was concerned with altering the generalized incentive framework in favour of exports, rather than with specific products and specific markets.

In an interesting study on the industrial competitiveness of ten developing countries (namely India, Brazil, Mexico, Korea, Malaysia, Taiwan, Thailand, Singapore, Hongkong and Kenya), Lall (1990) concludes that the main difference between the more successful countries, such as Korea, and the less successful countries, such as India, is to be found in the 'quality' of state intervention. In the two decades of the 1960s and 1970s, the share of factor productivity in the growth of value added was negative in India. In the average developing country, the corresponding figure was 31 per cent. In Korea the share of total factor productivity in output growth was as much as 47 per cent. All the ten countries, with the exception of Hongkong, sought to direct the nature and content of industrial activity. However, while countries like Korea were able to enforce competitive inducements to efficiency, the protected and over-regulated policy environment in India, compounded by slow growth, held back the efficient use of input and improvements in technology.

Interestingly, Lall also found that government interventions, despite their dismal record in many countries, had a vital role to play in promoting industrialization in the ten sample countries. According to him, the formulation of an adequate policy package for developing countries must include—apart from providing corrective incentives for healthy industrial activity—measures to build up human capital, technological activity, and supporting institutions. It is not one set of policies that matters to the exclusion of others, but the complex interaction of incentives, endowments, institutions, and technological effort.

Public Sector, Privatization, Targeting

The government's role as an investor in and manager of public enterprises is probably the most crucial issue for the future. It is also the most controversial and difficult. However, not even the most ardent defender of public enterprises can ignore the substantial inefficiencies that afflict government's management of these enterprises.[14] Nearly half India's commercial public enterprises are making losses. These losses are being met by borrowings or taxation, which reduces the resources available for development. In a recent critique of management failure, P. N. Dhar observes that

> the disabilities of a public-sector enterprise start right from its conception and birth; from the first stage when it is identified, appraised and selected for inclusion in the public investment programme . . . In theory, public-sector enterprises are owned by the people and run in their interest; in practice, they have spawned a number of economic interests and political constituencies which wield formidable power (Dhar, 1989, pp. 14-15).

There are, no doubt, good public enterprises as well as bad—even though all of them face the same political and institutional constraints. But the role of powerful political and other interests in perpetuating the inefficient operation of public enterprises cannot be denied.

As a solution to the problem of public enterprises in developing countries, the 'privatization' of such enterprises in developing countries has attracted a great deal of attention in recent years. In principle, in view of the overextension of public enterprises to all spheres of activity, as well as the limitations on government's capacity to manage them, a good economic case can be made out for privatization of public-sector enterprises. However, as we shall see below, wholesale privatization is not a practical or feasible alternative in India, nor is it likely to provide a viable answer to the problems of management. This does not rule out the sale of sick enterprises if buyers can be found, or the sale of units such as hotels, which are more appropriate outside the ambit of government.

'Privatization' is a term that can be used in many different senses. Ramanadham (1989, p. 62) lists as many as fifteen senses in which this term is used in the literature. These range from 'transition to private legal forms' to partial or complete denationalization or sale of assets. The objectives that privatization is seen to serve also cover a wide ground, including more efficient management of the enterprise, providing resources to government, broadening capital markets, and improving the allocational efficiency of investments (Ramanadham, 1989, p. 419). There is a flourishing literature now on the modalities of effecting privatization, its economic consequences, and the experience of countries which have implemented privatization policies.[15] The thrust to privatization as a policy tool, initiated by Prime Minister Thatcher in the U.K., picked up momentum in developing countries in the second half of the eighties, when a number of countries in Latin America and Africa adopted privatization as a means of solving the resource problems of debt-ridden and loss-making enterprises. In recent years the policy of privatization has also been supported by the World Bank and the IMF as part of their structural adjustment programmes in developing countries.[16]

While the ideological and efficiency arguments for privatization have been advanced vigorously by the proponents of privatization, it needs to be noted that there is no unanimity in the literature on the relationship between ownership *per se* and industrial performance. The experience of privatization in the U.K. has highlighted the importance of competition, rather than private ownership, in improving industrial performance (Kay and Thompson, 1986; Vickers and Yarrow, 1988). The performance of firms under private ownership was not found to be intrinsically superior. There were efficient and inefficient public enterprises, and efficient and inefficient private enterprises. It was found that if product markets were competitive, lower efficiency was penalized by a falling market share and low profits. However, if the environment was uncompetitive, private firms could enjoy high profits without any improvement in efficiency. A competitive environment, rather than ownership, promoted allocative efficiency. Further, the policy environment within which public enterprises operate, as well as their management structure, had more to do with their performance, relative to private enterprises, than the ownership of their assets (Levy, 1981). Nunnenkamp (1986) was unable to detect any statistically significant cross-country relationship between the relative importance of the public sector in GDP and gross fixed investment, employment, and level of industrialization.

There is also no firm evidence that privatization leads to better financial results. Fishlow (1990) has argued that the sale of public enterprises would not help unless the macro-economic environment is improved; and if economic policy is conducted better, then such sales might not be necessary. The sale of the most efficient enterprises may only reduce future net revenue, and a change of ownership alone will not make a crucial difference to the management of loss-making enterprises. It is also a matter of interest that holders of external debt in several Latin American countries have resisted a conversion of their debt into equity of public enterprises. They have preferred to use swaps for more attractive private assets.

The proponents of privatization overstate their case when they invoke ideological or 'allocative efficiency' arguments in favour of privatization. The really persuasive case for privatization is much more mundane, and lies in the limitations of administrative capacity and the inability of the political system to insulate commercial decision-making from political interference. By and large, financial outcomes of enterprise-level decisions are not a part of the 'objective' functions of most governments. Electoral compulsions and extraneous considerations are often the guiding factors in investment and production decisions, and the public sector has provided a relatively autonomous mechanism for the exercise of political patronage and power, with little or no real accountability.[17] Public-sector losses or inefficiencies impose no costs upon those involved in making decisions on behalf of public-sector enterprises. Since budgetary subventions are available to cover the losses, there is no effective compulsion or pressure to improve performance. These factors perhaps explain the reason for the indiscriminate expansion of the public sector in all sectors of the economy, regardless of cost and efficiency considerations, as well as for the continuation of loss-making enterprises in seeming perpetuity.

In India the central government alone controls about 250 public-sector enterprises.[18] This does not include enterprises in the banking and insurance sectors, which are entirely in the public sector, nor 'departmental' enterprises like the railways, posts and telecommunications. The total assets of 244 enterprises at book value were Rs 182,000 crores, and the share capital was about Rs 39,000 crores (see Table 3.1). Most of these enterprises were set up in the sixties and seventies, and the market value of land and replacement value of plant and machinery is likely to be several times higher than their historical cost. On the other hand, despite the impressive growth of capital markets in India in the 1980s, the total capital issues raised in 1989-90 were Rs 2610 crores, of which equity and preference capital was only Rs 504 crores. Total capital raised in a whole year (inclusive of debentures) was thus only 1.1 per cent of the book value of the assets of public-sector enterprises. Given the small size of the capital market in relation to the total assets of the public sector in India, it seems that, except at the margin, the sale of these assets through capital markets is simply not a feasible or practical proposition. The outright sale of only those enterprises which enjoy a monopolistic market or which generate super-normal profits, because of the price policy of the government, would similarly be tantamount to transferring public profits to private pockets, which cannot be justified on economic or social grounds. While the partial sale of equity (with proper valuation) is feasible, public-sector enterprises would in the foreseeable future still largely continue to be under the control of government.[19]

Whatever the merits or flaws of privatization policy, it is clear that solutions to the problems of managing public-sector enterprises have to be found primarily within the framework of public ownership. An important priority for the future is to reduce the managerial role of government in these enterprises, and to make it more consistent with available administrative capacity. It needs to be recognized that the number of decisions that the government has to make on a day-to-day basis needs to be reduced drastically. Given procedural requirements, each decision is likely to take time, involve a large number of steps, and involve a large number of decision-makers, irrespective of the intrinsic importance of a particular decision. The appointment of a chairman or a board of the largest enterprise will take the same amount of time, and involve the same steps and the same number of people, as that of the smallest enterprise. This is the key argument for the 'holding company' concept, i.e. the government should reorganize public-sector enterprises into groups, entrust the management of these enterprises to a holding company, and confine itself to appointments and to setting performance targets for the holding company. There is, however, a danger that if all the companies in a particular product group are under the control of the same holding company, this may strengthen monopolistic behaviour. In order to avoid this possibility, it is better that a number of holding companies be formed, with each of them controlling companies operating in different fields. The reorganization of the public sector along these lines is discussed further in Chapter 5.

Some pruning of the number of public-sector enterprises is a further desirable objective. In view of its different culture, the public sector is particularly ill-equipped to manage service industries and small, labour-intensive operations. In such sectors, a fruitful approach would be to grant management contracts to qualified managers on the basis of profit-sharing arrangements. A part of the shareholding can also be transferred to such managers over a period of time as reward for good performance.

There are three other important policy issues in respect of the public sector that require attention. These relate to personnel policy, financial policy, and the control mechanism over such enterprises.

In regard to personnel policy, a situation has developed in which the appointment of chief executives is subject to the pulls and pressures of various interests. Experience has shown that a number of public enterprises continue to operate without chief executives for considerable periods of time. An entirely new system for the appointment of chief executives, and for the termination of their services, has now become essential. For the appointment of government servants, the system of recruitment through the Union Public Service Commission (UPSC) has been found fairly effective. This system is also relatively free from political pressure. A similar arrangement should be evolved for the appointment of chief executives in public-sector enterprises. A new body, with similar terms of reference as the UPSC, could be created, and its recommendations for the appointment of chief executives taken as final. In other words the discretionary element in respect of such appointments will be significantly reduced, if not eliminated altogether. The termination or renewal of chief executives should also depend entirely on the performance of the enterprise, not on subjective judgement.

As regards financial management, it is important to introduce a 'hard' budget constraint with respect to the operations of public-sector enterprises. Various forms of budgetary and extra-budgetary support to loss-making enterprises must be completely eliminated. This means that the future growth of an enterprise, and its ability to survive, depend on its performance and its ability to finance losses through non-budgetary resources. This aspect is discussed in some detail in Chapter 5. In view of the fiscal crisis, commercial public-sector enterprises should be encouraged to raise fresh capital from the market for further investment. Access to the market will reduce the budgetary burden, without affecting public control of enterprises. A further benefit is that, in respect of profit-making enterprises, additional capital can be raised at a premium. This will reduce the cost of servicing the share capital. A greater dependence on the capital market is likely to provide an incentive to the management for improving the performance of enterprises under their control.

Public-sector enterprises are subject to multiple forms and layers of control. They are subject to ministerial control, parliamentary control, audit control, control by investigating agencies, budgetary control and control by the Bureau of Public Enterprises. With so many layers of control, it is not surprising that the performance of these enterprises in implementing projects and generating surpluses has been so poor. A major overhaul of the control system is therefore necessary. As suggested earlier, the control by administrative ministries should be confined to setting performance targets. Parliamentary control should be exercised only through the Committee on Public Undertakings. This will require a convention to be developed, namely that, except on matters of policy of vital public importance, questions and debates on individual public enterprises will be avoided. All other forms of control should simply be dispensed with. Each public-sector holding company and enterprise should be expected to develop its own internal system for vigilance and other matters, along the lines of normal commercial enterprises. Like these other commercial enterprises, public-sector enterprises should be expected to operate in accordance with the laws applicable to companies, and in accordance with the financial and fiscal regimes that happen to be in force from time to time.

In the light of post-independence experience, a wholly new approach to the management of public enterprises is necessary. The public sector must be made more self-reliant. If allowed to be managed properly, the public sector can contribute to the objectives of accelerating growth, absorbing technology, and providing a countervailing power *vis-à-vis* the private corporate sector. However, this role cannot be fulfilled if the public sector is weak and dependent on dwindling fiscal resources for its growth.

Given the absence of social infrastructure and the abysmal level of social services in the country, there is no option for the government but to assume direct responsibility for providing or augmenting such services in both rural and urban areas. Over time there has been a remarkable expansion of these services, even though per capita availability still remains low. It is also self-evident that, in poor countries, if the poor have to be provided even minimal access, government has to continue to provide these services. The real economic issues in this area are these two: (i) whether the subsidy and the government expenditure involved in the provision of social services can be 'targeted' and confined to the poor; (ii) whether the delivery of these services can be made more cost-effective.

In principle, the targeting of subsidized services to specific beneficiary groups is attractive and should help in reducing the fiscal burden. It also has obvious political appeal because, if it could be implemented, more poverty alleviation would be achieved with less expenditure. However, as pointed out by Kanbur (1988), this ideal solution suffers from severe administrative and informational costs in implementation.[20] In practice it is extremely difficult to confine benefits to the target group because of enumeration and identification problems. A further and perhaps more important problem, in very poor countries, is that although (in a strict statistical sense) the proportion of persons below the poverty line may be 40 or 50 per cent of the population, the proportion of what may be called the 'deserving poor' (or persons perceived to be poor) is closer to 80 or 90 per cent. The latter category includes industrial workers, small subsistence farmers, small shopkeepers, the partially employed, and the like. Their money incomes may be a multiple of the average per capita income, or several times the poverty line figure, but their real consumption levels in absolute terms are still quite low.[21] An acceptable programme of subsidized public services would have to cover this section of the population also, which means that the fiscal savings accruing from 'targeting' becomes relatively small.[22] A better and more fruitful approach for reducing the fiscal burden and the role of government in the provision of social services may be to reduce the 'menu' of subsidized services, and to standardize their quality to a minimum acceptable level.[23]

Controls

The role of government as a regulator of private-sector activity has been the subject of considerable debate in development economics in recent years. India has an all-pervasive system of controls on industrial investment, production, imports, exports, and the prices of key commodities. The control system has been liberalized somewhat in recent years. Also, small-scale industries, agriculture and services are by and large outside the purview of controls. However, in respect of the medium and large-scale industrial sector, foreign trade and foreign investment, the control system still remains extensive and detailed. The principal instruments of control and briefly outlined below.

(a) Industrial Licensing

Investments above a certain financial ceiling require an industrial license from the government, which specifies the list of items that can be produced by the unit and the maximum capacity of the plant. Expansion of the plant and diversification into unconnected production areas also require a license. The license is granted after taking into account domestic demand in the future, existing capacity, foreign-exchange implications, and other factors considered relevant. The industrial licensing system is buttressed by a number of other controls relating to financing, capital issues, and monopolies. All capital issues require government approval, and the financing of projects by financial institutions is subject to government guidelines. The Monopolies and Restrictive Trade Practices (MRTP) Act further regulates the entry and expansion of large firms in new areas.

The impact of the licensing system on India's industrial structure and its efficiency has been one of the most intensely discussed subjects in the literature on the development experience.[24] A number of government committees have also been set up since the mid-sixties to examine the working of the industrial licensing system (Government of India 1964, 1965, 1967, 1969, 1978a and 1979). As a result of these studies and reports, the licensing system has been considerably liberalized in stages since 1973. The reforms have included simplifications in procedure, a relaxation of licensing as a major constraint on the expansion of capacity, the system still has the effect of restricting competition and fragmenting capacity. Together with the tariff policy, which provides high and variable protection across industries, the licensing system remains a major instrument for promoting and protecting inefficient and inward-looking industrial units.

(b) Import and Export Controls

All imports are regulated through the import–export policy, which is announced every three years. During this period, however, the item-wise policy is subject to frequent changes. Exports are also subject to differential forms of regulation (see Chapter 4 for more details on the import-export policy). India's trade policy has been a subject of considerable academic research and study by government committees (Bhagwati and Desai, 1970; Wolf, 1982; Government of India, 1978b, 1984 and 1985a). Like the industrial policy, the trade policy is also highly complex and has been a major instrument of preventing competition and promoting 'inward looking' industrialization.

(c) Price and Distribution Controls

Although the coverage of commodities under price controls has been reduced over time, at present as many as sixty commodities are subject to some form of price control. Among these the important commodities are steel, sugar, fertilizers, drugs, and petroleum products. Steel and fertilizers are also subject to distribution controls. In addition to formal control, the government exercises 'voluntary' or informal control from time to time on certain commodities (e.g. vanaspati and cement). Price and distribution controls have sometimes had the effect of acting as disincentives for the production of essential items (e.g. essential drugs, which are subject to control, while the less essential drugs are exempt), or for increasing the burden of subsidies on the exchequer (e.g. fertilizers, where consumer prices are fixed at a low level but producer prices vary in line with costs).

(d) Financial and Credit Controls

The interest rates of financial institutions and banks are administered rates. On an average, the interest-rate structure has been highly positive in real terms in the 1980s. However, there are large sectors of the economy, particularly agriculture and small industries, where concessional interest rates are applicable. The allocation of credit is also subject to guidelines or policy announced by the government from time to time. Since the entire financial sector is in the public sector, the government exercises formal and informal control over the allocation of financial resources.

(e) Foreign Investment

All foreign investment and collaboration proposals, irrespective of size, are approved by the government. Normally there is a limit of 40 per cent on equity participation. Such investment is allowed in selected areas, subject to the inflow of technology. The rates of royalty payment and collaboration fees are subject to approval by government and the Reserve Bank of India.

(f) Foreign Exchange

All remittances of foreign exchange are regulated by the Reserve Bank of India under the Foreign Exchange Regulation Act (FERA). This Act also regulates the activities of companies with majority foreign holding of equity.

(g) Location, Environment and Labour Legislation

The location of industries is banned in the municipal areas of all towns and cities, as well as in specific areas around the largest twenty cities. The approved location of a new plant is specified in the industrial license. Environmental and pollution control clearance for all projects above a certain size is also mandatory. The rules regarding closure of units, retrenchment of labour, compensation, and sale of assets of a sick unit are governed by a comprehensive set of labour laws. At present there are about 100 regulations at the central and state levels which directly or indirectly affect employment and the retrenchment of labour.

This is a brief outline of the main pillars of the regulatory system. There are, in addition, tariff and excise laws, state laws, and other local regulations designed to influence or direct economic activity. Over the years, the regulatory system has become highly complex, overlapping, discretionary and unstable.

In the fifties the case for government regulation of economic activity had a compelling rationale, which also enjoyed considerable intellectual support among development economists at that time. It was believed that developing economies were characterized by widespread 'market failures', which resulted from structural rigidities and lack of responsiveness to price signals. As a result of these failures, the free-market economy was unable to function in society's interest and direct resources to uses where social rates of return (as distinguished from private rates of return) were high. In view of the savings constraint and scarce resources, it was considered necessary to ensure that allocation of investment, whether in the public or the private sectors, conformed to an overall plan of development and reflected the country's priorities. It was also felt that if resources were to be allocated in response to market signals, the result would be excessive consumption by upper-income groups, along with relative under-investment in sectors which were essential to the accelerated development of the economy.

The choice of instruments for regulating private-sector activity was determined by a strong suspicion that competition was the antithesis of planning. Thus, an important objective of the industrial and trade policies was to prevent 'wasteful' competition.[25] The Second Five Year Plan (1956) declared that 'a comprehensive plan which aims at raising the investment in the economy substantially and has a definite order of priorities in view cannot be seen through on the basis merely of overall fiscal and monetary control' (p. 38). It was, therefore, necessary to employ 'devices like export and import controls, licensing of industries or trades, price controls and allocations which influence and regulate economic activity in particular sectors or sub-sectors of the economy' (p. 38). The wide scope of the regulatory framework was also justified by appealing to certain other worthy objectives of development planning, such as a reduction in regional disparities, ensuring social justice, promoting self-reliance, and protecting the interests of the working classes.

A large number of other developing countries which embarked on the path of planned development at about the same time as India also relied heavily on a variety of controls to direct economic activity in the desired channels. The failure of many of these countries to generate either growth or equity has spawned a substantial neo-classical literature on the adverse economic effects of controls and indiscriminate state intervention. Two well-known contributions to this literature are by Krueger (1974) on 'rent-seeking', and by Bhagwati (1982) on 'directly unproductive profit-seeking (DUP) activities'. Krueger argued that quantitative restrictions on imports, for example, lead to an enormous waste of resources in rent-seeking activities as firms compete for import licenses and their rents. The welfare cost of rent-seeking to society is *in addition* to the standard economic losses on account of policy-induced distortions. Bhagwati (1982) extended the rent-seeking theory to cover directly unproductive profit-seeking activities that arise as a result of competition for rents. Rent-seeking activities (e.g. lobbying) uses up resources that are not available for production. These activities provide financial returns to those who engage in them, while producing no goods and services that enter a conventional social-utility function.

There is certainly a great deal of truth in the Krueger-Bhagwati formulations. A casual observation of economic life in many developing countries, including India, bears this out. However, there are also several problems with their thesis and its generalization. First, the theory does not explain why India and other developing countries failed to grow for almost a century under non-interventionist colonial states. Nor does it explain why developing countries registered an unprecedented growth for thirty years, between 1950 and 1980, under highly interventionist regimes. Second, as Fishlow (1990) has pointed out, 'no one has yet shown that the failure of government intervention *necessarily* outweighs market failure. On the contrary, effective state action is widely regarded as an underlying feature of successful outward-oriented Asian economic performance' (p. 66). There have been 'implementation failures', which need to be corrected, but this does not establish a case for laissez faire. Third, DUP activity is not the only distortion of free markets that occur. For example, world markets can be strongly oligopolistic, and the transfer of technologies may be highly restricted. Fourth, the rent-seeking literature seems better at explaining failures after these occur than in predicting the outcome of policies. As Stiglitz (1991) points out:

> How do we explain why alleged rent-seeking behaviour interferes with economic efficiency in Pakistan, but has much less deleterious effects in Korea; why corruption in Korea was a problem in some periods and not in others . . . why was there 'regulatory capture' in some states, in some industries and not in others?' (p. 139).

The rent-seeking theories seem to err in not being able to distinguish between different kinds of intervention, and in not recognizing the presence of externalities and the positive effects that selective and purposive intervention can have in exploiting these opportunities. The primary failure in several developing countries, including India, has been in implementation and in the tacit assumption that the state had an unlimited capacity to intervene. The direction for the future lies in changing the 'form' of intervention, and in limiting its scope to strategic and selected areas consistent with available administrative and managerial capacity. Some of the possible lines of reform within the regulatory framework in respect of the external sector are discussed in a subsequent chapter. Here, we briefly examine the changes that deserve to be introduced in the industrial licensing system.

It is well recognized and documented that the industrial licensing system has not achieved its avowed purpose (see Mohan and Aggarwal, 1990, and reports of committees set up by Government of India, cited earlier). Even as ardent a supporter of planning as Paranjape, who was a member of the Industrial Licensing Policy Enquiry Committee of 1969, says: 'in respect of licensing, the Committee has firmly concluded that the system had failed practically on all counts, whether it was regional dispersal, import substitution, or the prevailing concentration of economic power. Licensing could not even ensure the development of industries mainly according to Plan priorities.'[26] Raj (1986) observes: 'The industrial licensing system, as it grew over a period of nearly three decades, had accumulated much fat and filth. It had ceased to perform effectively most of the functions it was designed for earlier; it had become a major source of political and bureaucratic corruption . . . ' (p. 25). The adverse economic effects of the licensing system in fragmenting capacity, preventing competition and discouraging exports have similarly been recognized by other experts and government committees. The one positive result has been to ensure guaranteed domestic markets to investors. This is likely to have contributed to an increase in the rate of investment in the industrial sector by reducing 'risks'.[27]

The reform of the licensing system has to take cognizance of industrial priorities in the 1990s. In view of the balance-of-payments situation, the first priority is to ensure that industrial activity leads to a reduction in the trade deficit. The structure of industrial incentives has to be tilted in favour of exports, as against imports, for the domestic market. Second, in view of the overall savings constraint, the balance of advantage has to shift in favour of less capital-intensive projects. Third, in view of the resource constraint in the public sector, the ability of the public sector to provide subsidies to the rest of the industrial sector is limited (either in the form of supply of below-cost inputs or direct government subsidies). The question is whether these and other priorities of industrial policy in the nineties can be more efficiently achieved through the licensing system, or through an alternative intervention mechanism which relies more heavily on monetary, fiscal and financial instruments.

No unique or universally valid answer to this question is possible. The answer depends on the context. In the Indian context, and taking into account past experience, the limitation of administrative capacity, and political changes that are taking place,[28] my view is that the time has come to dispense with the industrial licensing system altogether. In its place, fiscal and financial instruments should be used more aggressively to achieve the objectives of industrial policy. As argued in Chapter 4, import policy and tariff policy can be used to shift the incentive structure in favour of exports. Tariff policy should also be re-oriented to reduce effective rates of protection for capital-intensive and import-intensive domestic production. This can be done, for example, by raising the rates of nominal protection on inputs and equalizing it with the rate of tariff on finished products.

The excise duty is a potent instrument for discouraging domestic demand. The excise-duty structure should be re-oriented in favour of labour-intensive production, and against capital-intensive or luxury production.[29] Similarly, the interest-rate structure should discriminate more actively in favour of exports and labour-intensive production. It is true that none of these, and for that matter any other, financial and fiscal instruments will generate a perfect fit between actual production and predetermined Plan targets. However, these instruments are likely to be more efficient, less discriminatory, and more flexible in guiding the allocation of resources. To the extent that they also reduce the scope for rent-seeking and unproductive profit-seeking activities, that would be an additional gain.

Conclusion

The role of government in development has to be redefined, not 'ended'.[30] As I.G. Patel has pointed out:

> It is not an accident that all countries that are held up as examples of successful development in recent years are by and large activists or interventionists in the economic sphere. This has been true as much of Japan as of South Korea, Taiwan and Singapore as indeed it was true in the last century of the United States, Germany and France (Patel, 1985, p. 14).

An important question for the future relates to the 'quality' of state intervention. As recent research has shown, Indian methods of intervention were much less efficient than, say, those in Korea, Japan and Taiwan. These countries were highly interventionist, but their intervention reinforced competitiveness and efficiency, while India's tended to impede the efficient use of resources. An improvement in the quality of state intervention must remain high on the agenda for the 1990s.

Notes

1. Even today, the Bank, which is otherwise a strong champion of free enterprise and market forces, does not lend without a government guarantee!
2. See Bardhan (1988), pp. 63-7, for a brief review of the literature. *The Journal of Economic Perspectives*, Summer 1990, contains a symposium on the 'State and Economic Development', with articles by Datta-Chaudhuri, Albert Fishlow, Westphal and Anne Krueger, among others. See also Srinivasan (1985).
3. At the end of the 1980s, the mood in the U.S.A. seems to have shifted slowly again in favour of more active government involvement. An early pointer is a cover story in *Time* magazine bemoaning the 'death' of government in America. See 'Is Government Dead? Unwilling to lead, politicians are letting

America slip into paralysis', *Time*, North American edition, 23 October 1989.

4. Both interviews by President Perez and Prime Minister Gonzalez are in *Time*, North American edition, 23 October 1989, pp. 50 and 54. A report on President Kaunda's speech to his party's annual meeting on the 'disastrous' economic results of past policies on Zambia's economy appeared in *Financial Times*, London, 14 November 1989, p. 8. Zambia has now embarked on a programme of liberalization.
5. *World Development Report*, 1989.
6. It is, of course, true that different countries with similar degrees of intervention and similar instruments of control have ended up showing very different results. There are also instances of the same country showing different results during different periods of its history, even though the extent of state intervention has remained broadly the same. It is likely that success or failure in particular cases, and during different periods of time in the same country, had more to do with the *type* and quality of state intervention rather than the *level* or the quantity of that intervention.
7. Bardhan (1988) has argued that the Indian example suggests that the state is much more powerful than is visualized in the Marxian or neo-classical political economy of class or pressure-group politics. 'In many developing countries, the State controls the "commanding heights" of the economy, owning a large part of the non-agricultural economy and regulating the flow of credit, foreign exchange, and investment licenses. To a large extent it can play one class against another, local capital against foreign, one transnational company against another, all for the purpose of furthering its own goals' (p. 65).
8. Nandy (1989) has analysed the growth of state power in India in a wider political and sociological perspective. Describing the Indian state as 'the hegemonic actor in the public realm', he says that

> Not only have the last forty years created an enormous vested interest in the concept, but almost the whole of modern India has come to see the nation-state as the only valid, possible concept of the state, as an institution that should have absolute priority over all other aspects of Indian civilization. The nation-state has acquired enough

clout to resist all demands of Indian society that clash with the needs of the state. The society is now required, in every instance, to adjust to the state (p. 5).

9. There is a substantial literature on planning and recent experience. For a comprehensive review of the planning experience, particularly in Latin America, see articles by Anglade and Fortin (1987), de Mattos (1987) and others in *CEPAL Review*, no. 31, United Nations Economic Commission for Latin American and the Caribbean, Santiago, Chile.
10. For a recent critique of Indian planning, see Gupta (1989). Also, Sundrum (1987), for a review of the planning process and its impact on development. The strengths and weaknesses of the planning process and India's planning experience were also the subject of a conference on 'The State and Development Planning in India', organized by the School of Oriental and African Studies, University of London, April 1989. Papers presented at this conference covered the historical and political dimensions of planning in India, as well as the technical and sectoral issues. A book containing these papers is being edited by Terry Byres, forthcoming from Delhi, Oxford University Press.
11. Dandekar, cited in Sundrum (1987).
12. See Mohan and Aggarwal (1990) for an account of the history of controls in India. They point out that the form and content of much of the control and regulatory apparatus governing Indian industry is based on the Defence of India Rules promulgated in 1939 under the Defence of India Act, which was brought into force after the outbreak of World War II. Most of the control legislation, for example, the Foreign Exchange Regulation Act (FERA), the Imports and Export (Control) Act, the Capital Issues Control Act, which affect industrial investment, was already in place before 1950. The legislative framework remains broadly unchanged even now.
13. For reviews of the Korean experience, see World Bank Country study (1987), Datta-Chaudhuri (1990), and Westphal (1990). In an interesting paper, Chakravarty (1987b) examined the Korean case from a Marxian perspective. He found that while growth was rapid, there were several contradictory characteristics of the Korean experience which could pose a problem in the future. Among these characteristics were: a high level of external indebtedness, relatively high inflation, and low per-

sonal savings. Chakravarty's study was apparently based on data upto the early 1980s. Since then, there has been a remarkable transformation in the Korean situation. External indebtedness has declined sharply (from about $ 46 billion in 1985 to $ 31 billion in 1988). The debt service ratio has declined from 24 per cent to 16 per cent during the same period. Personal savings have jumped to 30 per cent of GNP in 1988. Wholesale prices have been stable, showing a total increase of less than 4 per cent during the five-year period 1984-8.

14. Public-sector commercial enterprises of the central government earned a net profit of 4.5 per cent on capital employed in 1989-90, and paid a dividend of only Rs 311 crores, which was less than 1 per cent of the total share capital. For a review of the operating and financial performance of public enterprises, see Rao and Madhavi Latha (1990).
15. See Aharoni (1986) for a survey of the literature. Ramanadham (1989) and Cook and Kirkpatrick (1988) provide surveys of the issues and the experience of several developing countries with privatization. Levy (1981) and Nunnenkamp (1986) provide econometric and statistical evidence regarding privatization in developing countries. Also see the special issue of *World Development*, vol. 17, no. 5 May 1989, on privatization.
16. According to Kirkpatrick (1989), out of the forty structural adjustment programmes of the World Bank between 1980 and 1986, 73 per cent called for some action in the area of public-sector financial performance. The emphasis in these programmes was on deregulation and competition, rather than on divestiture. However, in more recent programmes, the World Bank has endorsed the policy of privatization as a specific policy objective.
17. There is, of course, a whole paraphernalia of rules and procedures for ensuring 'legal' (as distinguished from 'real') accountability. However, these rules and procedures have seldom provided an effective check against the arbitrary, and often whimsical, exercise of administrative and political discretion.
18. See Iyer (1991) and Reddy (1989) for a discussion of issues relating to the public sector, including privatization, in India.
19. An alternative to the domestic sale of assets is the sale of assets to foreign investors. Apart from the fact that, in India, this is likely to be politically unacceptable (except in a rare case), the economic case for doing so is also not clear. Foreign sales are

likely to be feasible only in highly profitable and protected areas, where the rates of return are high. These are also the areas where economic costs of foreign sales of assets will outweigh the gain (see Chapter 4).

20. Also see Pinstrup-Andersen (1988).
21. In India, in urban areas, the poverty line is defined in terms of a per capital consumption level of Rs 1600 per annum at 1985-6 prices. The average per capita wages of a public-sector employee is about Rs 30,000 per annum.
22. An interesting case of 'targeting' in the face of large numbers occurred in Sri Lanka. A general subsidy on rice was converted into a food stamp programme available to the poorer half of the population—and later inflation was allowed to erode the real value of the stamps. This solution involved obvious social and political costs.
23. Mexico has experimented with a programme to limit the 'menu' of food subsidies. Before 1983, subsidies were extended to most food items. After 1987, subsidies have been confined to sugar, tortillas and maize flatcakes, which are the staple of the poor. Two other programmes—for subsidized milk and subsidized rural food stores—were expanded. See World Bank (1988).
24. A comprehensive analysis of the licensing system and its economic effects is available in Bhagwati and Desai (1970). For more recent reviews, see Mohan and Aggarwal (1990) and Kelkar, *et al* (1990).
25. Mulji (1990) quotes an interesting passage from Jawaharlal Nehru's letters, where Nehru extolled the virtues of the First Soviet Plan, and observed that 'Under capitalism all [these] activities are left to individual initiative and chance, and owing to competition there is a waste of effort. There is no co-ordination between different producers or different sets of workers' (p. 129).
26. The report of the Industrial Licensing Policy Enquiry Committee (ILPIC), 1969, however, recommended continuation of the licensing regime despite the recognition that the system had led to a pre-emption of capacities and several other inefficiencies.
27. The evidence, however, is by no means conclusive. Several fast-growing countries were able to generate high rates of industrial investment without resorting to licensing.
28. See the Introduction.

29. One problem in curbing demand through high tariffs and excise duties is the possibility that it opens up smuggling. This, however, is also true of the licensing system, combined with high tariffs. The advantage of using excise duties in place of the licensing system is that excess domestic profits would accrue to the exchequer.
30. The article by F. Fukuyama, 'The End of History? (published in *National Interest*, vol. 16, 1989, Washington, D.C.) is the latest in the genre of papers of eschatology, or what one writer has called 'endism'. Fukuyama's paper has attracted a great deal of attention among political scientists and historians.

Table 3.1
CONSOLIDATED BALANCE SHEET OF 244 PUBLIC ENTERPRISES, AND CAPITAL RAISED BY NON-GOVERNMENT COMPANIES

I. Balance Sheet of Public Enterprises (31 March 1990)
(Rs crores)

Liabilities		*Assets*	
(a) Share Capital	38,957	(a) Fixed Assets	82,452
(b) Loans	60,358	(b) Investments	11,129
(c) Cash credit and short-term Advances	13,948	(c) Current and Other Assets	75,965
(d) Current liabilities & provisions	41,368	(d) Deficit	12,873
TOTAL	182,419	TOTAL	182,419

II. Capital Raised By Non-Government Companies 1989-90
(Rs crores)

(a) Equity and preference shares	504
(b) Debentures	2106
TOTAL	2610

SOURCE : Government of India, *Public Enterprises Survey*, 1989-90, vol. 1, and Reserve Bank of India, *Report on Currency and Finance*, 1989-90.

4

Towards Balance of Payments Viability

Since the beginning of the Second Five Year Plan, India has experienced balance-of-payments problems of varying intensity in twenty-nine out of thirty-five years.[1] Yet a viable strategy to tackle this problem has eluded India's planners. During the same period a number of developing countries, which started more or less with the same degree of industrialization and income level as India, have achieved remarkable success in increasing the share of manufacturing in total output and generating surpluses in their balance of payments. The cost for India has been heavy. Periodic crises have upset the planning process and reduced the room for manoeuvrability in fashioning macro-economic policies in response to the changing domestic and international environment. These crises have also increased the country's dependence on external capital markets and increased the country's vulnerability to external shocks. The conflict in the Gulf, which lasted for no more than six months, has amply demonstrated the fragility of the macro-economic balance in India after forty years of planning. A fresh look at the strategy to deal with the balance of payments is now needed.

In order to derive lessons for the future, it is useful to look at the nature of the balance-of-payments problem in the past, and the reasons why it has proved so difficult to find a lasting solution.

A Review of the Balance of Payments, 1956-7 to 1989-90

The period since 1956-7 can be divided into three sub-periods, depending on the nature of the balance-of-payments problem, the overall macro-economic environment, and the external aid situation. The three sub-periods are: 1956-7 to the 1975-6 (Period I) 1976-7 to 1979-80 (Period II) and 1980-1 to the present (Period III). Periods I and III were characterized by persistent balance-of-payments problems. However, there were important differences in the macro-economic environment, particularly in the fiscal situation. Period I was also characterized by large inflows of aid on concessional terms, while Period III saw a large recourse to commercial loans and a substantial increase in external debt. During Period II, which was relatively brief, there was a substantial improvement in the balance-of-payments and foreign-exchange-reserve position.[2] Table 4.1 provides the relevant macro-economic data for the three periods. In what follows, I concentrate on Period III (1980-1 to the present). A brief review of the macro-economic environment and balance of payments in the earlier periods has been undertaken primarily with a view to highlight the differences with the present situation.

(a) 1956-7 to 1975-6 (Period I)

The entire period was very difficult for India's balance of payments, partly because of slow export growth in relation to import requirements, and partly because of adverse external factors. This period was marked by three wars (in 1962 with China, in 1965 and 1971 with Pakistan), several droughts (including the disastrous droughts of 1965-6 and 1966-7) and the first oil shock in 1973. Despite tight import controls (through quantitative restrictions) and foreign-exchange regulations, the current-account deficit was 1.8 per cent of GDP. Foreign-exchange reserves were at a low level, generally less than necessary to cover three months' imports. Almost the entire current-account deficit (92 per cent) was financed by inflows of external assistance on highly concessional terms. There was hardly any commercial debt.

A striking feature of this period was fiscal conservatism. The fiscal deficit (of centre, states and union territories) constituted less than 6 per cent of GDP (as against

10.5 per cent of GDP in 1989-90, see below). The conservative fiscal policy also had implications for monetary policy. The average rate of growth of money supply was only 11 per cent (as compared with 19.4 per cent in 1989-90). The rate of inflation was also relatively low (6.7 per cent). A notable feature was the increase in public savings from 1.9 per cent in 1956-7 to 4.2 per cent in 1975-6. The average annual growth rate of GDP was, however, only 3.9 per cent during the period. There was also a significant increase in the capital–output ratio, partly because of low productivity and partly because of a shift in the structure of investment to more capital-intensive sectors.

(b) 1976-7 to 1979-80 (Period II)

These stand out as the golden years for India's balance of payments. There was a small current-account surplus (0.6 per cent of GDP on average) and foreign-exchange reserves equivalent to about seven months' imports. The export growth was good, but the primary reason for the sharp improvement in balance of payments was a dramatic improvement in net invisibles (mainly on account of remittances). Net invisibles increased from a paltry Rs 193 crores in 1974-5 to Rs 2486 crores in 1979-80.[3] The increase in foreign assets led to a substantial acceleration in the growth of money supply during the period (about 20 per cent per annum). However, the rate of inflation was surprisingly low. Excluding the drought year of 1979-80, the rate of inflation was barely 5 per cent per annum. Fiscal deficits, as a percentage of GDP, were also moderate (about 7 per cent on an average).

This period also saw the beginnings of a slow process of industrial and import liberalization. The import policy was gradually relaxed, and a greater 'automaticity' was introduced in the policy relating to the imports of raw materials and components for domestic production. The most important change in import policy was introduced in 1978-9, when all items not specifically restricted or banned were listed under an Open General Licence category; these could be freely imported for domestic production.[4] There were also some changes in the industrial licensing system which facilitated an expansion of output in important sectors (such as cement). The exemption limit for the requirement of an industrial licence was raised from Rs 1 crore (of investment in plant and machinery) to Rs 3 crores.[5]

The payments situation, however, changed significantly in 1979-80 because of the second oil shock and the deterioration in India's terms of trade. The full impact of the increase in oil prices was reflected in the trade balance in 1980-1. The trade deficit increased from Rs 2200 crores in 1978-9 to Rs 3400 crores in 1979-80, and further to Rs 6200 crores in 1980-1 (see Table 4.2).[6] The impact of the increase in the trade deficit on reserves was also moderate, because of the increase in remittances and net invisibles in 1979-80.[7]

(c) 1980-1 to 1989-90 (Period III)

In 1981 India entered into an arrangement with the IMF for a loan of SDR 5 billion under the Extended Fund Facility (EFF). The amount was to be disbursed over a three-year period. India, however, drew only SDR 3.9 billion and the arrangement was terminated in early 1984, at India's request, because of the improvement in the balance-of-payments position in 1983-4. The IMF loan helped to maintain reserves at a comfortable level in the first half of the eighties, even though the current-account deficit had increased after 1979-80. There was also a sharp increase in the indigenous production of oil, which reduced the growth in total imports. Domestic production of crude oil increased from 16.2 million tonnes in 1981-2 to 29.0 million tonnes in 1984-5. As a result, the share of domestic production in meeting consumption requirements rose from a little under 50 per cent to 75 per cent in 1984-5. The overall volume growth of imports during 1982-5 was only 2 per cent. However, exports were also sluggish and showed a growth rate of only 3.2 per cent during 1982-5.[8]

Another important feature of this period was the gradual decline in net receipts from invisibles.[9] As the trade deficit (on payments basis) was also rising sharply during the period, the contribution of net invisibles in financing the deficit declined, leading to a greater dependence on inflows of external capital. Thus, net invisibles, which financed nearly half of the trade deficit during 1981-2 to 1984-5, contributed only 20 per cent to meeting the financing requirements in 1988-9 and 1989-90 (Tables 4.2 and 4.3).

The eighties were also marked by a reduction in flows of concessional assistance to India, principally from the World Bank Group. The credits from the International Development Association (IDA) on soft terms declined, while loans from the World Bank on market terms increased sharply. As a result, the average interest rate on India's official debt increased from 2.4 per cent in 1980 to 6.1 per cent in 1982. Since World Bank loans are on a variable interest linked to market rates, the average interest rates on official loans to India have fluctuated since then (it was 5.6 per cent in 1989). The average maturity of loans declined from 40.8 years in 1980 to 32.6 years in 1982 and 24.4 years in 1989. The hardening of terms had an important impact on India's debt-service obligations on multilateral loans after 1985 (although the terms were hardened in 1981-2, the impact on debt service was felt later in view of the grace period on loans). The debt service payments on multilateral loans tripled from $ 371 million in 1984 to $ 1106 million in 1989.[10]

The large current-account deficit, particularly after 1984-5, was financed by substantial inflows of capital by way of commercial borrowings and deposits by non-resident Indians. Total external debt outstanding increased from $ 18.7 billion in 1980 to $ 26.5 billion in 1984, and to $ 56.3 billion in 1989 (or from about 10.8 per cent of GNP in 1980 to 21.5 per cent in 1989). The increase in debt to private creditors, including commercial banks and non-residents, was even more dramatic. Outstanding debt to private creditors increased from $ 2.3 billion in 1980 to $ 7.4 billion in 1984, and to $ 22.8 billion in 1989.[11] The increase in external debt has also sharply raised the debt-service ratio during the period. Debt service, as a percentage of exports of goods and services, increased from 9.1 per cent in 1980 to 18.1 per cent in 1984, and further to 26.3 per cent in 1989.

A major difference in the nature of the balance-of-payments problems in Periods I and III lies in the change in the sources of financing. In the earlier period almost the entire deficit was financed through inflows of concessional assistance, which kept the debt-servicing burden low. In Period III, almost the entire incremental deficit (in dollar terms) was financed through non-concessional loans on market-related terms. It is striking that total disbursements of loans on concessional terms (from multilateral and bilateral sources) to India in 1989 was almost exactly the same as in 1982 ($ 1.5 billion in both years).[12] This reflects the changing environment for development assistance, and the erosion in the commitment of industrialized countries and multilateral institutions to what was once referred to as a 'partnership in development'.[13]

Another important difference is that, in contrast to Period I, the macro-economic policy in Period III was highly expansionary. The combined fiscal deficit of centre and states was continuously rising, and reached 10.5 per cent of GDP in 1989-90 (it was less than 6 per cent in Period I). The average growth of money supply was 17 per cent (despite a substantial increase in the cash-reserve ratio). The ratio of domestic savings to GDP remained stagnant at around 21 per cent throughout the eighties. The rate of inflation averaged 8.2 per cent.

Period III was, however, marked by a significant acceleration in economic growth, particularly industrial growth. The rate of growth of national income in Period III was 5.6 per cent. There was acceleration in industrial growth, particularly after 1984-5. Industrial growth averaged more than 8 per cent per annum for the five-year period for the first time after thirty years.

An issue which crops up in a discussion of India's present problems is the extent to which the import and industrial liberalization of the 1980s has been responsible for the current crisis. Those in support of this view argue that imports have increased rather sharply in the second half of the eighties in rupee terms (see Tables 4.4 and 4.5).[14] According to this view, the surge in imports was facilitated by import and industrial liberalization. Those who hold the opposite view, on the other hand, argue that the import-intensity of domestic production in India has not really increased, and the ratio of imports to GDP has hovered around 8 to 9 per cent during the period 1985-90.[15] Imports have increased because growth has been faster. After allowing for the depreciation of the rupee, the average rate of growth in imports was 3.4 per cent per annum (in SDR terms). The growth rate of non-oil imports was 7.1 per cent per annum. This was mainly on account of a faster growth in export-related imports in 1988-9 and 1989-90, when exports were buoyant. Miscellaneous (or 'other') imports also increased, but they constitute a small proportion of total imports (see Table 4.6).

On the face of it, the latter view is supported by statistical evidence. It is also a fallacy to believe that the mere presence of bureaucratic controls and elaborate licensing procedures would have reduced the rate of growth of imports (assuming the rate of growth of industrial production to have remained the same). In India there was very little liberalization of imports which competed with domestic industry or consumer goods.[16] Import and industrial liberalization took the form of some reduction in administrative and discretionary controls. It is unlikely that a tighter or quota-based system of import allocations would have reduced the growth of imports, as long as such imports were required as inputs into domestic production.[17] Yet the fact remains that India has imported more than what could be supported by its own exports, other receipts, and normal aid flows. The growth in imports was financed by commercial borrowings or other borrowings on hard terms. This could be sustained only as long as such loans were freely available. The economy was plunged into a crisis as soon as these sources of finance dried up. The roots of the crisis, therefore, do not lie in import liberalization *per se*, but in the overall framework of macro-economic policies, including the fiscal policy, which permitted an expansion of internal demand for the home market without generating adequate exports during a period when the external environment for aid to India was deteriorating. Such liberalization as there was, was 'inward looking', and the higher growth of the domestic economy was financed by external loans on hard terms. This has proved to be a mistake.

In some respects the present situation in India has some similarities with the situation which prevailed in several heavily indebted Latin American countries at the beginning of the eighties.[18] The crisis has been brought about by an excessive dependence of the economy on 'new money' from commercial sources which are not forthcoming. India's total debt and debt-servicing burden in relation to the size of its economy is, at present, substantially lower than that of the heavily indebted Latin American countries at the beginning of the 1980s. However, as a proportion of exports, the ratios are similar. Further, India has a large trade deficit. Latin American countries, such as Mexico, Brazil and Venezuela, on the other hand, had a trade surplus, even though the current account was in deficit on account of interest payments. The fiscal crisis in India is also similar in nature to that of several heavily indebted countries in Latin America.

An important question that needs to be answered is: why was action not taken earlier to anticipate the crisis and prevent it emerging? The available published documents show that the emerging balance-of-payments scenario, and the consequences of high fiscal deficits and commercial borrowings, had in fact been anticipated by the government for quite a long time. Since 1983-4 when the balance-of-payments situation was quite comfortable the Economic Surveys of the ministry of finance have been highlighting the likelihood of a difficult balance-of-payments situation in the second half of the 1980s, and the need to reduce the reliance on commercial borrowings for financing consumption and low-productivity domestic investments. Thus, the Survey for 1983-4 observed that

> India has been able to avoid debt problems of the type witnessed in several other developing countries because of prudent management of the foreign-exchange situation . . . Commercial borrowing and IMF financing used in the Sixth Plan have already added to the debt-service profile of the country and it would be unwise to stretch it much further (Economic Survey 1983-4, p. 75).

A similar assessment of the situation was contained in the Economic Survey for 1984-5. The Economic Surveys of subsequent years also continued to highlight the need for reducing fiscal deficits, containing external commercial borrowings, and improving the trade balance.

The budget speeches of finance ministers during this period reflect a similar concern about the emerging balance-of-payments problem. For example, while presenting the budget for 1985-6, the finance minister observed:

> some of the factors that have worked in our favour in the Sixth Plan will not operate with the same vigour in the Seventh Plan. Oil production, which had increased by about 18 million tonnes during the last five years, may not increase at the same rate in the future. Repayments of the International Monetary Fund loan and external commercial borrowings would also increase sharply . . . There can be little doubt that if we have to reconcile a manageable balance-of-payments situation with a tolerable debt profile, export earnings would have to finance a larger and larger proportion of our imports so that the deficit in our balance of payments is reduced (Government of India, 1990, p. 539).

By the end of 1987 the balance-of-payments situation had become quite difficult. In his budget speech for 1988-9 the finance minister pointed out:

> as anticipated, the balance-of-payments situation has been under strain because of several factors. These include higher imports of edible oils and pulses, increase in imports of crude oil and petroleum products, increasing protectionist tendencies abroad, and an unfavourable climate for official development assistance . . . India has followed

a prudent policy in debt management and has avoided problems of the kind faced by several other developing countries. We remain committed to ensuring long-term viability in our balance of payments. (Government of India, 1990, p. 584).[19]

The reasons why the actual evolution of the balance-of-payments policy has been other than planned lie in the political economy and the growing uncertainty of electoral politics in India after 1983-4. The impact of political factors in determining economic policy during this period has been analysed by Rubin (1985), Kochanek (1985), Harriss (1987) and Kohli (1989), among others. Their analysis suggests that there were three factors which greatly influenced the course of economic policy in the eighties. The first was the rise of populism after 1983-4. A number of new expenditure programmes were introduced in the name of the landless, the rural poor, the urban poor and the homeless. Despite rising fiscal deficits and declining public-sector surpluses, Plan investments were increased sharply and a large number of new projects started in different parts of the country. After the elections in late 1984, and the massive electoral victory of the party in power, for a couple of years government policy seemed to move away from populism. However, the situation changed once again after the loss of the state elections in Haryana in May 1987.

A second factor has been the role of the domestic industrial establishment in the 'dominant coalition'. This was reflected in industrial and import liberalization of a type which encouraged domestic production for the protected home market, without any threat of external competition or any reduction in tariff protection. Access to imports was made liberal, but only in respect of those items which were not produced at home. In fact there is evidence that effective protection increased in respect of products manufactured indigenously (Kelkar *et al.*, 1990). External commercial borrowings were permitted liberally to meet foreign-exchange requirements of capital-intensive investments. Commercial borrowings became a substitute for domestic savings to finance low-productivity investments, with no export potential, in public and private sectors. Finally, the middle classes were the major beneficiaries of the industrial and consumer boom in the second half of the eighties. These sections, which included educated professionals in the public and private sectors, were influential in determining the course of public policy. Their influence was, for example, reflected in substantial and periodic increases in the exemption limits for income tax and a further narrowing of the base of direct taxes. Excise duties on consumer durables, electronics and automobiles, etc. were also kept at a relatively low level, which encouraged the setting up of new units with a high import content, and high rates of effective protection.

As the severity of the balance-of-payments problems became evident, an effort was made to increase exports, after 1987. These efforts succeeded to some extent. However, the current-account deficit and financing requirements could not be reduced, as imports, particularly of crude oil, also increased. After late 1988, effective action to reduce fiscal and trade deficits was further thwarted by electoral concerns (as the general elections were expected) and political uncertainties.

Review of Export Performance and the Trade Regime*

India's trade regime and export performance have been the subject of a number of studies. Singh (1964), Nayyar (1976) and Wolf (1982) provide an account of the evolution of exports and trade policies in the 1950s, 1960s and 1970s, respectively. Panchamukhi (1978) examines India's overall trade and trade policy from a theoretical point of view. Ahluwalia (1986) and Rangarajan (1990) deal with development in India's balance of payments since the mid-seventies. There is also the pioneering work by Bhagwati

* This section is mainly descriptive. Readers who are familiar with India's export performace and trade regime may like to skip this section.

and Dèsai (1970) which provides interesting insights into the impact of India's trade policy on the pattern of industrialization and the actual implementation of policies. International institutions, particularly the World Bank, have carried out several studies with a view to making recommendations for policy reform.[20] On the basis of these studies, it is possible to briefly summarize those aspects of India's trade performance, incentive structure and control mechanism which are relevant in future formulations of policy.

(a) Export Performance

India's long-run export performance has been poor in comparison to that of other developing countries, and also in relation to the growth of world trade. India's share of total world exports declined from 0.98 per cent in 1965 to only 0.45 per cent in 1988, and its share of world manufacturing exports declined from 0.65 per cent in 1965 to around 0.4 per cent in 1988. (In a comparative study of the export performance of thirteen countries during 1965-80, Agarwal (1988) found that India was the only country, apart from Pakistan, which saw a reduction in her share of manufactured exports even to developing countries.) Export performance was particularly dismal in the period immediately after the second oil shock of 1979. For the period 1979/80–1985/86, total exports grew around 0.4 per cent per annum, while manufactured exports grew around 1.2 per cent per annum, and primary exports actually declined at around 0.7 per cent per annum. [21] After 1985-6, upto 1989-90, export growth picked up due to a number of policy initiatives taken by the government. The overall growth of exports was about 15 per cent per annum, with manufactured and primary exports growing at 20 per cent per annum and 6 per cent per annum respectively. The stagnation of exports during the period 1979-80 to 1985-6 is one of the important factors which explain the emergence of an acute balance-of-payments crisis towards the end of the 1980s. During that period India enjoyed the advantage of a sharp increase in domestic oil production. It had also borrowed SDR 3.9 billion from the IMF, and was benefiting from the boom in the Middle East because of the increase in workers' remittances. In the second half of the eighties, oil production and workers' remittances did not increase much, and the IMF loan had to be repaid. The higher export growth during this period was not sufficient to make up for the stagnation in exports during the earlier period.

The decline in India's share of world exports in textiles provides an interesting case history of the policy-induced anti-export bias in India's trade policy. India was the earliest among the developing countries to have a thriving indigenous textile industry. The industry is labour intensive, and India's low wages in the clothing sector should have provided a natural comparative advantage in exports. The evolution of India's textile exports has been examined in detail in a recent study by Misra (1991). Even as late as 1971-4, India's share in world markets for textiles and clothing exports was the same as that of China (4.5 per cent). Korea's share was 7.7 per cent and that of Pakistan only 1.7 per cent. By 1983-6, China's share increased to as much as 14.6 per cent and that of Korea to 13.6 per cent. Other developing-countries, like Pakistan, Thailand and Hongkong, also increased their shares substantially. India was the only country among major developing-country exporters, whose share actually fell from 4.5 per cent to 3.8 per cent during this period. India's value of textile and clothing exports in 1986 were only two-thirds of the value required to just maintain its market share in 1971.[22]

India was unable to maintain her already low market share in the world's exports of textiles between 1971 and 1986, partly due to the fact that it exported relatively stagnant items (cotton textiles instead of man-mades) to relatively stagnant markets (quota instead of non-quota markets). It is well known that India's policy had a distinct bias against the competitive manufacture of man-made fibres or of their imports for export production. Other factors which inhibited India's exports were the high costs of manufacture and non-price factors, such as reliability and quality. Misra also found that demand-side factors had, at best, a very marginal role to play in India's poor export performance in textiles and clothing. The phenomenal export growth of other Asian textile producers was due to their conscious policy of strengthening international competitiveness and their exploitation of the shifting comparative advantage in world textiles and clothing manufacture. India's failure to maintain its initial advantage in textile exports illustrates the role of 'micro-economic' policies in inhibiting exports success, in addition to the macro-economic policy environment.

(b) Export Profitability and Protection

India has an extensive system of incentives for exports. These include the Cash Compensatory Support (CCS), a duty drawback on customs duty and excise duty paid on inputs, replenishment licenses for imports (REP), a tax exemption on export profit, and credit subsidies. The data compiled by the Industrial and Investment Corporation of India (ICICI) and the World Bank, however, show that even after taking these incentives into account, export profitability remains well below domestic profitability. Profitability was negative on a total-cost basis, but positive on a variable-cost basis (see Table 4.7). The data show that firms in India are likely to be interested in exports only if there is a surplus available after domestic sales. It may be mentioned that export profitability is highly variable across industries. It is also variable over time for the same industry.

There is enough evidence to show that high profitability in domestic markets as compared to export markets is on account of high nominal as well as high effective protection.[23] In nominal terms, India's average protective tariff is estimated to be about 116 per cent, with a standard deviation of 37 per cent.[24] The actual 'collection' rate is lower on account of specific exemptions, based on end-use, and duty-free imports for export production. (The actual collection rates are less than one half of the legal nominal rates.) Another important feature of tariff rates is that these are generally the highest for commodities which are also subject to quantitative restrictions (QRs) because of indigenous availability, and the lowest for commodities which are on Open General Licence (OGL) and freely importable. This implies that production for the home market enjoys the double benefit of tariff as well as quantitative protection. Data on effective protection compiled by the World Bank from various sources also show that the levels of effective protection (on value added at world prices) are also high and vary widely across industries without any apparent rationale.[25] The high nominal and effective protection rates have ensured that domestic prices were generally much higher than international prices, and the consequent profitability of investment for sales in the home market was also higher.

The economic effects of highly variable and high rates of protection were analysed more than two decades ago by Bergsman (1970), among others, in his well-known study of industrialization in Brazil. He pointed out that while there was enough justification for deviation from free trade in order to shift a country's production structure, indiscriminate protection over too long a period could lead to widespread inefficiency and a preference for the 'quiet life'. As Bergsman put it,

> quiet life effects seem more important per se when we realize that economic development is a process taking place over time. A large part of growth in output—especially output per capita, which is an essential part of development—is caused by increases in technological efficiency. If protection reduces the search for better methods, better organisation, better maintenance of equipment and all other elements of technological efficiency, the economy will suffer a permanent and increasing cost (Bergsman, 1970, p. 179).

This is what seems to have happened in India.

The effect of the protective regime on the industrial structure is an important economic issue and can be illustrated by an analysis of the performance of the Indian electronics industry in recent years. This is the most prominent of the so-called 'sunrise' industries, in which India is generally assumed to have a comparative advantage in view of the easy availability of skilled manpower and a strong technological base. Since 1981 a number of policy measures have been taken to promote the growth of this industry. These include the removal of capacity constraints, the liberalization of industrial licensing for foreign firms, the liberalization of foreign collaboration and equity investment, the liberalization of import policy for components and raw materials, and a sharp reduction in import duties on inputs. However, there has been very little or no reduction in tariffs or quantitative reductions on imports of final electronics products, except those which were not indigenously produced. As a result, the effective protection rates have been very high. For example, in respect of televisions, one of the fastest growing sectors in India, the effective protection rates were 150 per cent (for black and white and colour T.V.s as a group).[26] These policies succeeded in attracting foreign investment in a large number of units, but the scale of production in each unit remained low by international standards, and costs of production remained high. For example, in respect of ten major electronics products, India's factory prices in 1986 exceeded world prices by 20 per cent to 170 per cent, and many were also of inferior quality.

The impact of these policies on the development of the electronics industry has been analysed by Joseph (1989). The growth in production in the post-1980 period was spectacular. The highest growth rate was observed in consumer electronics (39.6 per cent), followed by professional electronics (30.9 per cent), and components (26 per cent). In the consumer electronics sector most of the increase in production was contributed by television receivers, where output increased by 66 per cent annually. Much of the growth in output occurred in units set up with foreign collaboration; these were largely dependent on the import of components. The growth of domestic employment in the industry, which is generally considered relatively labour-intensive, lagged far behind the growth of output. The growth of employment was only 11 per cent per annum in the post-1980 period.

The developments in respect of the imports and exports of the electronics industry are striking. According to Joseph's calculations, total imports as a percentage of production increased from 33 per cent in 1975-80 to 45 per cent during 1981-6. As imports increased faster than output, the share of imports in total demand increased from 25 per cent during the 1970s to more than 32 per cent in the 1980s. The industry was also highly dependent upon imported capital goods. These are estimated to comprise 85 per cent of total requirements. It is interesting to note that during the same period, the share of imports in total demand in South Korea declined from 43 per cent to nearly 35 per cent, and the bulk of production went into exports. Exports of the electronics industry in India, on the other hand, have been low and amounted to only 7 per cent of production during the 1980s. As a result, the industry became a large drain on foreign-exchange resources.

(c) The Incentive Structure

India provides a variety of incentives for exporters. There are as many as seven important incentives, administered by more than one agency. These are:

The Cash Compensatory Support (C.C.S.), which is designed to compensate for unrebated indirect taxes paid by exporters on inputs, higher freight rates, and market development costs. The rates vary from product to product, and often from exporter to exporter. The CCS involves the largest single budgetary outlay for exports. In 1990-1, the total budget provision was Rs 2100 crores.

The Duty Drawback, which reimburses exporters for customs duty and excise duty paid on inputs which enter for export promotion.

Replenishment Licences, which are meant to provide access to exporters to restricted raw materials and components. These are in addition to normal 'Actual User' licences, and are freely saleable in the market. These licences normally enjoy a premium and provide important flexibility to exporters in meeting their import requirements.

Advance Licences, which facilitate imports of specified raw materials without payment of any customs duty. These licences are available only against confirmed export orders and/or letters of credit.

Free Trade Zones and 100 per cent 'Export-Oriented Units', which provide facility for unrestricted imports of raw material, components and capital goods without payment of any customs duty. Free Trade Zones also enjoy certain special tax benefits. Because of complex procedures and infrastructure problems, these schemes have not been very successful in promoting exports.

Subsidies on Domestic Raw Materials. The most important scheme in this category is the International Price Reimbursement Scheme (IPRS) for Steel, which equalizes the difference between international and domestic prices of steel obtained from domestic sources.

Profit Tax and Credit Subsidies. Profits from exports are exempt from income taxes. There is also preferential access to credit for exporters, and pre-shipment and post-shipment interest rates for exporters are highly concessional.

Export incentives have raised the average profitability of exports and narrowed the difference between domestic and export profitability, and have played an important role in promoting exports. However, the multiplicity and complexity of the incentive structure have had three unintended effects, which have reduced their efficiency: (a) the actual combined benefit from the incentive structure is not transparent, and difficult to calculate. Thus, there is no clear relationship between the cost to the government of providing these incentives, and the actual net foreign exchange earned from different products; (b) the collection of these incentives involves important transaction costs for exporters because of delays in disbursement and disputes in interpretation; and (c) pressure lobbies have developed to protect, preserve and enhance one or the other incentive. 'Incentive-bargaining' becomes a more important determinant of export profitability than the expansion of exports and the search for new markets.

(d) Administrative Complexity

The trade regime, both in respect of imports and exports, is a veritable jungle of administrative rules, regulations and exemptions. Tariffs, duties and incentives are generally product-specific and can vary widely even for similar products, depending on end use and other factors. They are also highly variable over time, and subject to change without notice by administrative action. Both the implementation as well as the substance of the rules, regulations and rates are thus highly discretionary. The main instrument for regulating imports is the import-licensing policy, which determines whether a particular product can be imported, to what extent, and for what purpose. There are several lists, e.g. the 'banned' list, the 'restricted' list, the 'limited permissible list', the 'Open General Licence', and the list of 'canalized' items. In addition to physical non-tariff controls, imports are subject to customs duties which vary widely from product to product.

Exports, particularly agricultural exports, are also subject to licensing controls. There are about 170 products which are subject to the export control order. The products subject to export control generally fall into one of the following categories: (a) exports are completely banned; (b) exports are allowed 'on merit'; (c) exports are allowed, subject to 'limited quantitative ceiling'; (d) exports are canalized through a state agency; and (e) exports are permitted subject to prescribed conditions.

In addition to the control exercised by the Chief Controller of Imports and Exports (CCI&E) and the customs authorities, exports and imports are also subject to rules and regulations for repatriation and the remittance of foreign exchange under the Foreign Exchange Regulation Act (FERA), which is administered by the Reserve Bank of

India. The adverse impact of complex rules and procedures on India's exports have been analysed in detail in a recent study by Desai, *et al.* (1990).

Issues in Trade Policy: A Review of the Evidence

In considering options for the future, it is necessary to devote some attention to the results of theoretical and empirical research on certain trade-policy issues which have been discussed extensively in the literature, and which are of some relevance to India. Important among these issues are:

(a) Is the so-called 'outward-oriented' or 'export-oriented' strategy, in the sense in which these terms are defined in the trade-policy literature, a necessary condition for viability in the balance of payments?

(b) Is 'import liberalization' a necessary condition?

(c) Can trade reform be brought about gradually or is 'shock treatment' essential?

These issues are dealt with briefly. As the literature is extensive and easily accessible, only those aspects are highlighted which seem pertinent to policy formulation in India.

(a) Export Pessimism of the Fifties

After World War II, an export pessimism characterized the thinking of most influential development economists. An important reason for this was the experience of the Great Depression, when prices of primary products dropped precipitously and private capital flows ceased completely. Primary producing countries were badly affected because of their dependence on foreign markets. Trade expansion continued to look bleak in the early 1950s, while Europe was rebuilding its economy and its currencies were still not fully convertible. A conviction grew that a necessary corollary of domestic development was a less outward-oriented strategy, and many countries shifted their economic focus to the domestic market. The economic arguments in support of this view were put forward most forcefully by the two pioneers of development economics, Raul Prebisch and Ragnar Nurkse.

Prebisch (1950) postulated that the terms-of-trade of developing countries have a tendency to deteriorate over time *regardless of the policies of developing countries*.[27] While in the developed countries productivity improvements were said to be translated into higher wages, in the developing countries labour-supply pressure was said to keep wages unchanged, thus leading to lower prices. Correspondingly, Prebisch claimed that 'the great industrial centres not only kept for themselves the benefit of the use of new techniques in their own economy, but are in a favourable position to obtain a share of that deriving from the technical progress of the periphery' (1950, p.14).

The Prebisch thesis had a profound effect on development planners in the newly-independent countries of Asia and Africa, as also in South America, which was heavily dependent on the exports of primary products. It seemed to strengthen the Rosenstein-Rodan argument for co-ordinated investment in a balanced growth pattern (Rosenstein-Rodan, 1943). In his view, a balanced and co-ordinated pattern of growth required a planning framework that would allow the realization of external economies from the simultaneous establishment of several complementary industries. Without such planning, there would be no effective inducement to invest and no 'big push' to overcome rural underdevelopment.

Soon after the publication of Prebisch's work on the terms of trade, Nurkse published his book on the problems of capital formation in developing countries, followed by his famous lectures on several aspects of trade and development (Nurkse, 1953 and 1959). Nurkse believed that for the newly-emergent countries international trade could no longer serve as an 'engine of growth'. Nurkse's export pessimism arose from the notion that foreign markets simply could not accommodate imports on a sufficient scale as developing countries accelerated their development. In this situation, in order to grow, developing countries needed to undertake a balanced pattern of investment in a number of different industries. A pattern of mutually supporting investments in different lines of production would enlarge the size of the domestic market and thus support industrialization.[28]

These powerful economic arguments were buttressed by political perceptions and the ideas of political and intellectual leaders in developing countries. For them, industrialization was the key to social and economic progress, and the existing patterns of trade between metropolitan powers and primary producers constituted a major impediment to the expansion of industry. Industrialization represented diversification, high wages and development. Above all, it meant economic independence and freedom from colonial exploitation. It was also widely believed that British imperialism was sustained by the British advocacy of free trade, which was designed to prevent or at least slow down the rise of competitive production abroad (see Kindleberger, 1980, p. 294). The name given to these trade policies was 'free trade imperialism'.[29]

Meier (1990) has advanced a less benevolent view of the political compulsions that were operating in developing countries in favour of an inward-looking strategy. He argues that

> the promotion of a sheltered home market had a common appeal to the bureaucratic-authoritarian state, urban manufacturers, and multinationals that supplied technology and capital. Protection also met the state's objectives of pursuing revenue- and expenditure-maximizing activities through maximum revenue tariffs and export taxes (p. 156).[30]

Both the economic and the political contexts are very different now from what they were in the forties and fifties. While trade relationships continue to be highly political, the fear of domination by industrial countries through enhanced trade has receded. In fact the protectionist sentiment is now stronger in the developed countries because of the pressure of indigenous political lobbies. The emergence of Japan and Germany as major economic powers has also demonstrated that export success can strengthen economic independence rather than undermine it. In contrast, the recurring balance-of-payment crises in developing countries and the persistence of debt problems have made these countries more dependent on the industrial powers.

Economically, the export pessimism of the post-War period has proved to be unjustified. World trade in the 1950s and 1960s grew faster than world income. Several developing countries showed dramatic increases in their share of world trade. The post-War world has also seen a dramatic shift in the export composition of developing countries towards manufactures. Developing-country exports grew threefold in the 1955-78 period, and represented one-fourth of overall exports. Manufactures are now close in magnitude to the other non-fuel exports, such as food, minerals and agricultural raw materials. In fact exports of manufactures from developing countries grew twice as fast as the industrial countries' incomes in the 1960s, and four times as rapidly in the 1970s (Bhagwati, 1988b, p. 30).

There are, of course, some new arguments to justify export pessimism, but it is clear that the weight of international evidence is in favour of those who see substantial possibilities of expansion in trade because of specialization, technological innovation, andthe changing patterns of demand and comparative advantage.[31]

(b) Growth, Trade, and 'Outward Orientation'

There is a mass of literature on the relationship between growth and trade.[32] Several studies have attempted to establish a correlation between the growth of incomes and the expansion of exports. Important among these are studies by Michaely (1977), Balassa (1978), and Feder (1983). Most of these studies have found a high correlation between the growth of exports and the growth of incomes, although specific conclusions are dependent on the period, the sample countries, and the variables chosen. These statistical studies, based on cross-country regressions, do not however throw light on the causal link between exports and growth. It is plausible to argue that the high growth rates of exports may have been caused by the high growth rates of output—which, in turn, may have resulted from other exogenous factors, such as a higher savings effort—rather than the other way round.

A number of detailed country studies have also been undertaken to illuminate the effects of development policy on the growth of trade, and the impact of trade policy on growth. Two such multi-country studies, sponsored by the Organisation for Economic Co-operation and Development in the 1960s, and the National Bureau of Economic Research in the 1970s, are of particular interest.[33] Much of the material in these studies is concerned with incentive structures, especially with respect to how they affect the profitability of producing for the domestic market *versus* exporting, and of investing in urban manufacturing activities rather than in rural areas in general and agriculture in particular. Generally, these studies confirm the existence of a highly distorted structure of protection which has impeded the growth of exports as well as output. There has been considerable loss of efficiency, without any evidence of compensating gains in terms of improved equity or better income distribution. Paradoxically, an inward-looking strategy was promoted on the grounds that it would imply greater industrialization. However, exactly the opposite happened in several countries where discrimination against exports reduced the size of the market, imposed protectionist costs, and impaired the growth rate of industry. The strategy was more successful in expanding the industrial base in the earlier stages of development, when exports consisted primarily of non-manufactures.

Several writers have questioned the conclusion of these country studies, namely that a more open and outward strategy is necessarily more conducive to growth. Bruton (1990) has emphasized the importance of 'initial conditions' in determining the pace of growth. These conditions include differing resource endowments, the opportunities in international trade, the stock of technical knowledge, the prevailing economic and social links, and so on. Frances Stewart (in Fransman and King, 1984) notes that 'in trying to explain why some societies innovate effectively and others do not, the fundamental and underlying explanation often seems to lie in the realm of history and interests, rather than particular policies' (p. 88). Similarly, after examining the historical evidence, Kindleberger (1980) also concludes that 'in the long run, national export shares are determined by deep-seated changes in comparative advantage, originating in the forces that make for more rapid or slower growth. Policy can do little to mould these' (p. 297).

Bruton, Stewart and Kindleberger are right in reminding us of the importance of initial conditions, historical factors, and the political environment in determining the outcome of policy. However, the inter-country evidence and detailed studies of the particular ways in which trade policies have operated in different countries do point to the importance of the incentive structure in determining the pattern and pace of development. Trade policy by itself is not sufficient in promoting or retarding development, but it is surely important in influencing the eventual outcome. As regards the superiority of the export-promotion strategy over inward-looking strategies, Balassa's (1990) conclusion seems valid. He has argued that the inward-oriented strategy of development is likely to permit rapid economic expansion initially. However, it will eventually run into difficulties as the limitation of domestic markets leads to shifts into new activities that do not conform to the country's resource endowment and circumscribe the possibilities for the exploitation of economies of scale. Another problem with continued inward orientation is the emergence of the foreign-exchange bottleneck, and the inability of the economic structure to respond adequately to changes in the pattern of domestic and international demand. This may lead to a widening current-account deficit and to financing difficulties in the subsequent stages of industrialization. The Indian experience and the economic history of several other developing countries would seem to confirm this conclusion.[34]

There are several reasons why greater outward orientation may be conducive to a more efficient use of resources. Bhagwati (1988b) has emphasized the gains from trade on account of allocative efficiency. An export-promoting trade strategy brings incentives for domestic resource allocation closer to what will generally produce efficient outcomes. He has also argued that such a strategy is less likely to trigger what economists now call directly unproductive profit-seeking (DUP) activities. Sundrum (1990) refers to the dynamic advantages of trade through greater innovation and a knowledge of products and new techniques.[35] A particularly important form of the dynamic advantages of trade is that which arises from increasing returns to scale. As exports grow, there is an increase in the scale of production with its attendant economies, leading to a continuous increase in the efficiency with which resources are used.

Another way in which exports might contribute to economic growth is by relaxing the foreign-exchange constraint on growth. The precise argument has been most clearly spelt out in the 'two gap' theories of Chenery, Bruno and Strout.[36] In their models the foreign-exchange constraint is said to be binding if the foreign-exchange gap is greater than the investment-savings gap. Under this condition, for any given amount of foreign aid, the rate of growth determined by the foreign-exchange gap will be lower than that determined by the investment-savings gap. An increase in exports, by reducing the foreign-exchange gap, will enable the country to achieve a higher rate of growth. Other advantages claimed for an export-oriented strategy include gains in total factor productivity, a fuller utilization of under-employed resources, and an inducement to higher levels of investment arising from the expansion of demand.

What exactly is meant by an export-promoting trade strategy? The question is important, because different writers have used the term to describe different kinds of trade regimes. The definition offered by Bhagwati, which is now being increasingly used by trade theorists, is probably the most precise and quantifiable (Bhagwati, 1988b).

An export-promoting strategy (EP) is defined as the adoption of an effective exchange rate for the country's exports (EER_x) which is equal to that for imports (EER_m). An import-substitution (IS) or inward-looking strategy is defined as one where EER_x is less than EER_m. EER_x would include all export subsidies, tax credits, special credits, and any other subsidy on inputs used in export production. Similarly, EER_m would include import duty, import premia resulting from quantitative restrictions, and other charges. The adoption of an export-promoting strategy thus amounts to the adoption of a 'neutral' strategy and the elimination of the bias against exports. (A bias *in favour* of exports, which obtains when EER_x is greater than EER_m, is described by Bhagwati as an 'ultra-EP strategy'.)[37] Bhagwati has stressed that the pursuit of either the EP or the ultra-EP strategy does not preclude import-substitution in selected sectors. Nor does the EP strategy imply an absence of government intervention. Several economies (such as Korea or Taiwan) that have come close to the EP strategy have been characterized by considerable government intervention in the economy. An EP strategy also has to be distinguished from the traditional concept of 'export-led' growth, in which the country's exports generate an income expansion attributable to direct gains from trade and indirect beneficial effects. The incentive-related EP strategy, according to Bhagwati and others, has nothing to do with such beneficial external phenomena.

(c) Import Liberalization

The recent research in trade policy has enhanced our understanding of the impact of the incentive structure on growth. It has also established a *prima facie* case in favour of import liberalization and 'openness'. This view has been enthusiastically adopted by the IMF and the World Bank in the design of their balance-of-payments and structural-adjustment programmes, particularly after the second oil crisis of 1979. At that time, a number of developing countries found themselves in severe external difficulties and had to approach international financial institutions for assistance. By the mid-eighties a new orthodoxy had emerged, and a 'good' or 'strong' development strategy became synonymous with import liberalization and outward orientation. The change in approach was crystallized by the World Bank in its 1987 World Development Report, when it categorized individual countries according to the degree of the inward or outward orientation of their trade incentives.[38] There was a clear implication that countries belonging to the former group were better managed and had shown better economic performance. The IMF–World Bank programmes of assistance to developing countries in the 1980s have routinely included import-liberalization as a test of good performance.

However, it was soon noticed that several World Bank–IMF programmes had run into trouble and that the actual results were well below expectations. A few programmes had succeeded, but quite a number ended up with countries no better off than before (or worse off than before). In order to study the matter further, a number of studies of country experiences with IMF–World Bank stabilization and structural adjustment programmes were initiated, including some by the institutions themselves. Among the recent studies, those by the World Institute for Development Economics Research (WIDER),[39] IMF–World Bank Symposium on Growth-Oriented Adjustment Programmes (1987), Shapiro and Taylor (1990), Helleiner (1990), Rodrik (1990) and Sachs (1989) are noteworthy. These studies have raised several questions about the efficacy of the liberalization package in the context of balance-of-payments stabilization.

In considering trade-policy options for India in the 1990s, an important issue which needs to be considered is whether the viability of the balance of payments is dependent on greater 'openness' and the policy of import liberalization. What constitutes openness and import liberalization has not been precisely defined in the literature or by the

IMF–World Bank.[40] Generally, however, trade liberalization is assumed to imply the conversion of quantitative restrictions to low and uniform tariffs, and the use of the exchange rate (rather than quantitative restrictions or tariffs) for bringing about balance-of-payments equilibrium.[41] A likely consequence of the import-liberalization policy is the increase in the ratio of imports and foreign trade to GDP. Briefly, the main advantage claimed for import liberalization is that the implied reduction in the effective rates of protection would induce a more efficient allocation of investment along the lines of a country's comparative advantage. In addition to reducing the bias against exports and capital intensity, import liberalization is also likely to remove the bias against agriculture. The removal of quantitative restrictions would also eliminate costs associated with intrusive bureaucracies and wasteful rent-seeking.

Before we discuss the case for import liberalization in India, it is useful to look at the relevant empirical evidence. The cases of Japan, Korea and Taiwan are of special historical interest, as these countries are the leading success stories of outward-oriented and efficient industrialization. After examining the historical experience of East Asian countries, Sachs (1987) concludes that an export-promotion policy can be pursued by the *dirigiste* government even in the presence of tight import controls and tight regulations in capital markets. According to Sachs, in all these countries the post-War period began with an initial phase of macro-economic instability, followed by several years of stabilization and import substituting growth and eventually by a turn to export-led growth in the early sixties. In none of these countries was there a sudden removal of tariff or quota protection for domestic industry, or indeed anything approaching the adoption of a low and uniform tariff. As Lin (in Sachs, 1987, p.19) notes with regard to Korea and Taiwan:

> In fact, systematic decontrol of imports did not occur in either country until the late 1960s, well after the success of their export promotion efforts. In the interim, trade liberal-

> ization measures consisted primarily of allowing imports of intermediate products duty-free for use in export processing and of requiring domestic producers of import substitutes to reduce their prices relative to potential imports in order for their products to remain under import control.

On the basis of the experience of Japan, Korea and Taiwan, Sachs has suggested that a practical distinction needs to be made between export-promotion policies and trade liberalization. The experience of other developing countries between 1962 and 1984 also does not show that fast-growing countries, on an average, had either high or increasing shares of exports in GDP (McCarthy, Taylor and Talati, 1987). The WIDER study on the varieties of stabilization experience (Taylor, 1988) also suggests that the liberalization packages were not generally successful. In fact Taylor argues that 'the risk of economic collapse under liberalization seems to be non-trivial, if recent history in the Southern Cone, Mexico and African countries such as Zaire provides a guide' (p.168). In some less extreme cases, Taylor found that trade liberalization during the period of balance-of-payments difficulties widened the trade gap rather than narrowed it. This happened in Tanzania, Ghana, Sri Lanka and Argentina, where a substantial share of new imports, after trade barriers were lowered, took the form of consumer goods instead of capital goods or intermediates. Domestic productive activity, except in the import-handling service sectors, was not enhanced.

Rodrik (1990) has also advised caution in embarking upon programmes of import liberalization. He found that the efficiency gained from economic liberalization was generally small relative to the high hopes placed on liberalization. The negative effects made the policy 'unsustainable', and the resulting uncertainty compounded the problem. In his view:

> Particularly to be avoided are liberalization measures likely to create a big bang in terms of income redistribution, but a whimper in terms of the efficiency with which resources

> are utilized. The ratio of economic benefits to political opposition engendered by such policies, can be very small indeed, rendering the reforms unsustainable (Rodrik, 1990, p. 939).

After reviewing the conflicting claims of proponents of liberalization and their critics, Shapiro and Taylor (1990) conclude that 'the best summary so far is that the debate is inconclusive: an a priori case for either an open or closed trade policy regime can never be fully proved' (p. 870). This is a fair conclusion, and this is as far as one can go.[42]

It is obvious that there are no magic solutions or policies that can work regardless of the context. In the Indian context, as pointed out below, there is a strong case for a rationalization of the import regime, and for simplifying the incentive structure. There is also a need to make exports more profitable, and to reduce the area of administrative discrimination. However, given the balance-of-payments constraints operating now, and the financing options currently available, import liberalization as a strategy does not seem to be a feasible option over the next few years. This is a pragmatic view: it is not dependent on the theoretical validity (or otherwise) of the liberalization argument. By implication, import liberalization would have the effect of raising, even in the short run, the ratio of imports to GDP. This may not be undesirable in itself, but it would require larger inflows of external capital in the next few years, and this is not available *on appropriate terms*. Past experience shows that further commercial borrowings to finance import liberalization—even if these were available in sufficient amounts—would also be undesirable, given the high level of external debt. In this situation, import liberalization would be unduly risky, and could lead to a repetition of the unfortunate experiences of several other developing countries. Tariff reductions, combined with the elimination of import controls, could also prove counterproductive if there is an asymmetrical response to the new incentive structure (Cooper, 1971). Sectors subject to new negative signals may pick these up more quickly and effectively than do sectors that should be expanding in response to positive signals. As a result, if the losses are immediate and the gains are in the future, there could be strong political opposition which would make the policy unsustainable.

An appropriate response in the Indian situation, at the present juncture, is to aim at what Fishlow (1985) has aptly termed 'export-adequate' growth as distinguished from 'export-led' growth. Policies which tilt the balance of advantage in favour of exports are likely to be more sustainable than those which call for import liberalization as part of a new strategy of development. There is also need for a bold programme of simplification, administrative reform, and shift to non-discretionary import controls. Administrative reform needs to be achieved without raising the import ratio in the short run. The objective of policy reform should be to try and eliminate the balance-of-payments crisis in the near future, and to make crisis management less of a preoccupation for policy-makers in the nineties.

(d) 'Shock treatment'

A gradual change in the trade strategy and other elements of a stabilization programme are contrasted in the literature with programmes for making 'once and for all' large changes in policies, or giving 'shock treatment' to the economy. Currently, this seems to be the accepted dogma in the IMF and the World Bank. It is argued that the credibility, and therefore the sustainability, of the reform package is enhanced by strong action at the outset. Smaller, more gradual changes are likely, in this view, to be easily rolled back, and indicate a lack of governmental commitment. According to Helleiner (1990, p. 893) this view is purportedly supported by unpublished research by World Bank economists on thirty-nine liberalization episodes in developing countries. In a different context, the shock treatment has figured prominently in several anti-inflationary 'heterodox' stabilization packages in Latin America in the 1980s (for example those in Argentina, Brazil and Peru).[43]

The 'shock treatment' approach (which is also sometimes referred to as the 'big bang' or the 'radical' approach) has been put forward rather forcefully by the IMF–World Bank and other associated institutions in their recent study of the U.S.S.R.[44] The study recognized that a strong macroeconomic stabilization programme, accompanied by immediate price decontrol and other measures, could increase the price level rather sharply, and could also lead to large unemployment and a sharp fall in output. It was, however, argued that a more conservative programme of policy reform and stabilization would also fail as the gains from

> the surge in productivity that market-determined prices and enterprise initiative could deliver would not be forthcoming, output would still fall and inflation increase substantially. Lack of confidence could become self-fulfilling as disappointing results discredit the goal of a market economy, and lead to a loss of policy direction and collapse of the strategy at a fairly early stage (IMF *et al.*, 1990, p. 18).

It is believed that previous reform processes in Czechoslovakia and Hungary did not succeed because they proceeded in a deliberately slow and cautious manner, thereby failing to provide a momentum for growth. Reforms in different sectors were interdependent, and reforms in some sectors could not succeed without a simultaneous reform in other sectors.

On the other hand, in defence of a gradualist approach to reform, it may be argued that the problems and risks during the transition period can be more easily handled if targets and policy changes are modest, but firm and realistic. Some of the argument in favour of a gradualist approach were pointed out by Little, Scitovsky and Scott (1970).[45] For example, a shift in the structure of production towards exports would take time and require supporting infrastructure, the acquisition of new skills, and the development of markets. Similarly, large changes in relative prices would imply quick and large shifts in income distribution. These changes would be resisted by those losing from them, and the result might be social unrest and inflation, leading to a reversal of the changes as well as a loss of output, and a decline in business confidence and investment. Reflecting on the costs of recent changes in the economic system in Eastern Europe, Galbraith (1991) has observed: 'what has been called shock therapy is politically acceptable only to those not experiencing it; in consequence, much welcome liberalization in politics and personal expression is being associated with painful economic deprivation and hardship' (p. 45).

There are two crucial assumptions in the proposals for a radical approach to reform. First, it is assumed that after the initial fall in output and a rise in prices, the situation will stabilize and there will be immediate gains in productivity and efficiency because of radical reforms. Second, it is argued that society is passive, and large losses of employment and real incomes will be acceptable to people without political and social protest. Both assumptions are not likely to be valid. Whether the potential gains in productivity can be realized would depend, among other factors, on the institutional structure of the economy, including production, marketing and distribution mechanisms. The prevailing institutional structure cannot be changed outright by decree.[46] Similarly, the political and social acceptability of the reform package is an essential condition for its sustainability. The distributional questions, and the relative sharing of the burden of adjustment by different regions and groups, have to be carefully worked out. It is also likely that a radical change in trade strategy would have to be supported by larger flows of external assistance. If such assistance is not forthcoming, the reform process may itself be discredited and discarded.

There does not seem to be a logical way of deciding in favour of a gradualist or a radical approach. The correct approach can only be determined in the light of circumstances prevailing in the country. If the disequilibria are large and have persisted for too long, then small and modest changes are unlikely to work. It is then more likely that the political acceptability of a radical package will be greater; i.e. the larger the initial disequilibrium the greater the likely acceptability.[47] It is also important to distinguish between the 'content' of a programme and the 'pace' of its implementation. So far as the pace of implementation is concerned, there is considerable merit in a programme which can be implemented quickly. This will impart greater certainty, and also preclude the possibility of subsequent stages of the programme being scuttled because of inertia or vested interests. So far as the 'content' of the programme is concerned, it is important to ensure that the programme is sustainable and that it is backed by adequate financing.

By international standards, the size of the balance of payments correction required in India is relatively modest —between 1 to 1.5 per cent of GDP under normal circumstances.[48] A programme of shifting the structure of production in favour of exports (as against the domestic market), along with other administrative and policy reforms, should be able to accomplish this task within two to three years, without imposing intolerable social and political costs.

Balance of Payments Policy: Future Directions

India's Five Year Plans have been consistent in underestimating the current-account deficits implicit in the Plan projections of investment and income growth (see Table 4.8). Except for the Fifth Plan, import requirements have been consistently underestimated.[49] This may have been partly due to underestimation of growth in maintenance imports and partly due to over-optimistic assumptions regarding the possibility of import substitution. Industries which were expected to substitute imports in fact registered large increases in their own import requirements of raw materials and components (e.g. petrochemicals, automobiles and electronics). The underestimation of the current-account deficit has resulted in frequent balance-of-payments crises, the under-funding of projects; delays, and cost-escalation. For the future, an important requirement is to make a more realistic assessment of the balance-of-payments implications of the Plan, and of its financing.

It is also now fairly well established that widening fiscal deficits in recent years are a primary cause of balance-of-payments problems. An important priority in the immediate future is to reduce the government's fiscal deficit. In addition, certain modifications in the import–export policy and the policy for commercial borrowings are necessary.

(a) Fiscal Deficits

As pointed out earlier, a major difference in the balance-of-payments crises of the sixties and the eighties is the prevailing macro-economic environment in the country, particularly the deteriorating fiscal situation. The rising fiscal deficit in the eighties has adversely affected the balance-of-payments situation in two ways. First, the fiscal deficit and the increasing recourse of the government to the banking sector and the Reserve Bank of India for financing these deficits is the primary cause of the expansion in the aggregate money supply in the economy.[50] The expansion of aggregate demand has resulted in higher inflation and a higher import demand. Second, the increase in fiscal deficits has led to a greater reliance on external commercial borrowings to finance public-sector investments. About 90 per cent of the approvals for external commercial borrowings (in value) were given to meet public-sector requirements during 1985-6 to 1989-90.[51] While the bulk of the external debt is a liability of the public sector (and government), the public sector's contribution to exports has been marginal.[52] The large external commercial borrowings of the past have added to the debt-servicing burden, and rendered the task of balance-of-payments management more difficult.

There is substantial evidence to suggest that in countries characterized by high fiscal deficits and macro-economic instability of the type which prevails in India, a necessary condition for balance-of-payments viability is a reduction in fiscal deficits. For example in countries like Argentina, Brazil, Peru and Zambia, it is the inability to bring fiscal deficits under control which made the task of balance-of-payments management virtually impossible (Sachs, 1987 and Rodrik, 1990). On the other hand the experience of countries like Japan, Korea and Taiwan demonstrates the vital importance of maintaining fiscal stability for success in export markets. In these countries government budgets were generally maintained near balance, often with large surpluses on the current account of the budget. Inflation rates were low and fairly stable. This meant, among other things, that nominal exchange rates could be maintained at fairly stable levels without jeopardizing export profitability. Government savings contributed to rapid capital accumulation, and also provided the government with the resources and flexibility to use subsidies and other fiscal incentives to promote particular sectors of the economy.[53]

The formal link between the monetary sector, the fiscal account and the balance of payments was established by Polak (1957) in the famous 'Polak Model', which has determined the approach of the International Monetary Fund in formulating its stabilization packages.[54] In its simplest version, the Polak model stipulates that, under certain open-economy assumptions, the sum of reserves and domestic credit must equal the value of output divided by velocity. Thus, if credit creation exceeds a value consistent with money demand treated as a function of national income, then international reserves will fall. A crucial assumption is that the demand for money is effectively independent of changes in domestic credit, and that it bears a predictable and stable relationship to a limited set of variables (such as real income). The model further stipulates that if absorption (i.e. the value of domestic spending) exceeds nominal income, then there must be more credit creation (net of capital inflows) than new money demand. This will result in a deficit on the current account. The connection between fiscal deficit and the deficit on current account is established by assuming that the government must finance any deficit by increasing its net borrowings from abroad, or by increasing its net borrowings from the domestic banking systems (in other words, there are no sales of government debt to private non-bank sectors).

This is a simple model, based on monetarist assumptions, which are not entirely valid in any actual situation. However, it provides a useful analytical framework for integrating balance-of-payments concerns with domestic fiscal concerns. At the same time, it has to be recognized that policies for reduction in the fiscal deficit will have important implications for output, employment and income distribution in the short run. The fiscal package, therefore, has to be carefully devised and balanced so that the burden of adjustment is shared equitably by different classes in the society, and its adverse impact on output minimized.

In a statement in Parliament in December 1990, India's finance minister announced his intention to reduce the fiscal deficit of the central government to 6.5 per cent in 1991-2 from the level of 8.3 per cent of GDP in 1990-1.[55] (The 'fiscal deficit' measures the difference between the revenue receipts and total expenditure, including capital expenditure. This has to be distinguished from the other measures of the budget deficit.) This reduction in the fiscal deficit was expected to be the beginning of a transition to a sustainable regime over a three-year period. The government's intention was to reduce the fiscal deficit to 3 to 4 per cent of GDP, which was broadly the level of deficit in the mid-seventies. In order to examine the impact of reduction in fiscal deficit (of about 1.8 percentage points in one year) on various macro-economic variables in India, a simulation was carried out on the basis of a macro-economic model of the Indian economy developed by the National Council of Applied Economic Research (NCAER).[56] It was found that on the assumption of a normal monsoon in 1991-2, the fiscal squeeze of 1.8 percentage points could lead to a reduction in the rate of growth of output by 0.6 to 1 per cent. The growth of industrial output was likely to be lower by 1 to 1.5 per cent, and the rate of inflation was likely to be lower by 2 to 3 per cent. The simulation exercise showed that the effect of the fiscal adjustment would be favourable on the balance of payments, but not to the same extent as the nominal reduction in the deficit. The fiscal adjustment would lead to an improvement in the current account, which was only about one-third (in rupee terms) of the reduction in fiscal deficit (in rupee terms).[57] Thus, while fiscal contraction would be helpful in reducing the current-account deficit, it would not be adequate to correct the balance of payments. Additional trade policy measures would, therefore, also be necessary.[58]

The simulation exercise also showed that a reduction in the fiscal deficit would reduce the growth of money supply by about 3 to 3.5 percentage points because of reduction in the growth of reserve money. The reduction in government expenditure was, however, likely to lead to a reduction in the real incomes of the poor, which was larger than the reduction in income of other classes. It would also result in some unemployment in the unorganized sectors of the economy. The organized sectors would be relatively unaffected because of job security and the protection provided by labour laws. Compensatory programmes and policies were, therefore, necessary to cushion the impact of the fiscal squeeze on the poor and the weaker sections. A programme of fiscal correction should go hand in hand with a programme of productive employment. Measures for adequate distribution of food, and for keeping their prices stable, were particularly crucial.

In its quest for balance-of-payments viability in the 1990s, India must give first priority to measures for reducing the fiscal deficit. However, the fiscal package has to be supplemented with other measures.

(b) Export–Import Policy

Earlier sections dealt with certain basic issues of trade strategy, i.e. outward orientation, import liberalization, shock treatment *versus* gradualism. Within the broad framework of existing import/export policy, there are a number of changes which can be made to tilt the balance in favour of exports as against production for the domesticmarket. As Diaz-Alejandro (1975) has pointed out, it is *not* necessary to dismantle totally the prevailing trade regime in order to achieve a rapid growth in exports. As shown in several cases, including that of South Korea, many administrative rules can be turned around to encourage new exports, just as they were used earlier to promote new import-replacing activities. During a period when the availability of external finance is extremely limited, the least-risk strategy is *first* to get exports up and then to think of liberalizing imports. Import liberalization without adequate export growth or an abundant supply of external finance can be self-defeating.

The first task of reform in export–import policy should be to shift the balance of profitability in favour of exporters. In order to achieve this objective, it is not necessary to destroy the import-substituting industry, but to shift its focus to the export market. Many import-substitution industries developed during the last forty years are not as uncompetitive and technologically backward as the extreme critics of import substitution suggest. With a proper incentive structure, which rewards exports adequately, the existing productive capacity can be made to contribute to export expansion. The main reason for the relatively low profitability of exports, as compared with domestic sales, is the high level of tariff and non-tariff protection granted to import-substituting industries. This raises domestic prices substantially above export prices. The existence of budgetary constraints, and also the prevailing international GATT rules, make it easier to tax imports than to subsidize exports. As budgetary constraints are likely to continue in the future, the best instrument for increasing the profitability of exports is to shift the additional burden of export subsidization to importers. This can be done by a more aggressive use of the replenishment licence mechanism (REP) for financing imports.

The prevailing import-control system permits imports of raw materials and components by domestic manufacturers, irrespective of whether sales are at home or abroad.

These are generally referred to as imports by 'Actual Users' (AU). Such imports can be under the Open General Licence (OGL), or under the restricted list. The former does not require prior clearance or a licence. Items on the restricted list are, however, subject to administrative scrutiny and quantitative restrictions, and can be imported only against a licence. (In addition, there is a 'banned' list.) The principal criterion for the classification of items into different licensing categories is indigenous availability. Replenishment (REP) licences provide an additional import facility to exporters, which is linked to the value of exports. Imports under REP and other export-related schemes do not affect the entitlement of the manufacturer for imports under the AU scheme.[59] REP licences can be used to import a wider range of commodities (including banned items, to a certain extent). They are also freely transferable. On transfer, REP licences generally enjoy a 'premium' in the market, which provides some additional subsidy to the exporter.

The subsidy available to the exporter from the sale of REP licences varies according to the restrictiveness of the AU policy and the size of the REP market.[60] The subsidy is paid by the importer to the exporter, who forgoes his right to import. It follows that if all imports were to be permitted only against flexible REP licences, an explicit link would be established between exports and imports. Exporters would earn a higher subsidy and gain, and the costs of sale of goods in the domestic market would go up, depending on their import content. *Ceteris paribus*, export profitability would go up while domestic profitability would go down.

According to data compiled by the ministry of commerce, the total value of AU licences issued in 1989-90 was Rs 2900 crores (excluding OGL and other non-licensed imports), and the value of REP licences was Rs 3500 crores (excluding 'gems and jewellery').[61] Given the relative size of the two types of imports, it is not feasible to transfer in one stroke all AU imports to the REP market. This could severely affect domestic production, and also raise domestic costs very sharply in the short run. A more workable scheme may be to transfer initially, say, 50 per cent of the entitlements under AU licenses to the REP market. This would increase the demand for REP licences by 40 per cent (assuming that licenses issued in a particular year are used in that year, and there is no carry-over). If this is considered too high, the entitlement of exporters for REP licenses may be increased by, say, 10 to 15 per cent. Imports under OGL, which do not require a licence, need normally not be disturbed. These percentages are illustrative, and can be varied to generate the desired degree of subsidization of exports.

As can be seen, this scheme and its variants would substantially shift the incentive structure in favour of exporters *without* increasing imports. This is not a 'first best' or 'optimal' strategy of export promotion, but it is a relatively risk-free strategy under conditions of financial stringency. Several advantages are likely to accrue fairly quickly. First, the export profitability would improve. Second, those who do not export goods are likely to find their profits squeezed. Third, the area of administrative licensing of imports would be reduced, as part of the allocation function would be transferred to the market. Fourth, differentials in the rates of effective protection across industries will tend to narrow. The import cost of raw materials and components for domestic manufacture would go up, which would reduce the rate of protection on final products (which are currently very high), and increase the rates of protection for components and raw materials (which are relatively low). A possible disadvantage of the scheme is that premium rates, and the implicit subsidy on exports, may become unstable over time with changes in import policy and changes in domestic and external demand. Until more experience is gained in the operation of the scheme, it would be prudent to introduce this scheme without disturbing the prevailing effective exchange rate for exporters inclusive of all export incentives. It would also be desirable to keep the import policy stable.

As pointed out earlier, the effective protection granted to different industries is highly variable and has no obvious rationale. Industries which are supposed to be 'priority' receive low protection, while those regarded 'non-priority' receive high protection. This encourages the expansion of the latter group of industries at the cost of the former. The reason for this awkward structure of tariff and effective protection rates is that tariffs in India are generally 'cost based'. The policy is to provide sufficient protection based on the domestic cost of production, however high this may be, and however low the value added at world prices. This policy has induced domestic firms to enter areas of production irrespective of the consideration of comparative advantage and relative costs of production. Such uneconomic investments, in turn, generate tariff escalations and higher costs of production for all user industries. It is necessary now to move away from a 'cost based' system of protection to a 'normative system', where the tariff rates are more uniform across industries.

Another important area of reform is the duty-drawback system. A simple and liberal duty-drawback system has proved highly effective as an export-promotion measure in several countries, including Korea. The duty paid on capital-goods imports by exporters should be brought within the ambit of the drawback system by enhancing their rates across the board. The indirect exporters, i.e. those who supply domestically manufactured inputs to exporters, should also be covered by the drawback system. This can be done through the introduction of domestic letters of credit, which have been tried in other countries. The duty-drawback rate structure should be simplified, and should not be based on a firm-by-firm scrutiny of duty paid.

Finally, there is urgent need for an administrative simplification of rules and regulations, and for making the system more stable. The case-by-case administrative scrutiny of imports/exports deserves to be totally eliminated over a period of time. On the import side, as suggested earlier, all items which need to be restricted should be shifted to REP licences or OGL with higher tariffs over the next two or three years. On the export side, there should be no quantitative or quota restriction on exports. In many cases these restrictions are redundant as domestic prices are substantially higher than international prices. The one area where they are effective is agricultural exports. Quota restrictions on agricultural exports have the effect of reducing the total income of farmers in cases where world prices are higher than domestic prices. This is not equitable. Another important administrative measure is to move towards uniformity of rates from a system of highly differentiated rate schedules. This would make the system more transparent, and less amenable to sectional pressures.[62]

A realistic exchange rate is obviously crucial to export performance. There is some evidence that in earlier years this instrument was not used sufficiently to support India's exports. Fortunately, the management of the exchange rate has ceased to be a matter of controversy in India in recent years.[63] While there may be a difference of views among experts regarding the exact point at which the rupee exchange rate should be placed *vis-à-vis* other currencies, at present the area of difference is not very large. Apparently, the exchange rate was also not an issue in the loan negotiated by India with the IMF in January 1991. In the past few years, the exchange-rate management has supported exporters. This should continue. There is also a case for the replacement of fiscal subsidies, such as cash assistance by a one-time adjustment of the exchange rate.[64]

There are, of course, some who regard the existence of any current-account deficit in developing countries as an evidence of the misalignment of exchange rates, and recommend frequent and often large depreciations to tackle the problem. Such a policy can become counter-productive if short-run supply elasticities are not as high as assumed, or if the primary cause of the payments deficit lies in the fiscal imbalance. As Latin American experience shows, frequent depreciations of the exchange rate can create substantial problems for fiscal management, as debt-service payments in home currencies escalate along with the cost of public-sector imports. The exchange rate is an important instrument and deserves to be used fully. However, a mechanistic and narrow approach must be avoided.

(c) Invisibles

As pointed out earlier, the net receipts from invisibles provided valuable support to India's balance of payments for nearly a decade after 1975-6. After 1985-6, although there was some growth in private transfers, this was not sufficient to offset the increase in interest payments on external debt (Table 4.3).[65] In 1989-90 the contribution of invisibles to financing the trade deficit declined to about 20 per cent, as against nearly 50 per cent in 1984-5. Among net invisible receipts, two main sources are foreign travel and private remittances. Net receipts from foreign travel have also increased substantially in the eighties, and accounted for about 30 per cent of total net invisible receipts in recent years.

Non-residents in the Middle East and Gulf countries are estimated to account for roughly 45 per cent of total private remittances in India. The future flow of remittances (as against non-resident deposits) is heavily dependent on the growth of the economies of the Middle East after the recent Gulf War, and their policy towards Indian immigrants. There are considerable uncertainties at the present time on both counts.

There is very little empirical research on macro-economic factors affecting remittances into India (beyond unreliable anecdotes). In the absence of such research it is difficult to come to any firm conclusions on the policies to be adopted by India to encourage the flow of such remittances. Obviously the exchange rate is an important factor, particularly the differential between the 'official' exchange rate and the unofficial exchange rate.[66] If the divergence is too great (in favour of the unofficial rate), then flows of remittances through the banking channels are likely to be affected adversely. In such an event, there is a strong case for narrowing the gap between the two rates by depreciating the official rate. In India there is no evidence, although data are very poor, that the divergence is too large or has been consistently widening. The differentials have remained fairly stable and the unofficial rate has moved in line with the official rate. In a regime of import and exchange controls, the elimination of the differential is not feasible, as unsatisfied demand for foreign exchange will spill over to the unofficial market, whatever the *level* of the official exchange rate.[67]

Another issue which arises is whether some special incentive (say in the form of cash subsidy) should be provided for inward remittances. The argument is that merchandise exports enjoy a higher effective exchange rate than the nominal exchange rate because of the existence of various incentives, including cash-compensatory support. It is argued that, on the same analogy, there is a case for providing a higher-than-nominal exchange rate for remittances. There is, however, an important problem with this proposal, leaving aside the question of the fiscal burden. This would involve an indirect subsidization of the *users* of foreign exchange, as they would be buying the foreign exchange at the nominal exchange rate.[68] It is possible to counteract this effect by imposing a countervailing tax on users of foreign exchange. But then a better alternative may be to simply move the nominal exchange rate itself, for all transactions, rather than resorting to a subsidy-cum-tax system for altering the effective exchange rate. So far as the effect of incentives to exporters are concerned, the relevant variable is the profitability of exports, particularly relative profitability *vis-à-vis* domestic sales. This, as we have seen, is still heavily biased against exports.

In respect of remittances, the most effective response may be to follow a realistic and competitive exchange-rate policy, and to provide efficient and cheap banking services. Gifts in foreign exchange already enjoy tax exemption. This fiscal concession should be extended to other forms of receipts in foreign exchange by residents.

(d) Capital Account

The structure of the capital account in India has undergone considerable changes in the last three decades. In the sixties and seventies the main sources of financing the current-account deficit were official loans on concessional terms. In 1980 nearly 90 per cent of India's outstanding debt was to official creditors, and 85 per cent of it was on concessional terms. By 1989, however, the picture had changed dramatically and the official loans accounted for 61 per cent of the total outstanding debt, and the proportion of concessional loans had fallen to 47 per cent. Incidentally, almost the whole of the decline in concessional assistance was due to a change in the composition of World Bank Group lending to India. India is the poorest among the developing countries, and on objective grounds India's claim for concessional assistance is unquestionable. Nevertheless, the World Bank Group has reduced flows of concessional assistance to India. Aid to India is also one of the lowest in volume among developing countries in per capita terms.[69]

STRUCTURE OF INDIA'S LONG-TERM DEBT, 1970-89
(IN US $ MILLIONS)

	1970	*1980*	*1989*
1. Total Debt Outstanding	7837	18,322	54,776
2. Total Official Debt	7507	16,315	33,371
of which, concessional	7013	15,475	25,732
3. Total Private Debt	330	2,007	21,405

SOURCE: World Bank, *World Debt Tables, 1990-91*. The figures above do not include private non-guaranteed debt (estimated to be $1.5 billion in 1989).

The subject of capital flows has been of immense academic interest in development economics. The focus in the sixties, and during the better part of the seventies, was on official capital flows and direct foreign investment, which constituted the major part of capital flows to developing countries. Towards the end of the seventies and in the eighties, the attention shifted to issues relating to commercial debt, particularly lending by banks, in the context of the debt crises in several developing countries. The academic analysis of the issues pertaining to capital flows has generally proceeded along four lines. In respect of official flows, in the sixties, there was considerable interest in the analysis of the role of foreign aid as a supplement to domestic saving. Chenery and Strout's 'two gap' model, for example, was developed in this context. A second area of interest has been the analysis of the *effects* of foreign capital flows on development. Third, several theoretical models have been put forward with a view to explaining the determinants and effects of capital flows at the aggregate level. A further area of interest has been the quality of particular forms of capital flows, and allocative and welfare effects of such flows on the recipient country. Excellent reviews of research in these and other areas are available in Lal (1990), Cardoso and Dornbusch (1989) and Eaton (1989). Cline (1984) provides a useful analytical framework for the discussion of policy issues in relation to external debt.[70]

In India's case the issues of relevance from the balance-of-payments point of view relate to direct foreign investment and commercial borrowings. Official multilateral and bilateral flows are, of course, also important. However, these flows are mainly supply-determined, and India can hardly do much to affect the volume of such flows.[71] The volume of foreign direct investment in India is very small. It was of the order of Rs 200 crores (or about $100 million) on an average in the last three years (compared with $ 3.4 billion in China in 1989).[72] India has followed a restrictive policy with regard to foreign investment on the grounds of promoting the growth of indigenous capital. The main restrictions relate to the percentage of equity that foreigners can hold, and the areas in which foreign investment can take place.

The intense academic debate regarding the effects of direct foreign investment remains inconclusive (see Dornbusch, 1989, and Lal, 1990). The opponents of foreign investment have drawn attention to several imperfections and deleterious effects, such as the capital intensity of such investment, inappropriate technology, the possible adverse effects on income distribution, transfer pricing, and the negative contribution that such investment often makes to the balance of payments. The proponents of foreign investment, on the other hand, have highlighted the beneficial effects in terms of encouragement to the development of technology, managerial expertise, integration with the world economy, exports, and higher growth. It has also been claimed that debt financing generates fixed debt-servicing obligations, while equity needs to be serviced only after profits are made. There is also substantial empirical evidence which can be presented to support both points of view. For example, in recent years, foreign private investment seems to have contributed enormously to the growth of several Asian semi-industrializing countries (e.g. Thailand, Malaysia and Singapore). There are also examples, particularly from Latin America and Africa, where the contribution of foreign investment has not been so benign.

There is, however, one point on which both the proponents and opponents seem to agree. This is that direct investment may actually be harmful to the recipient country if the economy is highly protected and foreign investment takes place behind high tariff walls. Bhagwati (1986), for example, has referred to the work of Uzawa and other Japanese economists to show that capital-intensive, protection-induced capital flow may actually reduce incomes in recipient countries. This type of investment is generally referred to as the 'tariff jumping' variety of foreign investment, whose primary objective is to take advantage of protected markets in the host country. Lall and Streeten (1977) also found that the welfare effects of foreign investment are, by and large, negatively co-related with the degree of effective protection provided to a particular industry.

This is not an argument against foreign investment *per se*, but against foreign investment of a particular variety. In India there is a strong case for simplifying the laws relating to foreign investment, and for eliminating the bias against equity investment. The volumes are presently so small that even a many-fold increase can do no harm. With the globalization of production in the world economy, and the integration of capital markets, the case in favour of equity investment has become stronger. The only thing which needs to be ensured is that such investment is positive in terms of foreign exchange, and is internationally competitive. In respect of competitive investments, the rules governing entry should be made automatic and transparent. However, it is likely that new equity investment will flow into industrial projects for setting up new capacity. In so far as the present balance-of-payments difficulty is one of financing maintenance imports and debt-service obligations, it is realistic to assume that higher equity investment by itself will not provide an adequate source of financing.

DEBT RATIOS IN HEAVILY-INDEBTED COUNTRIES AND INDIA

	India	*17 Heavily indebted countries*	
	1989	*1982*	*1987*
Debt/GNP	21.5	45.6	58.0
Debt/Exports	303.5	254.2	317.9
Debt Service/GNP	1.9	7.9	6.2
Debt Service/Exports	29.3	43.9	34.1
Interest/GNP	1.1	4.8	3.9
Interest/Exports	17.8	26.9	21.4

NOTE: The Seventeen heavily-indebted countries are: Argentina, Bolivia, Brazil, Chile, Colombia, Ecuador, Ivory Coast, Mexico, Morocco, Nigeria, Peru, the Philippines, Uruguay, Venezuela, Yugoslavia, Costa Rica and Jamaica. Data for these countries are from Dornbusch (1989), p. 24. Debt data for India are from *World Debt Tables, 1990- 91* (World Bank).

From a low level of about $ 2 billion in 1980, India's commercial debt (excluding official debt) reached a level of $ 21.4 billion in 1989—a tenfold increase. Within barely a decade India has become one of the largest debtors among the developing world in terms of outstanding commercial debt. The preceding table shows the debt ratios for India and seventeen heavily indebted middle-income countries. These countries experienced increasing debt-servicing difficulties after 1982. Their position has improved somewhat in the last three years, as India's has deteriorated.

The ratios of debt and debt service to GNP are relatively low in India. However, in view of the low ratio of trade to GNP and the high share of agriculture in GNP (which is virtually a non-tradeable sector), more relevant indicators of the debt burden in India are the ratio of debt to exports and the ratio of debt service to exports.[73] Dornbusch and Fischer (1985) have provided a useful framework for a discussion of the debt problem in terms of the debt/export ratio. The dynamics of the debt problem can be analysed by starting from the following debt accumulation equation:

$$D_t = (1 + i_t)\ D_{t-1} - NX_t \qquad (1)$$

where, D is the dollar value of outstanding debt
i is the nominal interest rate on outstanding debt
NX is the non-interest component (measured in dollars) of the current account (the 'resource' gap)

Equation (1) can be transformed into an equation for the debt service ratio 'd' (with exports measured in dollars):

$$d_t = K_t d_{t-1} - nx_t \qquad (2)$$

$$K_t \equiv (1 + i_t)/(1 + gx_t)$$

where, gx is the nominal (dollar) growth rate of exports and nx is the ratio of NX to exports, or the resource gap measured as the fraction of exports.

Equation (2) points to the four determinants of the debt/export ratio. Assuming a positive outstanding stock of debt, the debt/export ratio at the end of period t is higher, the higher the nominal interest rate and the inherited debt/export ratio. A high growth rate in the value of exports, or a positive non-interest current account, tend to reduce the ratio. While it is not possible to specify a critical level of debt-service ratio or debt/export ratio (at which debt-service difficulties are likely to occur), it is clear that an ever-rising debt/export ratio is not likely to be viable. This situation may arise if non-interest current-account deficits are rising, and if export growth in relation to the growth of interest payments is not sufficiently high.

In India the factors affecting the debt-service ratio in the 1980s have been unfavourable, leading to a sharp rise in the debt/export ratio as well as the debt-service/export ratio. The following table shows the current-account deficit and the growth of interest payments in the 1980s (in dollars).

INDIA'S CURRENT-ACCOUNT BALANCE AND INTEREST PAYMENTS
(IN MILLIONS OF U.S. $)

	1980	*1985*	*1990*
1. GNP	172,533	212,969	262,089
2. Current Account Balance	-2,268	-5,536	-7,538
3. Interest Payments	503	1,311	2,954
4. Non-Interest Current Account (2-3)	1,765	4,225	4,584

SOURCE: World Bank, *World Debt Tables, 1990-1.*

The average nominal interest rate on loans from official creditors has moved up from 2.4 per cent in 1980 to 5.6 per cent in 1989. However, because of the decline in interest rates in the private capital market, the average interest rates on loans from 'all' creditors has not increased much (from 5.4 per cent in 1980 to 6.4 per cent in 1989). Total interest payments in dollar terms have nevertheless been increasing at a much faster rate than exports. Interest (in dollar terms) increased at a compound rate of 21.7 per cent per annum in the 1980s, as compared with 7.8 per cent growth per annum in exports (in dollars).

The debt/export ratio in India at the beginning of the 1990s had crossed 300 per cent, which is comparable to the value of this ratio in the seventeen heavily-indebted countries of Latin America, Asia and Africa. As a substantial part of the debt is in the public sector, the rising debt-servicing burden and rising fiscal deficits have led to the emergence of a vicious circle of deficit and debt. There is very little scope in the coming years to finance 'inward looking' investments through recourse to external commercial debt. The debt/export ratio must be first stabilized, and then reduced to more manageable levels in the course of the 1990s.

A fundamental reason why the debt financing of large projects in India is not economically viable lies in the low productivity of these investments. A good indicator of low productivity is the substantial delays and cost escalations that occur in the implementation of large projects. The following table shows the delays in respect of sixty-three projects in the public sector, costing Rs 100 crores or more (as of January 1991). All these projects were started before 1988.

FREQUENCY DISTRIBUTION OF TIME DELAYS IN SIXTY-THREE PROJECTS IN INDIA

Delay (in no. of months)	*No. of Projects*
No delay	12
1-12 months	10
13-24 months	18
25-36 months	12
Over 36 months	11
TOTAL	63

SOURCE: Government of India, Ministry of Programme Implementation

Most long-term commercial loans have to be repaid in five to eight years. The gestation period of most large projects in the public sector, according to the original schedule, is at least four to five years. If these projects are further delayed, the entire repayment liability has to be covered by the government before any financial or other benefit is available from the project. The fact that these projects add very little to exports, even after going into commercial production, has further compounded the debt-servicing problem.

In future, the recourse to commercial borrowing has to be highly selective. In addition to borrowings to meet external liquidity requirements (which are now unavoidable), only quick-gestation export-oriented projects should be considered for financing through external commercial loans. Both conditions, i.e. a low capital–output ratio and high exports, must be satisfied.

To sum up, in the 1990s India must find the means to move to a more viable balance-of-payments situation. Regular and persistent balance-of-payments problems, as witnessed in the last thirty-five years, are avoidable. There is sufficient international experience available to guide policy-makers towards devising a new strategy to deal with the problem, and for 'freeing development planning from the tyranny of avoidable payments crises'.[74] Fortunately, the magnitude of the balance-of-payments correction required is relatively small by international standards, no more than 1 to 1.5 per cent of GDP. This would require a big effort in the next two or three years, particularly in the fiscal field. This effort, in any case, is necessary to remove another important constraint on India's development, i.e. the savings constraint. It is necessary also to tilt the balance of policies in favour of exports, as against domestic sales. This can be done without destroying the established industrial structure. As the experience of several other countries, including Korea, demonstrates, the existing industrial capacity can be turned around to support export expansion with suitable changes in the incentive structure. At the present time, in view of external financing constraints, the least-risk strategy is first to get exports up, and to then think of liberalizing imports—and not the other way round. The simplification of the tariff system and other measures to reduce administrative forms of intervention, including the abolition of the capacity-licensing system, would make the task of export-promotion easier. In view of the high debt/export ratio, there is no further scope for financing inward-looking capital intensive investment projects through external commercial borrowings.

Notes

1. As a rough measure of the balance-of-payments problem in a particular year, two criteria were used: the current-account deficit in a particular year was more than 1 per cent and foreign exchange reserves were less than necessary to cover three months' imports.
2. During 1976-7 to 1979-80 (Period II), the current-account deficit was less than 1 per cent of GDP and reserves were sufficient to cover more than three months' imports. During Period I and III, on the other hand, the current account deficit was more than 1 per cent of GDP. During both periods, however, there were a few years when resources exceeded three months' imports, but the underlying balance-of-payments situation continued to be difficult.
3. The figures are from Reserve Bank of India's Reports on Currency and Finance for the relevant years.
4. This arrangement is generally referred to as the 'negative list' system in India, i.e. restrictions apply only to listed items and anything which is not listed is free from restrictions. See Wolf (1982) for details of changes in import and export policy during this period (pp. 115-19).
5. The overall impact of the changes in the industrial licensing system is, however, not clear. The liberalization in some sectors was accompanied by much greater restriction in others. For example, the physical reservation for the small-scale sector was vastly expanded. See Wolf (1982), p. 72.
6. The figures of trade deficit are on payments basis, as reported by the Reserve Bank of India. These are different from trade data reported by Directorate General of Commercial Intelligence and Statistics (D.G.C.I.S), which are based on customs data relating to shipments.
7. For a detailed account of the developments in India's balance of payments during the period following the two oil shocks, see Ahluwalia (1986).
8. See Rangarajan (1990) for details of developments in the balance of payments during this period.
9. The effect of the increase in the interest rates on India's borrowings during the period is reflected in the sharp rise in net payments on the 'investment income' account during 1985-6 to 1988-9 (see Table 4.3).

10. Data on terms of loans and debt-service payments are from World Bank, *World Debt Tables*, 1990-1.
11. The data on India's debt are also from World Bank, *World Debt Tables*, 1990-1.
12. Disbursement data, on a comparable basis, are from World Bank sources.
13. See Pearson Commission's Report, *Partners in Development*, New York: Praeger, 1969.
14. There is very little authoritative academic work on this subject. The debate has mainly taken place in newspaper columns, and has political overtones. 'Left' politicians and economists generally oppose liberalization (without necessarily defining what precisely is being opposed). Those in the 'centre' or 'right' of the political spectrum generally support liberalization, while at the same time supporting extreme forms of protection for domestic industry and extreme state intervention in fixing prices and guiding allocation.
15. According to unpublished estimates of Government of India, based on national account statistics for value of industrial output (registered sector) and D.G.C.I.S. data for value of imports of capital goods and industrial raw materials, the import-intensity of industrial production was 10.6 per cent in 1973-4, 15.7 per cent in 1981-2, and 11.2 per cent in 1987-8.
16. In fact this is a major complaint of those who favour 'genuine' liberalization. See, for example, Wolf (1982), Harriss (1987), Kelkar, *et al.* (1990).
17. In the sixties, when all imports were subject to strict licensing, the elaborate administrative scrutiny was generally confined to ensuring that imports were required for 'actual' production, and that imports did not compete with indigenous industry.
18. For example the debt-service ratio in India in 1989 was 26.3 per cent, as against that of 81.3 per cent in Brazil in 1982. World Bank, *World Debt Tables*, 1990-1. See Dornbusch (1989) for further details of the Latin American situation.
19. The need to keep commercial borrowings within prudent limits is also contained in several other documents of the government since the early eighties, including the Sixth and the Seventh Plans.
20. The studies by international institutions, including those by the World Bank, are unpublished.
21. The figures of export growth in this section are as reported by

D.G.C.I.S. on the basis of customs returns. These are different from those reported by the Reserve Bank of India.

22. All figures are from Misra (1991). The study is not yet published.
23. See Bhagwati and Desai (1970) and Panchamukhi (1978). Comparable studies of effective rates of protection for Indian industry are not available for the recent period, except from unpublished sources.
24. World Bank estimate. This figure does not include the incidence of countervailing excise duties. Inclusive of countervailing duties, the average tariff is estimated to be 142 per cent.
25. The effective protection rates varied from 162 per cent for synthetic fibres to 92 per cent for electronics and (-) 16 per cent for aluminium products in mid-eighties. Interestingly, hand tools and bicycles enjoyed effective protection rates of only 33 per cent and 24 per cent respectively. Kelkar and Kumar (1990) have pointed out that metal-based sectors of capital goods, other engineering industries, transport, etc. have been receiving very low or negative protection. This is despite the fact that the Plans have always given the highest priority to the production of capital goods. The protection rates provided to chemical-based industries, on the other hand, have been high even though they are supposed to enjoy a lower priority. The result has been that chemical industries have shown very high rates of growth, whereas the engineering sector has suffered from low growth.
26. The average effective protection rates are from World Bank sources. The average effective rates are weighted by value of production of different types of TVs.
27. For a detailed discussion of the terms-of-trade controversy and the statistical findings on this question, see Balassa (1990). Also see Love (1980).
28. Mahalanobis' closed-economy model for India represents an extreme case of elasticity pessimism (Mahalanobis, 1953).
29. Gallagher and Robinson (1953) have argued that 'responsible government, far from being a separatist device, was simply a change from direct to indirect methods of maintaining British interests. By slackening the formal political bond at the appropriate time, it was possible to rely on economic dependence and mutual good feeling to keep the colonies bound to Britain while still using them as agents for further British expansion' (p. 4).

30. Also see Hirschman (1968) and Findlay (1986) for political-economy explanations of the inward-looking strategy.
31. The so-called 'second wave of export pessimism' is based on the protectionist threat in industrial economies. Other arguments rest on the existence of labour-market imperfections (Fields, 1984), and on the inflexibility of resource movements in developing countries (Bhagwati, 1988b).
32. Recent reviews of the theoretical literature and empirical evidence on various aspects of the relationship between trade and growth are available in Bhagwati (1988b), Balassa (1990), Bliss (1990), Meier (1990) and Sundrum (1990).
33. See Little, Scitovsky and Scott (1970), Krueger (1978, 1982), and Bhagwati (1978).
34. See, for example, Diaz-Alejandro (1970). Commenting on economic policy in Argentina under Peron, Diaz-Alejandro observed: 'The economic history of Argentina since 1930, but especially since 1943, should be required reading for planners of countries beginning their industrialization. It is a dramatic example of the dangers arising in the development process when a balance between the production of exportables, importables, and home goods is neglected. In an economy with a severe exchange bottleneck, not even a gross savings rate of 20 per cent will bring rapid growth, as the Argentine experience shows' (p. 138).
35. Thus, Lockwood (1954), in his study of Japan, spoke of trade as the 'highway of learning'. Haberler (1959) considered trade as 'the most important vehicle for transmission of technological knowhow' (p. 705).
36. There are several interpretations and extension of the 'two gap' theory. For a discussion of different models, see Bliss (1990).
37. It may be mentioned that Chenery and his associates have used the IS (Import Substitution) and EP (Export Promotion) terminology in a different fashion. They have used these terms to decompose observed growth of output into components attributable to export promotion, import substitution and other categories (Chenery *et al.*, 1962).
38. See World Bank (1987), p. 78. Also, Helleiner (1990), for a critique of the methodology used by the World Bank for their categorization of countries according to trade strategy.
39. For the conclusions of the WIDER study, see Taylor (1988).

40. Trade theorists have defined export-oriented or outward-oriented strategies as being those where the average effective exchange rate for a country's exports (EERx) equals the average effective exchange rate for a country's imports (EERm), taking into account all duties, taxes, subsidies, etc. In theory, this condition can be fulfilled in a tariff-cum-subsidy regime where effective tariffs on imports is the same as effective subsidy on exports, even though both tariffs and subsidies are high. This case has to be distinguished from the policy of import liberalization, which implies a reduction in average effective import tariffs, and a greater penetration of imports into the economy.
41. Normally, the import liberalization packages also include reduction in all other forms of market intervention by the government, in capital markets, factor markets, and in the level of government taxation and expenditure.
42. For an exposition of the principal theoretical arguments against the policy of liberalization, also see Hamilton (1989).
43. These 'heterodox shock' packages generally consisted of various structuralist measures, including wage, price, exchange-rate freezes and caps on interest rates, etc. None of these experiments has proved be successful or sustainable. See Taylor (1988), pp. 121-33 for some case histories. More recently, the shock therapy has also formed a part of monetarist stabilization and liberalization packages, such as that introduced by President Collor in Brazil in 1990, whereby bank deposits and money supply were reduced drastically in one bold stroke. This package has also run into rough weather because of large-scale unemployment, and a rise in the inflation rate after a temporary decline.
44. See *The Economy of the USSR: Summary and Recommendations* pp. 16-18 (Washington, D.C., 1990). This study was undertaken jointly by the IMF, the World Bank, the Organisation for Economic Co-operation and Development, and the European Bank for Reconstruction and Development, in response to a request by the Houston Economic Summit of seven industrialized countries.
45. See Chapter 10, 'Problems of Transition', in Little, Scitovsky and Scott (1970). See also Diaz-Alejandro (1975), pp. 133-4.
46. For example, President Gorbachev's economic adviser has said that even the relatively modest reforms introduced in the Soviet

Union could lead to a slump in output by 40 to 50 per cent. This would happen because of the 'rigidly connected economic structure' between enterprises and the central government. This structure has been disturbed without putting an alternative viable structure in its place. In its annual survey for 1990-1, the United Nations Economic Commission for Europe has also cautioned against the 'big bang' approach to economic restructuring. Output of all goods, excluding services, fell by 11 per cent in East Europe and by 4 per cent in the Soviet Union in 1990. The Survey forecasts a big rise in unemployment in 1991, which will create further social and political tensions. (Reported in *Financial Times*, London, 27 March and 5 April 1991).

47. What constitutes a 'large' disequilibria is also likely to vary from country to country. For example, if the country is used to an inflation rate of 50 or 100 per cent, and different social groups are adjusted to it, a radical programme to reduce the inflation rate may be as unacceptable as in another country which is 'used to' an inflation rate of 7-8 per cent.

48. The current-account deficit, on payments basis, in 1990-1 was about Rs 10,000 crores (this is a rough estimate based on trade statistics, as balance-of-payments data are not available at the time of writing). Inflows of net external assistance were about Rs 4000 crores. The difference between the two figures was equivalent to about 1.2 per cent of GDP. Even allowing for zero net inflows of commercial borrowings and other non-resident deposits, a correction of 1.2 per cent of GDP will be sufficient to protect reserves at their present level. Positive inflows of commercial loans or a further reduction in the current-account deficit would allow some build-up of reserves.

49. In the Fifth Plan, there were considerable savings in imports due to an increase in domestic oil production and a low growth in consumption.

50. See Reserve Bank of India (1990), pp. 119-25.

51. See Government of India, *Economic Survey*, 1989-90, p. 128. Out of total approvals of Rs 13,300 crores during the period 1985-6 and 1989-90 (upto September 1990), about Rs 12,000 crores was in respect of the public sector, including public financial institutions.

52. The exports of non-petroleum manufacturing public sector enterprises were about 2 per cent of total sales. This was much

below the average for all manufacturing industries (which was itself very low at 5 per cent of sales). See Government of India (1990), *Public Enterprises Survey*, 1989-90, Highlights, p. 29.

53. See Sachs (1987) for an account of the fiscal policies pursued by Japan, Taiwan and Korea, and their impact on the balance of payments.
54. For a full description of the Polak Model and its extensions, see International Monetary Fund (1987). For a mathematical treatment of the fiscal and monetary approaches to the balance of payments and some empirical results, see Bartoli (1989). Also see Taylor (1988), pp. 154-64 for a critique of the Polak Model.
55. Statement made by the finance minister in the Lok Sabha on 27 December 1990. It may be noted that the actual deficit in 1990-1 was 8.6 per cent of GDP, and not 8.3 per cent, as estimated in December 1989.
56. The specifications of the NCEAR model for India are available in Sarkar and Panda (1990).
57. This estimate is to be interpreted broadly as the external sector specification in the NCEAR model, as in other models of the Indian economy, is very limited. It has been assumed that the fiscal squeeze affects Indian imports mainly through a lower domestic inflation rate and lower GDP growth. The main effect of the fiscal adjustment on exports is expected to operate through a lower domestic inflation rate, and a larger exportable surplus because of lower domestic demand. The effects of the fiscal squeeze, therefore, depend upon the assumptions regarding price and income elasticities of Indian imports and exports. Available estimates on these elasticites are not very firm.
58. In the extreme versions of the Polak Model, a reduction in fiscal deficit should lead to a one-for-one correction in the balance of payments.
59. See *Government of India*, Import-Export Policy for 1990/1 to 1992-3 (in 3 volumes), for details.
60. No systematic data are available on market premia on REP licences. With liberalization of the import regime in the 1980s, it has been reported that these premia have been generally small, about 7 or 8 per cent of the value of the licence. On an average, the cash value of this incentive has been less than 1 per cent of the value of exports. The situation, however, changed dramatically after the Gulf War and the introduction of new

curbs on imports. According to newspaper reports, the premia on these licences shot up to 30 per cent after September 1990.

61. 'Gem and jewellery' is a special case, as these exports are entirely based on imports, and involve only processing and finishing in India. REP licences issued for this sector would have to be excluded from the purview of the proposed scheme. The figures of AU and REP licence mentioned in the text exclude licences for capital goods, imprest and advance licences for exporters, and certain other categories.
62. According to an unpublished report, it was not even possible to classify 20 per cent of imports under the harmonized system of classification used by the customs authorities.
63. As is well known, the 1966 devaluation of the rupee became a matter of great controversy in India, as it was believed to have been effected under external pressures. The move also proved ineffective because of its wrong timing (it coincided with a drought), and lack of adequate financial assistance to support import liberalization (see Denoon, 1986).
64. Exchange-rate management is another under-researched area of economic policy in India. The basket to which the rupee is linked is secret, and the variables which are used to adjust the exchange rate are not known.
65. I am grateful to O.P. Sharma for Tables 4.3 and 4.8.
66. The 'unofficial' rate at which the rupee can be exchanged for other currencies through non-banking sources is generally referred to as the 'hawala' rate in India. No systematic published information is available on the movement of this rate over time. In the recent period, according to newspaper reports, the unofficial rate of the rupee has been 20-25 per cent higher than the official rate. Biswas and Nandi (1986) examined the long-run behaviour of the unofficial exchange rate in India during the period 1954 to 1980 in a monetarist framework. They found that disequilibrium in the domestic market had a spill-over effect on the unofficial exchange rate. Also see Patton Culbertson (1989) for a discussion of the theoretical issues involved in predicting the behaviour of the unofficial exchange rate.
67. Some pioneering research was done by Bhagwati and others on the impact of trade regimes on generating illegal transactions in foreign exchange. This work has enhanced our understanding of how illegal markets work and why. It is also likely that trade regimes characterized by import and exchange con-

trols are more vulnerable to corruption and evasion. However, what can be done to minimize these effects in the 'second best' or third best situations (when elimination of these controls is not feasible) is not clear. See Bhagwati (1974). For a review of the more recent literature on parallel markets, see Jones and Roemer (1989).

68. A subsidy-cum-tax system on current transactions is tantamount to a multiple exchange -rate practice, and is in any case not permissible under the Articles of Agreement of the International Monetary Fund.
69. See Little and Clifford (1965) for a discussion of the rationale and criteria for distribution of aid. This still remains one of the most authoritative treatments of policy issues relating to aid flows.
70. There is, of course, a substantial literature on theoretical and policy issues concerning debt crises, including a special issue of *Journal of Development Planning* (no.16, 1985), United Nations.
71. The utilization of outstanding commitments of aid to India is, however, an important problem. According to the ministry of finance, Rs 43,000 crores of total committed aid was unutilized at the end of March 1990, of which Rs 16,000 crores was from the USSR. The utilization of aid from the USSR aid poses some special problems. As far as other bilateral and multilateral aid is concerned, there is scope for further action to accelerate its disbursement. Much of this aid is tied to projects. The utilization is dependent on the pace at which such projects can be implemented.
72. Data on actual direct investment are available with a considerable time lag. The data on approvals given by the government show that direct foreign investment was Rs 107 crores in 1987, Rs 234 crores in 1988 and Rs 316 crores in 1990 (India Investment Centre, New Delhi).
73. In recent years, the international practice has been to include exports of both goods and services in calculating the debt-service ratio.
74. See Diaz-Alejandro (1975), p. 141.

TABLE 4.1
MACRO-ECONOMIC INDICATORS DURING THE THREE SUB-PERIODS

	Macro-economic indicators	*Units*	*1956-57 to 1975-76*	*1976-77 to 1979-80*	*1980-81 to 1989-90*	*1989-90*
1.	Current-account deficit	Per cent of GDP	1.8	-0.6	1.9	2.4
2.	Foreign-exchange reserves	Per cent of imports	20.5[1]	57.9	28.9	14.7
3.	Net external assistance	Per cent of current - account deficit	91.8[2]	N.C[3]	36.7	21.7
4.	Imports (dollar values)	Annual growth rate	9.6	22.3	8.4	7.5
5.	Exports (dollar values)	Annual growth rate	8.7	12.5	8.7	20.1
6.	Fiscal deficit[5]	Per cent of GDP	5.6[4]	7.0	9.9	10.5
7.	Centre's fiscal[5] deficit	Per cent of GDP	4.3[4]	4.7	7.5	8.0
8.	Money supply	Annual growth rate	11.2	20.4	17.2	19.4
9.	GDP	Annual growth rate	3.9	2.3[6]	5.6	5.2
10.	Industrial growth	Annual growth rate	5.9	5.0	7.4	8.6
11.	Inflation	Per cent change in GDP deflator	6.7	7.5[6]	8.2	6.7
12.	Gross domestic investment	Per cent of GDP	16.0	21.2	22.1	24.1
13.	Gross domestic savings	Per cent of GDP	14.1	21.8	20.2	21.7

	Macro-economic indicators	*Units*	*1956-57 to 1975-76*	*1976-77 to 1979-80*	*1980-81 to 1989-90*	*1989-90*
14.	Incremental capital-output ratio	Value	4.1	9.2[6]	3.9	–

NOTES: 1. For the years 1957-8 to 1975-6.

2. For the years 1956-7 to 1974-5. In 1975-6, the figure was negative.
3. Not computed since the current-account deficit was negative in 1976-7, 1977-8 and 1979-80.
4. Relates to 1960-1 to 1975-6.
5. Fiscal deficit is computed as a residual by deducting revenue receipts and recovery of loans from total expenditure of the government, including capital expenditure.
6. The rate of growth of GDP, the rate of inflation and the incremental capital-output ratio during this sub-period, excluding the drought year (1979-80), works out to 4.7, 4.7 and 4.4 respectively.

SOURCE: Computed from various Government of India and Reserve Bank of India publications for the relevant periods.

TABLE 4.2
YEARLY MOVEMENTS IN NET INVISIBLES AND TRADE DEFICIT
(IN RS CRORES)

Year	*Net Invisibles*	*Trade Deficit*	*Ratio*
1973-74	- 104	510	- 20.4
1974-75	+ 193	1287	+ 15.0
1975-76	+ 527	1183	+ 44.5
1976-77	+ 827	310	+ 266.8
1977-78	+ 1388	597	+ 232.5
1978-79	+ 1508	2212	+ 68.7
1979-80	+ 2486	3440	+ 72.3
1980-81	+ 3539	6211	+ 57.0
1981-82	+ 3356	6494	+ 51.7
1982-83	+ 3100	6719	+ 46.1
1983-84	+ 3216	6925	+ 46.4
1984-85	+ 3274	6721	+ 48.7
1985-86	+ 3323	9586	+ 34.7
1986-87	+ 2999	9354	+ 32.1
1987-88	+ 2471	9296	+ 26.6
1988-89	+ 2908	14003	+ 20.7
1989-90	+ 2700	13771	+ 19.6

NOTE : Net invisibles are excluding official transfers.
SOURCE: Reserve Bank of India.

TABLE 4.3
AVERAGE ANNUAL NET RECEIPTS OF INVISIBLES ON CURRENT ACCOUNT
(IN RS CRORES)

	1971-72 to 1973-74	*1974-75 to 1979-80*	*1980-81 to 1984-85*	*1985-86 to 1988-89*
1. Foreign travel	+ 23.4	+ 385.0	+ 852.4	+ 1212.3
	(19.9)	(32.3)	(25.8)	(36.3)
2. Transportation	+ 43.6	+ 64.9	+ 183.8	- 176.3
	(37.2)	(5.4)	(- 5.6)	(- 5.3)
3. Insurance	+ 2.3	+ 10.6	+ 12.3	+ 4.1
	(2.0)	(0.9)	(0.4)	(0.1)
4. Investment income	-243.7	- 43.4	- 199.2	- 1602.8
	(-207.8)	(-3.6)	(-6.0)	(-48.2)
5. Govt. not elsewhere classified	- 2.6	- 14.9	- 19.9	- 41.5
	(-2.2)	(- 1.3)	(-0.6)	(-1.3)
6. Miscellaneous	- 33.9	+ 19.6	+ 374.3	+ 123.6
	(-28.9)	(1.6)	(11.3)	(3.7)
7. Transfer payments	+ 93.6	+ 769.5	+ 2464.0	+ 3806.4
	(79.8)	(64.6)	(74.7)	(114.4)
i) Official	- 14.0	+ 12.3	+ 22.9	+ 522.3
	(-11.9)	(1.0)	(0.7)	(15.7)
ii) Private	+ 107.6	+ 757.2	+ 2441.1	+ 3284.1
	(91.7)	(63.6)	(74.0)	(98.7)
Total net (1-7)	- 117.3	+ 1191.3	+ 3300.0	+ 3325.8
	(100.0)	(100.0)	(100.0)	(100.0)

NOTE : Figures in brackets indicate percentage to the total.

SOURCES: Ministry of Finance, Economic Survey (various issues) and *Reserve Bank of India Bulletin* (Bombay: February 1991).

TABLE 4.4
GROWTH RATES IN IMPORTS
(IN PER CENT)

	Net oil imports (oil import-oil export)		*Non-oil imports*		*Total imports*	
	In Rs	*In SDRs*	*In Rs*	*In SDRs*	*In Rs*	*In SDRs*
1985-86	21.0	11.7	25.1	15.5	14.7	5.9
1986-87	-44.8	-53.8	17.8	-1.6	2.2	-14.5
1987-88	43.8	29.7	6.0	-4.4	11.5	0.6
1988-89	12.1	-0.3	30.1	15.6	25.9	11.9
1989-90	49.1	29.9	22.3	10.3	25.6	13.2
Annual average growth						
1985-86 to 1989-90	15.2	3.4	20.3	7.1	16.0	3.4

SOURCE : Rangarajan (1990) for the period upto 1988-9. Growth rates are based on trade statistics released by the Directorate General of Commercial Intelligence and Statistics (DGCIS). The same source has been used to update the data.

TABLE 4.5
NON-OIL IMPORTS : ANNUAL GROWTH RATES
(IN PER CENT)

	In Rupees					
	1985-86	*1986-87*	*1987-88*	*1988-89*	*1989-90*	*Annual average 1985-90*
Total non-oil imports of which:	25.1	17.8	6.0	30.1	22.3	20.3
1. Bulk consumption goods	5.5	-19.6	17.1	26.0	-47.5	-3.7
2. Other bulk imports	28.9	- 6.4	-16.9	45.4	40.0	18.2
3. Capital goods	35.3	51.4	-3.1	9.9	27.9	24.3
4. Mainly export-related imports	15.9	20.7	15.4	56.1	32.2	28.1
5. Others	25.7	21.7	46.6	28.8	11.9	26.9

SOURCE: See Table 4.4.

TABLE 4.6
STRUCTURE OF IMPORTS : 1984-85 TO 1989-90
(DISTRIBUTION IN PER CENT)

Community Groups	1984-85	1985-86	1986-87	1987-88 PR	1988-89 PR	1989-90 PR
1. Bulk imports	59.2	54.8	39.9	39.4	39.0	39.6
a) Oil and petroleum products	31.6	25.4	14.0	18.2	15.5	17.7
b) Non-oil bulk consumption goods	8.1	7.5	5.9	6.2	6.2	2.6
c) Other bulk items	19.5	21.9	20.0	15.0	17.3	19.3
2. Capital goods	18.5	21.8	32.3	28.0	24.5	24.9
3. Mainly export related imports	11.9	12.0	14.2	14.7	18.2	19.2
4. Others	10.4	11.4	13.6	17.9	18.3	16.3
TOTAL	100.0	100.0	100.0	100.0	100.0	100.0

NOTE : PR = Partially revised.
SOURCE: See Table 4.4.

TABLE 4.7
DOMESTIC AND EXPORT PROFITABILITY
(GROSS PROFIT ON DOMESTIC AND EXPORT SALES)

	1978/79	1979/80	1980/81	1985/86	1986/87
			ON TOTAL COSTS		
Domestic profitability	12.0	12.4	13.9	16.1	13.2
Export profitability (without incentives)	-15.4	-12.7	-11.2	-27.3	-17.0
Export profitability (with incentives)	4.0	5.4	4.9	-8.8	-0.2
			ON VARIABLE COSTS		
Domestic profitability	–	–	–	27.9	25.1
Export profitability (without incentives)	-5.2	-2.8	-1.6	-11.5	-2.2
Export profitability (with incentives)	14.2	15.2	13.9	4.6	12.6

– : Not available
SOURCE: ICICI/World Bank.

TABLE 4.8
EXTENT OF VARIATIONS IN THE ACTUALS OVER PLAN ESTIMATES, FIRST TO THE SEVENTH PLAN
(IN PER CENT)

Plan	*Export*	*Import*	*Trade balance*	*Invisibles (net)*	*Current account (net)*
First	–	–	–	–	12.2
Second	1.6	38.0	116.7	29.8	136.5
Third	4.1	3.5	2.3	–	0.9
Fourth	-11.6	9.7	133.6	-674.3	181.9
Fifth	-26.0	-46.8	-113.2	167.8	-183.9
Sixth	-15.1	10.7	70.2	38.6	100.6
Seventh	7.8	38.9	93.5	-31.6	185.0

– : Not available
SOURCE: Computed from Five Years Plans and Economic Surveys of Government of India, and the Reserve Bank of India Bulletins for the relevant period.

5

Policies for Higher Savings

In Chapter 2 we noted that India's long-run savings performance compared unfavourably with that of fast-growing countries. The performance has been particularly poor in the 1980s. The gross-savings ratio has remained practically stagnant, and the net-savings ratio has actually declined. The behaviour of public savings has been dismal. Its proportion in total savings is falling; at constant prices there has even been a decline in the rupee volume of savings; and net savings have been negative at both current and constant prices (Tables 5.1 and 5.2). As pointed out earlier, an important consequence of the stagnation in the domestic savings ratio was the increasing dependence of the economy on external commercial borrowings to meet the country's capital requirements. This process cannot be sustained any longer. It is clear that a significant increase in the ratio of domestic savings, in addition to measures to increase productivity of investments, is a necessary prerequisite of sustained growth in the 1990s.

Household Savings

A satisfactory economic theory of savings behaviour in developing countries is not available. The 'life-cycle' theory of saving behaviour (Ando and Modigliani, 1963, and Modigliani, 1970), which has been found useful in understanding the savings behaviour of individuals in industrial countries, is clearly unsatisfactory in the context of developing countries. The general life-cycle model suggests that individuals smooth consumption over time by taking into account anticipated changes in household resources, as well as the expected rate of return on savings.

In this framework, private-sector savings behaviour is directly influenced by assessments of how the future pattern of income and consumption would be affected by age, government policy and other factors. An important implication of the life-cycle theory is that the savings rate changes systematically over the individual's lifetime. Clearly, the savings behaviour of households in developing countries does not fit well into this framework in view of the low capacity to save because of subsistence incomes, the large fluctuations in agricultural incomes, the lower importance of wage employment, a shorter life expectancy, and other social and cultural factors such as the importance of extended-family arrangements.[1] After examining the available evidence on determinants of savings and development, Gersovitz (1988) concludes:

> Empirical knowledge about saving seems to lag considerably behind the theory, so that most of the implications of the theories remain untested. Evidence is not yet available on the effects on savings of exogenous factors that influence nutrition, health, life expectancy, education, the availability of other investment opportunities and their returns, family structure, and bequests (p. 418).

Nevertheless, from the policy point of view, it is possible to make two generalizations about determinants of savings in developing countries.[2] First, policies that help improve the productivity of investment and raise the rate of growth of incomes will also help savings. The same initial rate of savings can yield different growth rates of income, depending on productivity and the incremental capital–output ratio. If productivity is low, the task of raising the marginal rate of savings out of low increments to income is likely to be difficult. The increase in the growth rate on account of a productivity increase, on the other hand, makes it possible to raise the marginal rate of savings while maintaining the past *rates* of growth in consumption. The causation between growth and savings is likely to run both ways—higher savings generate higher growth and vice versa.[3]

However, if the growth rate of income is the same as before, an increase in the domestic savings rate *ipso facto* implies a reduction in the *rate* of growth of consumption. This is the second important point about the savings rate. For example, if income is growing at a steady rate of 5 per cent per annum and consumption has been growing at, say, 13 per cent per annum (as was, for example, the case in India during the eighties), an increase in the domestic savings rate in the future, with the same growth rate, can be brought about only by reducing the growth-rate of consumption. This is difficult to achieve, particularly if the consumption of those below the poverty line needs to be increased—as should indeed be the case—through direct anti-poverty programmes. The objective of these programmes—and for that matter of any poverty-alleviation strategy—is to increase the incomes and consumption of the poor at a rate which is higher than the average. This means that if the rate of savings has to be raised at the same time, the growth-rate of consumption of the non-poor must be even lower (than the reduced average).

The need to increase savings by reducing the growth of consumption was a central consideration in early planning exercises.[4] This consideration, in fact, shaped many of the policies and priorities relating to inter-sectoral investment. A two-pronged approach was adopted to reduce the growth of consumption. First, investment was to be directed to capital goods, energy and other investment-related sectors, so that the supply of consumer goods was constrained. Since the bulk of investment in the heavy- and capital-goods sector was by the public sector, it was assumed that profits arising from such investments would be reinvested rather than consumed. Industrial licensing was actively used to ensure that there was no further private investment in consumer goods or consumer durables, except in the small-scale sector and in existing factories. Second, a set of fiscal, financial and tariff policies was used to restrain the growth of consumption. Typically, domestic taxes on consumer goods and consumer durables were substantially higher than those on investment goods (with important exemptions for consumer goods produced in the small-scale sector).[5] The financial and credit system provided little or no support for investment in, or purchases of, consumption goods. Imports of such goods were prohibited.

The Second Five Year Plan (1956) was explicit in articulating this strategy.[6] Among other things, it emphasized the need for using fiscal policy as well as direct controls, including the rationing of essential commodities, to reduce consumption and cope with shortages. On the question of different types of controls to restrain consumption and raise resources, it was argued that

> overall fiscal and monetary discipline, it would appear, can go a long way towards regulating the ebb and flow of economic activity, and differential taxation can assist in channelling resources at the margin in certain directions. There is little doubt, however, that a comprehensive plan which aims at raising the investment in the economy substantially and has a definite order of priorities in view cannot be seen through on the basis merely of overall fiscal and monetary control (p. 38).

The Plan, therefore, visualized the need for imposing direct controls on consumption. In order to meet the situation arising from shortages of consumer necessities, the Plan recognized the need to increase supplies, if possible. However, it went on to say that imports of necessities

> may involve diverting resources from other important uses. The same may hold for a diversion of domestic resources from investment into consumption. Physical controls may thus become necessary, if the entire plan is not to be disturbed. Thus, control on essential consumption cannot be ruled out in particular situations (p. 39).[7]

With some changes in emphasis, this approach towards increasing savings and reducing consumption continued in the 1960s. Thus, the Third Five Year Plan (1961) observed that 'in planning the pattern of production, care must be taken to avoid the use of the limited resources available in the production of non-essential goods and services' (p. 52).[8] The Plan also endorsed the desirability of continuing with physical allocations and direct controls in respect of essential goods as well as raw materials and intermediates.[9] The 1970s were dominated by the after-effects of the 1973-4 oil shock and the impact of several important political developments. There was, however, a growing realization that physical controls, price controls, and the industrial licensing system to curb conspicuous consumption were not working as expected. The growth rate was low, industry was stagnating, and the "parallel" or "black" economy was flourishing. While there were some changes in liberalizing and streamlining the system of industrial licensing in response to these concerns, the earlier policy framework in respect of production of consumer goods remained virtually intact.[10]

The Sixth Five Year Plan (1980) envisaged a substantial jump in the savings ratio (from 21 per cent in 1979-80 to 24.4 per cent in 1984-5). However, there was now a significant and explicit shift in the approach to the regulation and control of consumption. It was recognized that past policies with regard to physical controls and detailed industrial licensing had led to the emergence of several deficiencies in the management and utilization of assets. A much greater role was therefore assigned to the demand side in determining the pattern of investment and growth. In determining sectoral growth-rates, the Plan took into account 'the demand for and supply of different commodities and services either through the market mechanism or as a result of specific public policies adopted to clear specific markets' (p. 35). The output projections for the Plan reflected the projected consumption requirements,[11] and allowed for high rates of growth in consumer-goods industries. This pattern has continued since then, and, with the greater liberalization of industrial licensing and import policy in recent years, the allocation of investment has been primarily demand determined.

Policies designed to curb or restrain the growth of consumption directly through production controls and investment controls have not worked well in the past; they are unlikely to work well in the future. Indian planners, as well as their counterparts in centrally planned economies (e.g. China and countries in Eastern Europe) have come to this conclusion. The weight of historical evidence seems to support this view. In the initial stages of development these policies may work and succeed in raising the savings rates, and in building the industrial and manufacturing base. However, after some time these policies begin to yield diminishing returns as the production structure becomes less flexible and less responsive to changes in the economic situation. This happened in India, as evidenced by the widespread under-utilization of industrial capacity, particularly in the capital-goods sector over the last twenty years, combined with a slowing down in the growth rate of savings. The under-utilization of capacity and the rising capital–output ratios in turn affected public-sector savings and investment. Thus, a vicious circle developed. The slow growth in public investment led to a decline in the demand for capital goods, which in turn led to a decline in the growth-rate of the manufacturing sector.[12]

The question then arises: what, if anything, can the government do to promote household savings in future? In recent years considerable attention has been devoted to interest-rate policy in developing countries as an instrument for raising domestic savings.[13] In the context of the high inflation which prevails in several Latin American countries, and the failure to adjust interest rates in line with inflation rates, it has been argued that negative real-interest rates helped divert savings to informal financial markets, unproductive investments, and flights of capital abroad. The theoretical argument in favour of positive real-interest rates has been advanced forcefully by Mckinnon (1973), among others. Mckinnon has argued that positive real-interest rates are warranted to build up real money balances, an increased financial intermediation, and the unification of financial markets—thereby ensuring an efficient utilization of resources, particularly scarce capital.

The available empirical results on the relationship between the level of interest rates and the level of savings (as a proportion of income) are, however, ambiguous. This is partly due to the poor quality of data, and partly on account of the difficulty of isolating the impact of real-interest rates from the effects of other economic policies. Khatkhate (1988a) has examined the available cross-country evidence on the relationship between the *level* of the real-interest rate and savings, and the growth performance of sixty-four developing countries during the period 1971-80. He found that there was no difference of any statistical significance in the performance of two groups of developing countries above and below the mean real-interest rate. The evidence on the impact of a *change* in interest rates on the change in the savings ratio is also mixed due to the offsetting income and substitution effects of increased interest rates. For developing countries, Rossi (1988) has concluded that the net effect of changes in real-interest rates on savings is positive, but small in magnitude.

For India too, for the reasons given above, it is not possible to be categorical about the relationship between interest rates and the overall savings ratio. The available evidence suggests that there is a significant relationship between the level of real-interest rates and the *composition* of savings in favour of financial savings. Khatkhate's (1991) calculations show that, until the 1980s, interest rates were negative, but in recent years interest rates have been generally positive.[14] As a result, financial assets as a ratio to GDP have increased impressively, even as compared to some of the newly-industrializing countries like Korea. Datta Roy Choudhury (1990) has also found that the income elasticity of financial savings was significantly higher than the income elasticity of total savings in the eighties. An unpublished econometric study by Madhur (1990) for the period 1970-88 confirms the positive relationship between real-interest rates and the ratio of financial savings to disposable incomes of the household. While some ambiguities remain, there is sufficient evidence to suggest that it is desirable to maintain interest rates at a positive level in real terms.

A word of caution is also necessary. Pegging real-interest rates at too high a level, or linking them mechanically to changes in price level and exchange rate as part of a macro-economic stabilization programme, as monetarists often recommend, could have severe adverse effects on financial markets and the inducement to invest. In several Latin American countries (e.g. Brazil), interest rates were raised during the period of rising prices, but these were not adjusted downwards during the period of declining inflation rates (brought about by a contractionary monetary and fiscal policy). This raised the real cost of servicing debt for companies, leading to large-scale financial bankruptcies and a fall in output, which triggered off a fresh round of inflation. A good policy is to keep interest rates positive in real terms, taking into account both present and expected rates of inflation and the likely monetary growth, but to keep them flexible and adjustable in both directions.

A large number of countries provide fiscal incentives for savings. But the effect of fiscal incentives on savings is ambiguous. Theoretical and empirical research on the impact of tax incentives seems to indicate that such incentives increase savings in the form of specific assets, but not all the increase represents new savings. While tax incentives may raise private savings, their impact on national saving is less clear because they may reduce government saving (Smith, 1989). In the United States, for example, Munnell (1988) estimates that employer-sponsored pensions raised private savings by $ 57 billion in 1985, but 80 per cent of this increase was reflected in tax deductions. Venti and Wise (1987) came to a similar conclusion with respect to tax-sheltered Individual Retirement Accounts (IRA) in the United States.

In India there are substantial fiscal incentives available for investment in instruments such as National Savings Certificates, life insurance, provident fund, and the National Saving Scheme. Within certain limits, interest income from bank deposits, dividends from certain kinds of equity investments, investment in units of the Unit Trust of India, and certain other types of investments are also tax-exempt. The effect of these incentives is to raise the effective return on investment in these instruments at the cost of the exchequer. For example, a 9 per cent per annum tax-free public sector bond could yield about 20 per cent return per annum to a tax payer in the highest tax bracket; and the tax-adjusted return on National Savings Certificates could be as high as 32.8 per cent per annum for high-income groups. Many of these savings-related incentives effectively raise the exemption limit for personal income-tax and erode the base of direct taxation. The impact of these incentives is also regressive as the higher the taxable income, the greater the benefit. While a case can be made for limited tax incentives on social grounds for investment in personal- and family-security-related instruments, such as life insurance and provident fund, there is no case for providing fiscal incentives with a view to diverting household savings for government use. The direct financial and fiscal costs are high, and disproportionate to the returns on investment. These types of fiscal incentives deserve to be phased out.

There is some evidence that the most important contribution that the government can make to promote household savings is to ensure 'macro-economic' stability. A low and stable rate of inflation is particularly helpful. In Latin America, for example, inflation rates in the 1980s have been high, and countries in that region have shown the sharpest decline in the savings ratio over that decade. This is also true of the African region. In Asia, on the other hand, which has generally low rates of inflation, savings rates have increased and are 9 to 10 percentage points higher than those in Latin America.[15] The direction of causation between low inflation and higher savings, however, is not clear. Part of the explanation may lie in the fact that monetary and fiscal policies to control inflation lead to a sharper decline in national income than in the rate of growth of consumption. In other words, the fall in money incomes affects savings more than consumption.[16]

The most direct means by which governments can increase savings is to increase public savings. As noted earlier, the stagnation in the savings ratio in the recent period in India is largely on account of a decline in the ratio of public savings to GNP.

Public Savings

Public-sector savings, of both centre and state governments, was around 2.9 per cent of GDP at market prices in 1970-1. It reached 4.9 per cent in 1976-7, and then started declining. In 1989-90 it stood at 1.6 per cent, a level reached in 1955-6.[17] The decline in budgetary savings of government, as distinguished from those of public enterprises, was dramatic. The decline in government savings occurred despite an increase in the ratio of tax revenue to GDP (Table 5.3). The ratio was under 7 per cent in 1950-1, 11.5 per cent in 1970-1 and 17.4 per cent in 1989-90. The current expenditure of the government as a ratio of GDP rose from 11.5 per cent in 1970-1 to almost 23.1 per cent in 1989-90. As far as public enterprises are concerned, the after-tax profits of central government commercial enterprises as a ratio of capital employed was 4.5 per cent in 1989-90 (Table 5.4). The performance of state level PSEs has been even worse. These enterprises had net losses of Rs 1928 crores in 1990-1 (Table 5.5).

The growth in expenditure has given rise to large revenue deficits at the centre as well as the states in recent years. The revenue deficit of the central government had to be financed by government borrowings from both the Reserve Bank of India as well as banks. The revenue deficit of the state was financed through borrowings from other sources and by a diversion of resources for the Plan. Table 5.6 shows the revenue, monetized and fiscal deficits of the central government for recent years.

A recent study by Guhan (1991) on the budgetary position of the state of Tamil Nadu illustrates the perilous position of state finances in India. Tamil Nadu, which is traditionally regarded a better-administered state, has an outstanding record of mobilizing revenue with a current tax ratio (as per cent of state domestic product) of 12 per cent in 1984-7. Yet the budget has been in deficit and there has been a significant increase in consumption outlays. Consumption outlays were about two-thirds of gross outlays in 1960-70; these have gone up to three-fourths in 1985-90 with a corresponding decline in outlays on capital formation. (It should be stressed that all consumption expenditure is not unproductive, e.g. expenditure on health and education.) The bulk of the increase in consumption expenditure is accounted for by compensation to employees, which increased to 76 per cent of current outlays during 1985-90 (as compared to 33 per cent in 1960-70). Guhan estimates that the state recovered only 12 per cent of the cost of different types of services provided by it, and 88 per cent of the cost was unrecovered. A very large proportion of direct and indirect subsidies went to the non-poor category. For example, Tamil Nadu provided a subsidy of Rs 2650, on an average, on every agricultural pump set. About 91 per cent of the aggregate subsidy on pump sets went to large farmers. Public-sector enterprises, and particularly the state electricity boards, were large recipients of budgetary subsidies to cover losses. The electricity board enjoyed a subsidy of 40 per cent of its annual gross revenue during 1985-90. Among the state enterprises, thirty-three out of sixty-two showed large losses, and the rest barely broke even. A similar study by Bajaj and Agarwal (1991) for Uttar Pradesh shows that the state of overall finances, under-recoveries, subsidies and losses in the largest state of the Union is even worse.

The rising revenue deficit and declining public savings have had several adverse economic consequences. First, there has been a sharp increase in public debt. The macroeconomic implications of the growth of public debt have been analysed in several recent studies. Important among these studies are those by Seshan (1987), Rangarajan *et al.* (1989), Buiter and Patel (1990) and Chelliah (1991). While their assumptions differ, all these studies have concluded that the emerging profile of public debt in India is unsustainable. Thus, according to Rangarajan *et al.*, the overall debt GDP ratio is likely to increase very sharply—from 44.6 per cent of GDP in 1987-8 to the 100 per cent mark in 1995-6, and to 150 per cent of GDP by the end of this century. With the projected acceleration of debt accumulation, the interest burden on government debt will rise to 30 per cent of projected receipts of the government by the turn of the century (as compared with 12 per cent in 1987-8 and only 1 per cent in 1974-75). The more recent study by Chelliah has come to a similar conclusion.

Second, the fiscal crisis has led to the emergence of a balance-of-payments crisis. In their analysis of India's debt, Buiter and Patel (1990) concluded that

> unless measures to reduce the primary deficit are taken, a fiscal crisis is bound to come. Where and when it will strike cannot be predicted with certainty. Often, a fiscal crisis first manifests itself in the foreign exchanges. Actual or imminent international reserve exhaustion is a common trigger for emergency measures, including recourse to IMF standby financing and the conditionality that this implies. Such foreign exchange crises can happen even if, as in the case of India, the external debt burden of the country is quite modest (p. 50).

These words were prophetic as, by the end of 1990, India was indeed facing a major balance-of-payments crisis, necessitating recourse to the International Monetary Fund.

Third, because of the resource crunch, capital formation has suffered, particularly in the state sector. While the central government was able to fulfil its targets of Plan outlays by a greater recourse to borrowings, state governments showed substantial shortfalls in actual outlays (in relation to Plan projections), because of their more limited access to borrowings. Since the primary responsibility for investment in social sectors, agriculture and irrigation is that of the states, the impact of lower outlays in the state sector was mainly felt in these areas, which are crucial for India's development. Bagchi and Sen (1991) have calculated that, at constant prices, there was a shortfall of 18 per cent in irrigation, 14 per cent in water supply and sanitation, 9 per cent in health, and 2 per cent in agriculture.

These shortfalls occurred despite the fact that the original targets were themselves quite modest. There was also a shortfall of 22 per cent in power outlay.

Fourth, there has been a decline in the rate of growth as well as the quality of public services. This has affected the poor more because of their greater dependence on these services, and their lower capacity to substitute private services for public services. Bagchi and Sen (1991) estimate that, as compared with the Sixth Plan, while expenditure on general administration and interest payments increased as a proportion of total revenue expenditure in the Seventh Plan, the expenditure on social services actually declined (from 41 per cent to 39 per cent). The decline would have been much more precipitous but for the increase in wages and salaries of employees (e.g. teachers and doctors).

Fifth, the acute financial stringency and the inability of central and state governments to tackle it, has led to a scramble for resources, leading to an increase in real interest rates as governments are finding it more and more difficult to borrow from the market. The statutory liquidity ratio has had to be progressively increased (to 38.5 per cent of deposits). The effectiveness of monetary policy to control monetary growth has been eroded as the cash reserve ratio has also been increased to the maximum statutory level. Fiscal reform has been another casualty. Short-run revenue considerations have been dominant in fiscal policy formulation, with the result that the role of fiscal policy for macro-economic management and resource allocation has been neglected.

The costs of the fiscal imbalance on India's economy have been truly enormous. The adverse implications of the widening deficit have been recognized at the highest levels of government, particularly since 1985-6. While presenting the budget for that year, the finance minister took cognizance of the emerging resource constraints and said that 'the basic problem is that our non-plan expenditure has been increasing at a rate substantially faster than the growth of current revenues' (Government of India, 1990, p. 539). He observed that in the last few years the government was able to finance large increases in the Annual Plan largely through borrowings, both external and internal. He added that this process could not go on indefinitely, and the process of pruning budgetary expenditure had to begin immediately.

The Long Term Fiscal Policy (1985) presented to Parliament later in that year suggested certain specific measures to reverse the decline in public savings, including the containment of subsidies within a certain percentage of GDP, reducing unproductive administrative expenditure, and increasing the contribution of public enterprises through proper pricing and other policies. The Seventh Five Year Plan, which was finalized in October 1985, also drew attention to the problem of the growing borrowing requirements of government. The Plan proposed a reduction in deficit financing by reducing the growth of non-Plan expenditure. It specifically provided for a rate of growth in non-Plan expenditure, which was no higher than the growth of GDP. (In actual fact, however, the growth of non-Plan expenditure during the Seventh Plan Period was three times as high.)

In February 1987 the budget was presented by the prime minister, who reiterated that 'some hard choices have to be made to keep our expenditure within our means. Government is determined to make them. The situation requires a thoroughgoing review of our expenditure policy. Mere scratching the surface will not help' (Government of India, 1990, p. 571). In order to put a cap on the budget deficit, he announced that 'deficit in the Budget Estimates for 1987-8 shall not be exceeded'. Such a firm commitment in advance was given for the first time in India's fiscal history. It is interesting to note that this commitment, which was widely commented upon at the time as being 'unrealistic', was actually fulfilled. However, after 1988-9 the situation reversed itself, and deficits started increasing again.

There is also a fair amount of consensus on the measures necessary for containing the growth of non-Plan expenditure. Thus, the Long Term Fiscal Policy (1985) as well as the Seventh Plan had indicated the broad programme for containing expenditure. The main elements of an expenditure-reduction programme have also been highlighted by several experts, including Chelliah (1991). Among the measures suggested by Chelliah are: raising the income elasticity of taxes, increasing fees and user charges, reducing the growth of current expenditure, increasing the net return on lending by government, and reducing the interest burden on the budget. There is no major difference of opinion among experts, and indeed in Government, on these and other desirable areas for action. Yet, as the following Table shows, achievements have fallen far short of targets.

CENTRE'S PUBLIC SAVINGS : TARGET AND ACHIEVEMENT
(AS PER CENT OF GDP)

		1980-85	*1985-86*	*1989-90*	
		(Average)		*Target*	*Achieved*
1.	Balance from current revenue	0.7	-0.4	0.2	-1.1
2.	Resources of the public sector	2.1	2.9	4.1	3.1
3.	**Total Public Savings**	**2.8**	**2.5**	**4.3**	**2.0**

NOTE : Data for the period upto 1985-6 and the target for 1989-90 are from 'Long Term Fiscal Policy' (1985). The actuals for 1989-90 have been taken from the budget of the Government of India for that year.

An interesting question is why it has not been possible for government to check the growth in expenditure, even though there is a consensus regarding the desirability of doing so, as well as on the methods for bringing this about? Administrative action has not been lacking, and from time to time the government has introduced new mechanisms to bring expenditure under control. Thus, in the sixties, in addition to the Annual Financial Statements or the conventional budget, it was decided that each ministry would formulate a Performance Budget to be presented to Parliament. In 1985-6, a system of 'zero-based budgeting' was introduced, and it was decided that one-third of the government budget would be scrutinized each year over a three-year period, and all non-essential activities would be discontinued.[18] In 1990-1, the government announced its intention to present a four-monthly review of the annual budget to Parliament, so that the progress of actual expenditure could be monitored against the budget estimates. From time to time, high-level committees, including cabinet committees on expenditure, have been set up to prune expenditure. Yet, despite all these efforts, government expenditure has continued to grow at an unsustainable rate. The reasons for this phenomenon need to be scrutinized closely.[19]

The major components of government expenditure are: (i) government consumption expenditure; (ii) government's expenditure on capital formation; and (iii) financial investments and loans to the rest of the economy. The following Table shows the growth in expenditure of the central government under these heads in the 1980s.

TOTAL EXPENDITURE OF THE CENTRAL GOVERNMENT
(IN THOUSANDS OF CRORES)

	Consumption expenditure	*Gross capital formation*	*Transfer payments*	*Investment and loans*	*Total*
1980-1	5.2	1.9	8.2	7.2	22.5
1989-90 (BE)	19.7	8.4	41.3	19.1	88.5

SOURCE: Government of India, *Economy Survey*, 1989-90.

It is striking that the total expenditure and all its components have grown by about four times in nine years. The growth of transfer payments has been a little faster than the average because of the faster growth in interest payments, and that of loan and investments has been a little slower because of resource constraints. But all the major components of expenditure have broadly kept pace with the overall growth of expenditure.

An important reason for what looks like an autonomous growth in expenditure at a predetermined rate is that all expenditure by government ultimately constitutes a private benefit for some section of society, or for some specific person.[20] This is particularly true of direct subsidies or the unrecovered costs of providing government services. Most subsidies or below-cost services are ostensibly introduced for the benefit of the poor. A substantial part of the benefits, however, actually flow to the more affluent, who also have greater political power (see, for example, Mundle and Govinda Rao, 1990). The costs, on the other hand, are not easily identifiable, and in any case do not fall upon the decision-makers. The cost to society in terms of the higher potential rate of inflation and other economic distortions are, of course, recognized and debated. But the fact remains that while the benefits are immediate and sectional, the costs are generalized and occur in the future. This reality gives rise to the formation of powerful lobbies in favour of government expenditure at all levels.[21] In democratic societies, where governments are dependent on electoral goodwill, the restraint on government expenditure weakens in proportion to the closeness of an election. If governments are unstable or face the prospect of a mid-term poll, it is almost certain that there will be an even faster expansion of government expenditure. Burgeoning budget deficits in India during 1988-91 provide ample evidence of this.

Another important reason for the growth of government's administrative expenditure is the over-centralization of the decision-making process. The influence of this factor was recognized by Kornai as early as 1959 in his examination of the reasons for low productivity and efficiency in the Hungarian light industry. Kornai (1959) pointed out that

> the growth of the number of persons engaged in administration is one of the most significant social consequences

> of excessive centralization. It has a measurable impact on the composition of the labour force and thus on the social structure. The manpower withdrawn from the productive process by the growth of administration is excessive (p. 206).

In India too, over-centralization has played a part in the growth of government employment and administrative expenditure. Government employment in India has grown at an annual rate of 2.7 per cent, which is much faster than the growth of employment in general. The average wage rates within government employment have also increased at a faster rate than in the rest of the economy.

There are important functional reasons for the growth of both capital and current expenditure in government, in view of the poor availability of public services (and 'public goods'), and on account of the need for higher investments, particularly in the infrastructure sectors. The state has been regarded the primary agent of accumulation, so the pressure to increase government expenditure for financing the Plan has correspondingly mounted. The budget had to step in to make up for shortfalls in the internal generation of resources of public-sector enterprises through higher and higher borrowings.

Subsidies of various kinds, particularly food and fertilizer subsidies, represent a further autonomous factor in the growth of public expenditure. The fertilizer subsidy is determined on a cost-based formula. The selling price of fertilizers has remained constant in nominal terms since 1981, but costs are determined on the basis of actuals from year to year. This system has ensured an 'open-ended' system of growth in fertilizer subsidy. It has not been found possible to modify the system, despite a commonly-accepted view that the open-ended formula of subsidies needs to be altered drastically. A reduction in the food subsidy has also not been feasible, partly because this subsidy fulfills an important social purpose and partly because of the likely inflationary impact of the increase in food prices. The rate of growth in the food subsidy, however, has been much lower than that in fertilizer subsidy as the issue prices of foodgrains have, to some extent, been raised in line with increases in procurement prices. The export subsidy, which is another major subsidy, has also grown in view of the need to reduce the bias against exports in a highly protected domestic environment.

In a pioneering study, Mundle and Govinda Rao (1990) have provided estimates of the total volume and composition of government subsidies, covering the centre and fourteen states, for 1987-8. The study employs a broad concept of subsidy, and, in addition to direct subsidies, includes subsidies to households implicit in the provision of social and economic services below cost, as well as the unrecovered cost of loans given and investments made in non-departmental enterprises and co-operatives. They estimate the total cost of subsidies to centre and states at Rs 42,324 crores, which was 70 per cent of the total cost of providing all services. In terms of GNP, the subsidy worked out to nearly 15 per cent. About two-thirds of the total subsidy was provided by the states. The subsidy to public enterprises added upto Rs 15,000 crores, out of which Rs 9,200 crores went to central public-sector undertakings, and the rest to state enterprises. Mundle and Govinda Rao point out that much of this subsidy was not targeted towards disadvantaged groups. For example, in relation to education, which accounted for 23 per cent of the total subsidy, only less than half was spent on primary education. Similarly, in relation to health services, only about 20 per cent flowed to the rural sector where the vast majority of the poor live.

(a) Expenditure and Tax Policies

The obstacles in the way of implementing a programme of expenditure control are formidable. At the same time, it is also clear that unless revenue deficits are reduced, there is little prospect of an increase in the overall savings ratio and the rate of capital formation in the economy.[22] A decisive break from earlier methods of tackling the problem of declining public savings is necessary. The past approach to expenditure control has been gradualist and 'quantitative'. From time to time, the government announces either a certain fixed proportionate cut in all government expenditure, particularly non-Plan expenditure, or a predetermined target in terms of GDP for various types of expenditure. This quantitative approach has not worked. The limited success achieved in one or two years (as in 1987-8) has been quickly eroded by new pressures and compulsions. There is no alternative now but to take a bold and 'policy-based' approach to government expenditure, rather than a purely quantitative or marginalist approach.

Certain broad principles, which should guide the formulation of a 'policy-based' approach to government expenditure need to be stated here. First, past experience shows that the government wage bill cannnot be reduced or contained unless government reduces the areas of its activity. In addition to government ministries and production-based enterprises, a whole lot of service, research, study and promotional functions have been assumed by government, simply on the grounds that these functions deserve to be performed. In actual practice, while large numbers of organizations have been set up at both centre and state levels, they have not been able to fill the gap in services with any degree of effectiveness. These organizations have generally ended up becoming a source of employment. Government should now take a policy decision to close down all organizations which are being funded by the budget, but which do not directly contribute to production or to providing social services in the fields of health, education and welfare. Employees can be fully protected, and their wages can continue to be paid until they are absorbed elsewhere in the public or private sectors. Even in service or promotional organizations, wages and salaries seldom constitute more than 50 per cent of the total expenditure. All organizations, simply because they are there, tend to expand over time and use scarce resources (e.g. land, power and transport). A closure of unproductive organizations should result in substantial economies over time, in addition to releasing scarce administrative resources in government.

Second, the government should eliminate all subsidies, except those on food and, to some extent, on fertilizers. Compensatory policies will be necessary to cushion the adverse impact of the elimination of subsidies, and some time-phasing may also be desirable. But the policy in this respect should be absolutely clear and unequivocal. With regard to export subsidies, for example, the compensatory mechanism may be to shift the burden of subsidization to the market and to the importers through liberalization of replenishment licences for exporters (see Chapter 4). Currently, the cost of producing fertilizers is twice as high as the issue prices of fertilizers. The gap between the two represents the amount of subsidy provided by government. The fertilizer subsidy has increased by leaps and bounds, from Rs 381 crores in 1981-2 to Rs 4500 crores in 1989-90. In view of the large size of the subsidy, it is not feasible politics to try and eliminate the fertilizer subsidy altogether. Nor would it be economically desirable, as an abrupt end to the entire subsidy regime may affect the use of fertilizers by small farmers and, thereby, their incomes. A more feasible approach is to have a once-and-for-all adjustment in prices, and simultaneously announce the policy that fertilizer prices will be automatically revised annually in line with the increase in the cost of production on the basis of a fixed, verifiable and known formula, which pays due regard to efficiency considerations.[23]

A third principle to be followed in a policy-based approach is to ensure that the interest rate on savings or loans mobilized by governments—centre or state—which are then passed on to another entity, are not subsidized. In other words, the interest rate should be the same for both the lender and the ultimate borrower. There is no good reason why the intermediation function should result in explicit or implicit subsidies.

Fourth, with regard to public-sector enterprises, the budget should not provide any loans or grants to cover revenue losses.

A policy-based approach to expenditure control along the above lines is feasible, provided there is a national consensus in favour of it. A time may have also come for imposing a constitutional ceiling on government's overall borrowings. Article 292 of the Constitution contains a provision for the imposition of a statutory limit on the centre's borrowings. It reads as follows:

Fourth, with regard to public-sector enterprises, the budget should not provide any loans or grants to cover revenue losses.

A policy-based approach to expenditure control along the above lines is feasible, provided there is a national consensus in favour of it. A time may have also come for imposing a constitutional ceiling on government's overall borrowings. Article 292 of the Constitution contains a provision for the imposition of a statutory limit on the centre's borrowings. It reads as follows:

> The executive power of the Union extends to borrowing on the security of the Consolidated Fund of India within such limits, if any, as may from time to time be fixed by Parliament by law and to the giving of guarantees within such limits, if any, as may be so fixed.

This Article is not new, but is based on Section 162 of the Government of India Act, 1935, which provided that:

> Subject to the provisions of Part XIII of this Act with respect to borrowing in sterling, the executive authority of the Federation extends to borrowing upon the security of the revenues of the Federation within such limits, if any, as may from time to time be fixed by Act of the Federal Legislature and to the giving of guarantees within such limits, if any, as may be so fixed.

There are two important features of Article 292 of the Constitution. First, it is not a mandatory provision. The second is that the limit fixed under law would cover only the borrowing on the security of the Consolidated Fund, i.e. its coverage is restricted to borrowing through market loans, treasury bills and external loans which flow into the Consolidated Fund of India. It will not cover quasi-borrowings made by government, such as small savings, provident fund, deposits, and the like, which flow into the 'Public Account of India'. In the 1990-1 budget, while net Consolidated Fund borrowings are estimated at Rs 18,726 crores, quasi-borrowings in the Public Account are estimated at Rs 17,795 crores.

The Public Accounts Committee of Parliament has also in the past, more than once, recommended that a law be enacted to fix a ceiling on borrowings. The government has, however, been of the view that such ceilings would be difficult to operate in respect of borrowings through treasury bills, as these fluctuate widely during the course of the year. It has also been argued that the total expenditure approved by Parliament is in effect a limit. These arguments are valid, but only partially. The limit approved by Parliament at the time of the budget is not generally adhered to, as it is easy to cover additional expenditure through supplementary demands. The Reserve Bank of India also has no power or authority to limit the borrowings of the central government. Under the circumstances, the budget, as originally approved by Parliament, has served more as a floor for expenditure rather than as a ceiling.

Merely putting a limit on the issue of treasury bills by the central government cannot be a sufficient check. It would be more effective to put a constitutional ceiling on the central government's revenue deficit, rather than on borrowings against the security of the Consolidated Fund of India. The revenue deficit is, after all, what is desired to be controlled, and it is preferable to do so directly, rather than indirectly through a limit on particular forms of borrowings. It may be provided that the revenue deficit of the central government shall not exceed a certain percentage, say 1 per cent of GDP, upto 1994-5, and thereafter the central government shall not present a revenue-deficit budget to Parliament.[24] It may be argued that a ceiling will not be effective if the government is determined to spend, and that such a ceiling is not necessary if the government is determined to control its expenditure. This is true. However, past experience shows that in a multi-party Parliamentary system, electoral concerns play an important role in determining expenditure priorities. A constitutional provision which is applicable to all governments—present and future—is likely to be more effective.

In addition to measures to contain expenditure and reduce subsidies, there is a need to raise higher revenues from taxes. Tax revenues as percentage of GDP have increased over the years (Table 5.3). At the same time, several anomalies have developed. A number of studies are available on India's tax structure and its effects on equity, efficiency and allocative efficiency.[25] In relation to public savings, the most important issues relate to measures for reducing the possibilities for the generation of 'black money', and measures for increasing the buoyancy of the tax system, particularly direct taxes. From all accounts, the amount of incomes not disclosed to tax authorities is large and increasing. According to the estimates made by the National Institute of Public Finance and Policy (NIPFP) in its study of the black economy in India, around Rs 35,000 crores of taxable income evaded the tax net annually in recent years. The amount of income tax, which is liable to be paid but is not paid, is at least as large as the income tax that is actually paid (Rs 5,600 crores in 1990-1). The NIPFP study (Acharya and Associates, 1985) has itemized as many as eight causal factors and emphasized that these act together, and not independently. In addition to more efficient administration and enforcement, most fiscal experts agree that the discretionary system of controls and highly differentiated and complex tax system are the important causes for the generation of black money. The tax system is riddled with exemptions, complex laws, and elaborate administrative rules which erode the base of taxation, and also provide ample scope for corruption and evasion. From time to time, efforts have been made to simplify the system and to make it less discretionary. The actual results have not been very satisfactory so far. Further exercises in this direction remain an important priority for fiscal reform.

A striking feature of the composition of tax revenues in India is the decline in the share of direct taxes over the years, and the increasing dependence of the budget on indirect taxes, particularly revenue from customs duties. The share of direct taxes in total tax revenue has fallen from 37 per cent in 1950-1 to about 20 per cent in 1990-1, and that of personal income tax has fallen from 21 per cent to 9 per cent during the period. The share of customs revenue in gross revenue in 1990-1 was about one-third. The share of customs revenue in the centre's tax revenue was considerably higher at 47 per cent. (Customs revenue is not shared with states.) The economic effects of high nominal and effective tariff rates were discussed in the previous chapter. The decline in the share of direct taxes, which reflects the prevalence of large-scale tax evasion, further undermines the efficiency and equity of the tax system. As pointed out in the literature on public finance, both 'horizontal' and 'vertical equity' are affected, as the link between the burden of taxation and the ability to pay is broken at all levels of income. A more balanced tax structure is another important priority of tax policy in the 1990s.

Tax policy in developing countries presents a cornucopia of thorny issues. This is also an intensively researched area with a wealth of empirical data. It is not possible to do justice to the subject within the confines of a chapter (or even a book). The Government of India's 'Long Term Fiscal Policy' (1985), and the NIPFP's study on the black economy (1985) provide several valuable suggestions on the possible lines of tax reform. In recent years a number of developing countries in Latin America, Africa and Asia have embarked on a process of reform. Their experience provides some useful clues on the nature of desirable structural changes and the tax administration needed to implement them. Thirsk (1990) has analysed the experience of ten developing countries that have undergone at least one comprehensive tax reform during the last decade. The countries are: Indonesia, Korea, Mexico, Colombia, Jamaica, Bolivia, Turkey, Zimbabwe, Malawi, and Morocco. Despite important differences in their economic and cultural background, six trends are clearly discernible in the tax reforms implemented by them. These are: (i) the application of value added tax; (ii) lower personal and corporate tax rates, along with the abolition of most exemptions; (iii) a closer integration of personal and corporate income taxes; (iv) the alignment of the corporate and top-bracket personal income-tax rates in order to reduce evasion by unincorporated enterprises; (v) measures to broaden the base of personal and corporate income taxes; and (vi) inflation adjustment of direct- and indirect-tax rates.

The measures taken by several of these countries to broaden the direct tax base are of particular interest. These have included fewer exemptions and the inclusion of fringe benefits in the personal income-tax base, a greater use of presumptive methods of taxation applied to hard-to-tax-groups in the economy, an increased use of withholding taxes, and generally tighter tax administration. Presumptive taxes on small businesses and urban professionals have been levied on gross receipts, wealth or consumption as indicators of underlying levels of taxable income. Countries susceptible to inflation have also found it necessary to adjust both direct and indirect taxes to maintain real tax revenue and to avoid inflation-induced inequities. If indirect tax rates are not adjusted to inflation, larger revenue deficits occur which make the task of inflation-control more difficult. If personal tax rates are not adjusted to inflation, there is a stimulus to untaxed fringe benefits. An unindexed tax system can also reduce effective tax rates on corporate incomes (because of higher interest deductions), while raising the tax rate on wage incomes (because of 'bracket creep').

While the tax-reform measures taken by other countries cannot be applied wholesale to Indian conditions, their experience merits consideration in devising an appropriate system for India. An important prerequisite of an efficient tax system is its stability. The Indian tax system has been much too unstable. This has provided scope for evasion, litigation and administrative discretion. An unstable system also affects adversely the economic behaviour of corporations and individuals, as the tax liability arising from investments or any other economic activity is uncertain for more than a year or two. The programme for future structural reform should be carefully considered and extensively debated before it is introduced. Experience shows that a broad national consensus is necessary for the successful implementation of a fiscal reform programme.

(b) Budget and Public Sector Enterprise

The total investment in public enterprises is estimated at over Rs 300,000 crores, or almost equal to the country's Gross National Product in 1988-9.[26] Nearly 75 per cent of the total investment was in the central sector. The original case for a heavy reliance on public-sector enterprises was spelt out in the Industrial Policy Resolution of 1956. The Resolution stated:

> The adoption of the socialist pattern of society as the national objective, as well as the need for planned and rapid development, require that all industries of basic and strategic importance, or in the nature of public-utility services, should be in the public sector. The state, has, therefore, to assume direct responsibility for the future development of industries over a wider area.

The Resolution desired the public sector to occupy 'the commanding heights of the economy' as it perceived it, as an instrument for: (i) socializing the means of production in strategic areas; (ii) providing a countervailing power to the growth of large business houses; (iii) bringing about balanced regional development; (iv) generation of economic surplus; and (v) encouraging the development of a wide range of ancillary industries.

Another compelling consideration for the reliance on public-sector enterprises for promoting investment was that the private sector did not have the ability to mobilize the huge resources required for the development of basic and infrastructure industries.[27]

It should be recognized that the growth of public investment has provided important gains to the economy. Public-sector enterprises created the large infrastructure for economic development, and served as an important source of demand for the private sector. This helped to channelize some private investment into socially desirable directions. The public sector contributed, to some extent, in controlling the monopoly power of the private sector, and to reducing regional imbalances. Fair wages and liberal welfare provisions in public enterprises enabled the working class in the organized sector to improve their living standards, and to set an example for private-sector enterprises. Public-sector enterprises also contributed significantly to an increase in output in the core sectors of the economy. For example, after nationalization, the coal industry increased its output by nearly 40 million tonnes within a short period of four to five years. Similarly, it was the public-sector oil companies which helped to withstand the second oil shock by trebling crude oil output in the Sixth Five Year Plan. Similar examples exist in other high-technology sectors, such as BHEL in power equipment and IPCL in petrochemicals.

The most conspicuous failure of public-sector enterprises has been in the financial area. An important shortcoming has been the relatively low level of capacity utilization in many enterprises. This has increased the capital–output ratio, and reduced efficiency in the use of capital. The poor financial performance of several enterprises is traceable to a large extent to poor investment decisions. These are reflected in factors such as inappropriate location (e.g. the Nagaland Paper Project), inappropriate technology (e.g. the surgical equipment plant), an irrational product-mix (e.g. the Salem Steel Plant), and imposed marketing arrangements (e.g. the Kuderamukh Iron-ore Project).

Public-sector enterprises were also asked to assume several other responsibilities, including those relating to trade and services. The objective of stabilizing the food economy was entrusted to the Food Corporation of India; price stabilization in cotton and jute was assigned to the Cotton Corporation of India and the Jute Corporation of India; and the promotion of foreign trade was made the responsibility of the State Trading Corporation and the Minerals and Metals Trading Corporation. In response to various other pressures, public-sector enterprises increasingly became the instruments for meeting short-term or ad hoc demands, such as producing mass-consumption goods, stimulating growth in economically backward areas, or for using locally available raw materials. Furthermore, a large number of industries which became sick under private-sector management were taken over by government with a view to protecting employment. As a result of this indiscriminate expansion, the public sector today covers widely different types of enterprises, with investment ranging from Rs 3,000 crores in some cases to a few hundred thousand in others, and employment ranging from 20,000 to no more than 20.

Government departments have been ill-equipped to manage this vast range of enterprises which serve multiple purposes in almost all sectors of the economy. Evidence of management failure is government's inability to fill top-level vacancies in the public sector. Such appointments are entirely within the purview of government, and are not subject to external hurdles, such as trade-union pressures or parliamentary scrutiny. Several procedural innovations have been tried, but these have failed to improve the decision-making processes within government. A number of committees have provided comprehensive reports, but nothing much has resulted from these endeavours. A radically new approach to the management of public-sector enterprises is necessary in the nineties. The issues relating to personnel policy, financial policy and the control of public-sector enterprises were discussed briefly in Chapter 3. There are two issues relating to the government's budgetary policy and the re-organization of public enterprises along competitive lines which merit a longer discussion.

Janos Kornai, the eminent Hungarian economist, introduced the concept of a 'soft budget constraint' in the literature on economic management in socialist economies.[28] Kornai argued that the 'soft budget' syndrome is usually associated with the paternalistic role of the state towards economic organizations. Although the phenomenon is conspicuously apparent in socialist systems, it also appears in mixed economies with different degrees of stringency.

As Kornai's concept is of seminal importance, it is useful to re-state its full implications. According to Kornai (1990),

> the 'softening' of the budget constraint appears when the strict relationship between expenditure and earnings has been relaxed, because excess expenditure over earnings will be paid by some other institution, typically by the state. A further condition of 'softening' is that the decision maker expects such external financial assistance with high probability and this probability is firmly built into his behaviour (p. 21).

There are several different ways in which the Government can soften the budget constraint for a public sector enterprise (or for that matter, a private firm). Among these are:

(a) *Soft subsidies*: These are negotiable, open-ended, and subject to bargaining and lobbying. These could include automatic financing of losses and cost over-runs.

(b) *Soft taxation*: This refers to a tax system in which tax rates are not uniform, but tailor-made according to the financial situation of different sectors or different regimes. The fulfilment of tax obligations is not strictly enforced, and the possibility of obtaining exemptions is always open. It may be clarified that the softness of a tax system does not depend on the rate of taxation. Thus, even with a low rate, the taxation system can be 'hard' if rules are uniform and payment of taxes is strictly enforced.

(c) *Soft credit*: The credit system is soft if the fulfilment of a credit contract is not enforced, unreliable payments are tolerated, and postponement and rescheduling are allowed. Soft credit is often used to assist firms in financial trouble, without real hope of any repayment of debt.

(d) *Soft administrative prices*: This situation obtains when enterprises can pass on 'costs' irrespective of efficiency or market situation. An alternative means of softening the budget constraint is to permit enterprises to spend, expand, and invest without regard to their own profit–loss position.

Kornai points out that the stringency of the budget

constraint is not simply a financial matter; it reflects a certain social relationship between the state as patron and the enterprise as client. The immediate effect of the softening of the budget constraint is on the economic behaviour of the enterprise. Losses do not matter, and the efficient use of resources is of no consequence, for nothing depends on it. The survival and expansion of the enterprise depends on external assistance and decisions, not on its own capability and performance. This has several important economic consequences. The price responsiveness of the enterprise declines, and the capacity to adjust to relative prices, interest rates and exchange rates diminishes. The unit also becomes unresponsive to technological changes and to unfavourable external conditions. Another consequence is that the demands for inputs and investments become unconstrained, as the satisfaction of these demands depends on government decisions rather than on financial merit.

The doctrine of a 'soft budget constraint' seems to capture the Indian reality surprisingly well. All the different means of softening the budget constraint on enterprises have been in operation in India, and the economic consequences have been equally apparent. The future of these enterprises, and of those who run them, depends entirely and exclusively on outside forces, not on internal performance. A loss-making firm or an entire sector can not only survive but also expand with the help of budgetary subsidies, tax reliefs and preferential credits. In this situation it is clear that no tangible progress among public enterprises is feasible, unless a 'hard' budget constraint is introduced and adhered to. To begin with, various forms of budgetary and extra-budgetary support to loss-making enterprises must be eliminated. Losses, if any, should be covered in the normal way through working-capital loans from banks, as in the case of any other enterprise. If the financial position of the enterprise is such that it cannot raise loans, then there is no option but for it to reduce its operations, close down, or enter into a rehabilitation scheme. Thereafter, a hard budget constraint should be enforced in respect of government investments in the form of equity or loans for expansion. The government should insist on a commercial rate of return on its investments, and if this is not forthcoming the management should be changed.[29]

In Indian conditions, in view of conflicting pulls and pressures, it would be difficult to enforce a hard budget constraint without legislative authority. The revenue support to loss-making enterprises is generally provided by the government through what are called 'non-Plan loans'. A Constitutional amendment, or some other suitable legislative enactment, is necessary to prohibit central and state governments from providing grants or non-Plan loans to loss-making public-sector undertakings. Departmental enterprises, such as the Railways and the P & T, may be exempted from the application of this provision. The arguments for and against a legislative amendment to enforce budgetary discipline were discussed earlier. It is apparent that, in a multi-party democracy, a legislative enactment binding on all parties is likely to be an effective check on unproductive budgetary expenditure.

At the same time, it is necessary to remove all distribution and price controls over these enterprises. Without this measure it is not feasible or appropriate to introduce a hard budget constraint. The distribution and pricing decisions should be left to the enterprises, and these should emerge from market pressures rather than from administrative ministries. An important reason for their relatively poor financial performance in the past has been the delay in taking decisions on the pricing of public-sector products. Under-pricing has resulted in large subsidies and in the transfer of real resources from the public to the private sector. There is no governmental control over *costs*, which are determined by market pressures and collective bargaining. On the other hand, governmental control over the pricing of output has resulted in the erosion of profitability, for which public-sector enterprises themselves are not responsible. It may be emphasized that the removal of governmental control from distribution and pricing need not mean a faster increase in prices or an unacceptable distortion in the distribution pattern. Fiscal and monetary policies, and a competitive environment, should ensure that prices are kept at a reasonable level, and that there is greater efficiency in the utilization of resources. If there are special distribution requirements, or if certain interests have to be protected, the best course of action is for government to provide an explicit subsidy rather than to introduce distribution controls.

(c) Reorganization of Public Enterprises

The recent research on industrial competitiveness and industrial performance shows that ownership *per se* is less important for promoting efficiency than 'competitive inducements to efficiency' and the macro-economic environment (Lall, 1990). Large monopolies, operating in the domestic market without competition, tend to be inefficient and rigid in their response to changes in the pattern of demand or technological innovation. The success of countries like Korea and Japan in promoting productivity, exports and technological innovation is largely due to their success in realizing the scale economies in production and learning, while at the same time enforcing competition and imposing a market discipline on large enterprises. Many of these successful enterprises are organized as conglomerates which operate in diverse fields and compete with each other. Korea has perhaps carried this strategy the furthest by promoting and protecting the giant 'Chaebol'.

The Korean example, with appropriate modifications, provides a useful model for the reorganization of public-sector enterprises in India. These enterprises should be organized in such a manner that economies of large-scale production can be realized without reducing competitive pressure and market discipline. This can be done by setting up five or six multi-product conglomerates in the public sector by reorganizing the existing enterprises in different groups. At the same time, monolithic and monopolistic enterprises can be broken up into four or five separate companies which would freely compete with each other.

Through these mechanisms it is possible to visualize an arrangement whereby several conglomerates will operate in different areas, e.g. steel, oil, coal, telecommunications and engineering. These multi-product conglomerates could be organized with the largest company in a particular product at its centre, and several other associated companies operating in different areas. For example, Conglomerate A could consist of the largest steel plant as its flagship company, and several other associated companies in oil, coal and other fields. Similarly, there could be an 'Oil Conglomerate' and a 'Coal Conglomerate', and so on, each of them with a number of associated companies from different product groups. Each conglomerate should have complete operational freedom to manage its own business, and its board of directors should have the authority to merge or sell smaller companies, change the product mix, and diversify into other areas, as necessary. These conglomerates should be under the administrative control of different production ministries. The primary responsibility of the administrative ministry will be to undertake an annual performance review of the enterprise, and to present this review to Parliament.

In order for this procedure to work efficiently, the major goals of public-sector conglomerates should be set out clearly. As far as existing enterprises and activities are concerned, the most important goal for the next decade should be an improvement in financial performance and the generation of surpluses for further investment. The country has been passing through a major fiscal crisis, which has affected capital formation in several crucial areas of the economy. In the nineties the primary goal of public-sector managements should be to reverse this. As far as new investment is concerned, the Planning Commission should lay down the priorities, taking into account the considerations of regional dispersal and equity. These priorities should be discussed with the managements of the conglomerates. While the decision on overall investment priorities should rest with the Commission, the views of the enterprises regarding their implications for operations and profitability should be known to the public and to Parliament.

This sort of arrangement will radically alter the present dispensation *vis-à-vis* the management of public-sector enterprises. This will also run counter to two old premises that have guided the management of the public sector in India over the last forty years. It is generally believed that profits, if they occur, are all right, but that the public sector is generally not supposed to work for financial profits in view of its 'social' role—whatever that may be. Similarly, competition has been seen as the antithesis of planning, which consisted of setting targets for the industrial capacity of each product and distributing this capacity among a limited number of producers.

The suspicion of competition has been a guiding premise of India's Plans, although there has been some change in emphasis in our later Plans. There may have been an understandable reason for this view, for a country in a hurry, in the early stages of planning, when there was little experience to go by. But our experience since then, and the performance of public enterprises in India as well as in other countries, demonstrates that monopolistic structures and the lack of proper management structures are among the important reasons for the unsatisfactory behaviour of these enterprises.[30] The time has now come to make a radical departure, to put the old theories on their head, and reorganize public enterprises along competitive lines. The best method of implementing this change would be to appoint a Public Sector Reorganization Commission, with specific terms of reference, and with a political mandate to implement the reorganization within a given time frame.

This sort of organizational structure will remove what one writer has referred to as the 'dysfunctional interface' between government and public enterprises (Morris, 1991). Management responsibility will shift exclusively to professional managers, and competition will ensure accountability. This new structure will not, of course, solve all problems. It will, however, create the necessary conditions for a more functional and efficient organization of enterprises in the public sector.

The Second Five Year Plan (1956), which laid the foundations of growth in the public sector, had also visualized the need for experimentation and decentralization in respect of the public sector. The Plan stated:

> it is neither necessary nor desirable that the economy should become a monolithic type or organisation offering little play for experimentation either as to forms or as to modes of functioning. Nor should the expansion of the public sector mean centralization of decision-making and of the exercise of authority. In fact, the aim should be to secure an appropriate devolution of functions and to ensure to public enterprises the fullest freedom to operate within a framework of broad directives or rules of the game. The organisation and management of public enterprises is a field in which considerable experimentation will be necessary (p. 23).

Thirty-five years have passed since then; it is none too soon to put this precept into practice.

A correction of the fiscal situation, and a bringing about of higher productivity in public enterprises—these are the two most important elements in the strategy for increasing the rate of savings in the 1990s. This would require a radical rethinking regarding the role of governmental subsidies, administration, and the organization of enterprises. The behaviour of the Indian economy and the pattern of Indian development will depend crucially on how successfully and how quickly this challenge is met.

Notes

1. See Deaton (1989), Gersovitz (1988) and Haque and Montiel (1989) for a discussion of theoretical issues relating to savings behaviour in developing countries.
2. Uma Datta Roy Choudhary (1990) has tested two hypotheses regarding long-term savings behaviour in India over the period 1950-1 to 1986-7: (a) that the current year's income is the most

important factor influencing the level of household saving; and (b) the current year's saving of the household is influenced not by the current year's income alone but also by the expected average income, i.e. saving is a function of a composite 'permanent' component of income, which is independent of short-term fluctuations, and also of a 'transitory' component. She found that the latter hypothesis provided a better explanation of savings behaviour. However, she concluded that in view of many uncertainties regarding data, it was not possible to come to a firm conclusion.

3. See notes to Chapter 2 for a discussion of the theoretical literature on the relationship between growth and savings.
4. The perception that the savings constraint was the dominant constraint in development was a vital consideration in India's choice of development strategy. See Chakravarty (1987a), pp. 9-10. In an interesting paper written during a visit to India in 1960, Kalecki gave considerable importance to working out a policy of taxation which would restrain the consumption of non-essentials. Such a policy was expected to provide sufficient resources for the financing of investment. See Chakravarty (1987a), pp. 23-4.
5. In 1956 India also experimented with a direct expenditure tax, following a report by Nicholas Kaldor. This was, however, later abandoned because of its very low yield and administrative complexity.
6. See Chapter 1.
7. It is interesting to note that on the question of maintaining an adequate supply of necessities, planners took a somewhat different view than did Kalecki, who attached considerable importance to ensuring a rate of growth of supply of necessities which was consistent with the rate of growth of national income.
8. Although the words 'essentials' and 'non-essentials' are used very commonly in official documents in India, the exact definition of 'essentials' can be quite flexible, depending on the context. Strictly speaking, in terms of the commodities notified under the Essential Commodities Act, essential commodities are confined to foodgrains, pulses, edible oils, kerosene, and only five or six industrial items, such as clothing, vanaspati, and matches.
9. The Third Five Year Pan (1961), pp. 127-30.
10. The annual Economic Surveys, published by the ministry of

finance, for the years 1974-5 to 1979-90 give an account of the changes in industrial and licensing policies. Some steps were taken to liberalize licensing and import policies in 1975-6 and 1976-7 (e.g. raising the value limit for the delicensed sector, the introduction of a system of 'automatic' licensing for imports, and procedural simplifications). A new industrial policy statement was adopted in 1977, which emphasized the role of the small-scale sector and the decentralized sector in industrial development.

11. A good indicator of the change in approach is given by output projections for man-made fibres. The earlier Plans had sought to restrict output well behind consumption growth through the instrument of restrictive production licensing. The Sixth Plan provided for a doubling in the output of Polyester Filament Yarn and staple fibre—from about 33,000 tonnes to 73,000 tonnes. In the event, even this proved to be highly unrealistic.
12. A number of writers, including Raj (1986), have argued that the reason for the deceleration in industrial growth after the mid-1960s was on account of a stagnation in demand for capital goods and a low level of public investment.
13. See Khatkhate (1988a) for a review of the literature, and for cross-country evidence on the average relationship for sixty-four developing countries during the period 1971-80 between the level of the real-interest rate and some macro-economic variables, such as the rate of growth and the savings ratio.
14. Khatkhate's (1991) calculations take into account changes in prices as well as the nominal exchange rate. The measurement of the level of real-interest rates in developing countries presents several conceptual and data problems. See Khatkhate (1988b).
15. Dornbusch and Reynoso (1989) have cautioned against the use of inflationary finance on wider developmental grounds. The Latin American experience shows that 'the scope for deficit finance as an engine of economic development is extremely limited and extraordinarily hazardous. When overdone, inflationary finance acquires a dynamic of its own that can set back the development effort by a decade or more' (p. 209).
16. In the Indian context, Bhatty and Sarma (1977) have also highlighted the importance of price stability as a prime prerequisite for the growth of savings. Their study examined savings behaviour in India during the period 1950-1 to 1973-4.

17. Figures after 1980-1 are not strictly comparable with those before that date, because of the introduction of a new series of national-income account statistics.
18. For an account of Indian budgetary practices and the accounting system, see Swarup (1990).
19. The rest of the discussion in this chapter focusses on the central government. The nature of the problem and proposed solutions are, by and large, also applicable to state governments.
20. An early formulation of the tendency for government expenditure to rise autonomously is that by Adolph Wagner. Wagner predicted that as the process of economic development took place, 'government expenditure must increase at a faster rate than output'. See Peacock and Wiseman (1967).
21. The failure to check the growth of expenditure is the common experience of several other countries. Thus, Schick (1990) has observed that 'the plain fact is that industrialized democracies have not done very much to curb the upward spiral in public expenditure' (p. 45). He also points out that the failure to rein in public expenditure is primarily a political—not an economic—problem. 'Cutting expenditures means trimming services, taking away benefits, curtailing rights to payments, and allocating losses. None of these are easy for democratic politicians to do' (p. 46). Schick cites an interesting study published in the United States by the National Bureau of Economic Research, which correlated the debt/GNP ratio of democratic countries with various measures of political strength. The not-so-surprising conclusion was that 'strong governments have lower ratios than weak ones. While political weakness in the United States derives from the separation of power between the legislative and executive branches, in other countries it may be due to unstable coalitions, minority government, or frequent elections' (p. 51).
22. Chakravarty (1990) has raised the possibility that public savings and private savings may be interlinked, and the behaviour of household savings may not be invariant to the trend in government expenditure. The generation of incomes in the private sector is likely to be affected by revenue deficits of government. While this is true in principle, there is no evidence in India that rising revenue deficits of the government have contributed to an increase in the savings ratio in the private sector. The savings ratio in the household sector averaged 15.4

per cent of GDP during the period 1976-7 to 1980-1, when the revenue budget of the government was in surplus. This ratio remained practically unchanged during 1984-5 to 1988-9 when revenue deficits were increasing.

23. Parikh and Suryanarayana (1991) have explored the implications of an increase in fertilizer prices on the economy through simulations using a general equilibrium model, which accounts for changes in supply, incomes, prices and consumption. A 20 per cent increase in fertilizer prices should lower government deficit by more than Rs 1000 crores. The study points out that any adverse impact on the growth of agricultural output and incomes of poor farmers because of the partial or total withdrawal of the subsidy can be more than compensated for by using part of the resources for an additional rural works programme and investments in additional irrigation. The latter policy combination is 'unambiguously' superior to the policy of subsidizing fertilizers.
24. A similar provision exists in Indonesia, and has been found to be highly effective. The U.S.A., West Germany and Canada have different types of statutory ceilings on government borrowings.
25. A recent review of the literature and main issues relating to fiscal policy is by Acharya (1988). Acharya's paper also provides an account of the main thrust of the long-term fiscal policy announced by the government in 1985.
26. The GNP figure is at current prices, while investment figures are at historical cost. These figures are used only for purposes of illustrating the size of the public sector in the economy.
27. Another interesting argument advanced by Mahalanobis (1955) was the need to keep prices of capital goods low. He argued that 'for rapid industrialization of our underdeveloped country, it would be desirable to keep the cost of capital goods as low as possible. The further removed the type of capital goods under consideration is from the production of final consumer goods, the greater is the need to keep the price low. Heavy machinery, which would manufacture machinery to produce investment goods, is the furthest removed from the consumption end. It is essential, therefore, that government should have complete control over the heavy machinery industry so as to be able to fix prices to suit national needs' (pp. 51-2).
28. Kornai introduced the concept of a soft budget constraint in his

book 'Economics of Shortage' (1980), which put forward his theory of chronic shortage in socialist economies. The concept has since been widely discussed. Kornai's book, *Vision and Reality, Market and State* (1990), provides a reformulation and a succinct interpretation of the theory of the soft budget constraint.

29. See Chapter 3 for a discussion of the privatization issue in the Indian context.
30. It goes without saying that competition alone is not a sufficient condition for efficiency. In 1990, there were forty-three enterprises which were classified as competitive, but chronically sick, by the Department of Public Enterprises. Out of these twenty-seven were sick private-sector enterprises which were taken over by the government. The rest became sick because of various other reasons such as wrong technology, an inappropriate location, and a lack of demand. However, no remedial action could be taken because of management failure and the soft budget constraint.

TABLE 5.1
DOMESTIC SAVING (GROSS AND NET) RATIOS AT CURRENT AND CONSTANT PRICES, 1980-81 TO 1989-90

Year	*Gross domestic savings as per cent of GDP at market prices*		*Net domestic savings as per cent of NDP at market prices*	
	Current prices	*At 1980-81 prices*	*Current prices*	*At 1980-81 prices*
1980-81	21.16	21.16	13.47	13.47
1981-82	20.99	20.80	13.11	13.06
1982-83	19.39	19.19	10.92	10.94
1983-84	19.55	19.08	11.30	11.14
1984-85	18.70	18.21	10.10	10.11
1985-86	20.44	19.71	11.61	11.53
1986-87	19.53	18.69	10.39	10.43
1987-88	19.64	19.04	10.52	10.66
1988-89	21.09	20.36	12.42	12.33
1989-90	21.66	20.81	12.68	12.69

NOTE : Household sector saving in financial form at current prices has been converted into constant prices by using the private final consumption expenditure deflator; all other components of savings are converted into constant prices by using the deflator relating to aggregate gross domestic capital formation. See Shetty (1990). Figures in the Table above were recomputed and updated by Shetty by using latest available figures.

SOURCE: National Accounts Statistics, Different Issues.

TABLE 5.2
PUBLIC-SECTOR AND HOUSEHOLD-SECTOR SAVINGS
IN INDIA 1980-81 TO 1989-90

Year	Public sector		Household sector	
	At current prices	*At 1980-81 prices*	*At current prices*	*At 1980-81 prices*
(a) GROSS DOMESTIC SAVINGS (IN THOUSAND CRORES)				
1980-81	4.7	4.7	21.8	21.8
1981-82	7.3	6.5	23.7	21.0
1982-83	7.8	6.4	23.7	19.2
1983-84	6.8	5.2	30.5	19.7
1984-85	6.5	4.6	32.6	21.8
1985-86	8.5	5.3	39.8	25.0
1986-87	8.0	4.6	44.2	25.7
1987-88	6.9	3.7	52.7	29.0
1988-89	7.7	3.8	67.4	34.6
1989-90	7.6	3.4	78.9	38.3
(b) NET DOMESTIC SAVINGS (IN THOUSAND CRORES)				
1980-81	(-) 0.2	(-) 0.2	16.4	16.4
1981-82	1.4	1.3	17.1	15.3
1982-83	0.8	0.7	16.1	13.5
1983-84	(-) 1.3	(-) 1.0	22.1	13.7
1984-85	(-) 2.9	(-) 2.0	23.1	15.5
1985-86	(-) 2.9	(-) 1.8	28.9	18.6
1986-87	(-) 5.1	(-) 2.9	32.0	19.1
1987-88	(-) 8.1	(-) 4.2	39.1	22.3
1988-89	(-) 9.8	(-) 4.7	52.1	27.6
1989-90	(-)13.2	(-) 5.8	61.6	31.1

(c) GROSS AND NET DOMESTIC PRODUCT (IN THOUSAND CRORES)

Year	*Gross domestic product*		*Net domestic product*	
	At current prices	*At 1980-81 prices*	*At current prices*	*At 1980-81 prices*
1980-81	135.8	135.8	123.7	123.7
1981-82	159.4	144.6	145.0	131.8
1982-83	177.6	149.9	160.7	136.3
1983-84	206.9	161.0	187.6	146.5
1984-85	230.7	167.0	208.6	151.6
1985-86	262.6	177.4	236.4	161.1
1986-87	293.4	185.9	263.4	168.5
1987-88	332.6	194.4	298.7	175.9
1988-89	395.0	212.6	355.9	193.3
1989-90	442.8	223.3	397.2	202.9

NOTE : The deflators used for conversion to constant prices are: private consumption expenditure deflator for financial savings and the respective capital formation deflators for other components of savings (see Shetty, 1990). Figures have been rounded.

SOURCE : National Accounts Statistics, Different Issues.

TABLE 5.3
GOVERNMENT'S CURRENT RECEIPTS, CURRENT EXPENDITURE AND SAVING
(AS PER CENT OF GDP AT MARKET PRICES)

	1970-71	1975-76	1980-81	1984-85	1989-90
I. *Current receipts* of which:	13.2	16.1	15.9	17.2	19.0
Tax revenues	11.5	14.6	15.0	15.8	17.4
Non tax revenues	1.7	1.5	0.9	1.4	1.6
II. *Current expenditure* of which:	11.5	13.2	15.2	18.7	23.1
Defence	2.9	3.3	3.0	2.9	3.2
Interest payments	0.5	0.6	1.1	2.2	3.4
Subsidies	0.8	1.4	2.3	3.4	4.2
Others	7.3	7.9	8.8	10.2	12.3
III. Government savings	1.7	2.9	0.7	-1.5	-4.1

SOURCE: National Accounts Statistics, Different Issues.

TABLE 5.4
PROFILE OF THE CENTRE'S PUBLIC ENTERPRISES

	Units	*1980-81*	*1985-86*	*1988-89*	*1989-90*
1. Number of running public enterprises	Number	163	211	226	227
2. Capital employed	Rs Crore	18207	42965	67629	84437
3. Turnover	Rs Crore	28635	62360	93137	106078
4. Gross margin (profit before depreciation, interest and tax)	Rs Crore	2401	8230	13438	16410
5. Depreciation*	Rs Crore	983	2983	4866	5787
6. Gross profit before interest and tax	Rs Crore	1418	5287	8572	10623
7. Interest	Rs Crore	1399	3115	4167	5341
8. Net profit before tax	Rs Crore	19	2172	4405	5282
9. Tax	Rs Crore	222	1000	1411	1500
10. Net profit after tax	Rs Crore	-203	1172	2994	3782
11. Internal resources generated (gross)	Rs Crore	1225	5068	8915	10772
12. Net profit (after tax) to capital employed	Per cent	-1.1	2.7	4.4	4.5

* Includes deferred revenue expenditure.

SOURCE: Government of India, *Economic Survey*, 1989-90 (updated).

TABLE 5.5

FINANCIAL RESULTS OF DEPARTMENTAL COMMERCIAL UNDERTAKINGS OF STATES AND UNION TERRITORIES

(RS CRORES)

		1985-86	*1988-89*	*1989-90 (R.E.)*	*1990-91 (B.E.)*
1.	Departmental undertakings				
(i)	Forest	497.70	414.35	447.94	536.49
(ii)	Power projects	-75.04	-84.19	-48.34	-48.55
(iii)	Road & water transport services	-25.65	-56.51	-77.66	-79.67
(iv)	Dairy development	-99.29	-52.38	-380.48	-393.74
(v)	Industries	-14.10	-10.09	-130.28	- 77.18
(vi)	Mines & Minerals	40.06	51.83	53.57	57.59
(vii) (viii)	Irrigation & projects: (commercial) : Multi-purpose river projects :	-871.60	-1840.79	-1763.00	-1922.96
2.	Profit of profit-making under-takings	537.76	466.18	501.51	594.08
3.	Loss of loss making under-takings	-1085.68	-2043.96	-2399.76	-2522.10
4.	**Net financial results of departmental undertakings**	**-547.92**	**-1577.78**	**-1898.25**	**-1928.02**

SOURCE: Government of India, *Economic Survey*, 1989-90 (updated).

TABLE 5.6
REVENUE, MONETIZED AND FISCAL DEFICIT OF THE CENTRAL GOVERNMENT
(AS PER CENT OF GDP)

Years	*Fiscal deficit*	*Monetized deficit*	*Revenue deficit*
1980-81	6.54	2.61	1.50
1981-82	5.44	2.01	0.24
1982-83	7.04	1.90	0.74
1983-84	6.74	1.91	1.23
1984-85	7.71	2.62	1.83
1985-86	9.29	2.36	2.12
1986-87	9.50	2.42	2.65
1987-88	8.50	1.97	2.75
1988-89	8.18	1.66	2.69
1989-90	8.64	3.12	2.81

SOURCE: *Reserve Bank of India Bulletin.* June 1990 (Supplement).

Epilogue

> The liberation of spirit that has come to India could not come as release alone. In India, with its layer below layer of distress and cruelty, it had to come as disturbance. It had to come as rage and revolt. India was now a country of a million little mutinies.
>
> And—strange irony—the mutinies were not to be wished away. They were part of the beginning of a new way for many millions, part of India's growth, part of its restoration. — V.S. NAIPAUL*

In mid-1991 the short-term prospects of the economy look distinctly bleak. The budget, which was to be presented at the end of February 1991, was abandoned at short notice. In March 1991 the minority government which had taken office only four months earlier, resigned. These events ensured that no effective action could be taken to deal with the severe balance-of-payments crisis facing the country. India was left at the mercy of her foreign creditors and donors.

The immediate requirement is additional liquidity, and one way or another the immediate crisis will have to be taken care of. If additional liquidity is available, the cost in terms of loss of employment and output can be minimized. If it is not available, India will have to muddle through, as so many other developing countries in Latin America and Africa have done, with attendant high economic and social costs. Beyond the current crisis, India must also look ahead to the restoration of her economic health and her image —in her own eyes and in the eyes of the rest of the world. This is the challenge now.

The international environment is unfavourable to developing countries. The growth of world trade slowed down

* *India : A Million Mutinies Now*, pp. 517-18.

in the eighties (about 4.2 per cent per annum in volume as against 6.2 per cent in the 1970s), and indications are that this trend will continue in the foreseeable future. Multilateralism in trade is increasingly being replaced by bilateral and regional trade groupings among industrial countries. Net flows of external assistance to developing countries are declining, and several of them are now experiencing a negative net transfer of resources from developed countries. The problem of external indebtedness continues to be an obstacle to economic revival. The international banking system has become a highly uncertain source of funds even for those developing countries which have excellent track records. The exchange markets remain highly volatile and unpredictable. There has been no progress in the area of international monetary reform or in the creation of new mechanisms for meeting the balance-of-payment needs of developing countries. Eastern Europe and the U.S.S.R. are going through economic convulsions. This has special relevance for India, as a substantial part of India's trade is under bilateral arrangements with these countries. The North–South dialogue, which was uninspiring at the best of times, is subdued if not altogether dead.

In this environment the burden of adjustment is likely to fall upon India, and on India alone. While international assistance is needed, it is unlikely to be available in sufficient quantities on reasonable terms, and for a sufficiently long period, to ease the pain of adjustment. This is the recent experience of other developing countries in Africa and Latin America (despite these being more closely aligned politically with the Western powers). In Africa, real incomes in 1990 were about 10 per cent lower than in 1970. In Latin America, the cumulative decline in per capita consumption between 1980 and1987 was -8.4 per cent in Argentina, -36.4 per cent in Bolivia, -15.4 per cent in Chile, -18.9 per cent in Mexico, and -32.2 per cent in Venezuela. This period was also marked by a sharp acceleration in the inflation rate in heavily-indebted developing centuries. In the eighties, the average rate of inflation was nearly 150 per cent per annum in the group of fifteen heavily-indebted countries, as against 39 per cent per annum during 1970-81 (Dornbusch, 1989). Adjustment to an external crisis invariably involved either a voluntary or forced reduction in domestic absorption, which affected output, employment and prices. Another lesson of recent history is that a delay in taking corrective action invariably raises the costs of adjustment more than proportionately. Countries which delayed the necessary action in the hope of attracting larger external funds, or for domestic political reasons, suffered substantially larger falls in income than others.

Fortunately, the size of India's balance-of-payments problems is relatively small in comparison with several other developing countries. As pointed out earlier (Chapter 4), it is about 1 to 1.5 per cent of GNP, and is capable of being corrected in the next two or three years without imposing intolerable social and political burdens. Another advantage is the resilience of the 'real' economy. Industrial production expanded by 8.4 per cent in 1990-1 despite the balance-of-payments crisis. For the seven-year period 1984-5 to 1990-1, industrial growth has exceeded 8 per cent per annum on an average, which is one of the highest in the developing world. Agricultural production also reached a peak in 1990-1, and foodstocks are once again at a comfortable level (after the severe drought of 1987-8). Exports have increased by more than 10 per cent per annum in real terms during 1986-7 to 1990-1, as against less than 1 per cent per annum in the first half of the eighties. These are favourable developments which should help in minimizing the costs of adjustment.

In the previous chapters, in the light of India's own experience and the findings of theoretical and empirical research, I have tried to identify several priority areas for policy reform. Here I shall pull together these different strands and suggest a programme of action which can lay the foundations of sustainable growth in the 1990s. Such a programme, which can be implemented quickly, falls *within the constraints of the present political and economic system*. The detailed arguments appear in the relevant chapters.

1. *Foreign exchange* : Recent events have amply demonstrated the vulnerability of the economy to external shocks, and the underlying weakness of India's balance of payments. The likely emergence of a severe balance-of-payments problem was long anticipated, but remedial measures could not be taken because of domestic political developments since 1988. The cost to the economy has been heavy. The most pressing priority now is to take measures to reduce the trade deficit to more manageable levels. There is sufficient evidence to show that India's incentive structure is heavily weighted in favour of domestic sales and is biased against exports (Chapter 4). Such import liberalization as has occurred has been 'inward looking', and has promoted imports of non-competing raw materials, components and capital goods for domestic manufacture for the domestic market. An attempt has been made to shift the balance of advantage in favour of exports during the last four years. This process has to go much further and, in addition to other structural reforms, an explicit market-based link has to be established between exports and imports. A mechanism for achieving this objective was suggested in Chapter 4. There is also no option but to restrain the growth of imports of crude oil, petroleum products and fertilizers. This can be done by a combination of measures on the demand and supply sides. In the next two or three years, until such time as a better balance is achieved on the trade account, the country has to live with shortages of these products, if necessary. This will be economically less costly than borrowing more and more to pay for current consumption. For reasons mentioned earlier, there is also no scope for commercial borrowings for long-gestation projects for the domestic market.

2. *Public debt* : Several studies have established, beyond any doubt, the alarming profile of India's public debt, including its external debt. India has been borrowing, both internally and externally, to finance widening deficits in its revenue and capital accounts. This process cannot be carried much further without landing the country in financial

disaster. There is enough empirical evidence from the history of other countries to show that high inflation, including the possibility of hyper-inflation, lie ahead if the situation is not stabilized soon. India's external debt, in terms of GNP, is still relatively low compared with that of heavily-indebted countries in Latin America and elsewhere. However, in relation to exports, the size of the debt has now reached Latin Americans proportions. All the other variables which affect debt-servicing capacity, such as average interest rates on new borrowings and the pattern of non-interest current-account deficits, have been highly unfavourable for India in recent years (Chapter 4). The rate of growth of external debt must be reduced, and kept well below the rate of growth of exports, so that the debt/export ratio is brought down significantly in the next five years.

3. *Fiscal deficit* : A proper management of public debt as well as the balance of payments requires firm action to reduce fiscal deficits. A medium-term objective should be to eliminate the revenue deficit altogether, so that there is no need for government to borrow in order to finance current expenditure. The need to control expenditure has been felt by government for some time, but, for political-economy reasons, it has not been possible to make any progress. The situation in the last few years has become worse, instead of getting better, even as the public and political consciousness of the need to tackle the fiscal problem has increased. As suggested in Chapter 5, a 'policy-based' approach to expenditure control, approved by Parliament, is necessary. In a multi-party democracy like India, experience shows that nothing short of a Constitutional amendment, which is binding on all governments—present and future—will be effective in eliminating revenue deficits. In addition to expenditure control, measures to widen the tax base, simplify the tax system, and improve the revenue administration are important elements in a programme to reduce budget deficits. A more transparent system with uniform rules, and less product differentiation, will increase the buoyancy of the tax system.

4. *The public sector* : The management of the public sector is a key issue. In view of its large size, a sustained improvement in the savings available for investment is not feasible, without higher productivity. As the size of the capital market in India is only about 1 per cent of the value of the total assets of the public sector (at historical cost), it is clear that a wholesale privatization of public-sector units is not a feasible option in the Indian situation in the foreseeable future. All commercial enterprises should, however, be required to raise equity and loans for their further growth from financial and capital markets. Sick units and smaller units with low profitability could be sold through public offers. Beyond these measures, the solutions to the problems of the public sector in India will have to be found primarily within the framework of public ownership. In addition to streamlining the administration and a proper management of the public sector (Chapter 3), it is necessary to impose a 'hard budget' constraint on the public sector. Central and state governments should be prohibited, by law, from financing the losses of public sector units. It does not make sense for the government to borrow at a high cost to finance public-sector losses as well as its own revenue deficits. In this respect the situation is fundamentally different from that prevailing in the sixties or seventies when the revenue budget was in surplus. Henceforth, public-sector units should depend on existing banking and financial mechanisms to meet their credit requirements, in accordance with normal policy. As pointed out in the previous chapter, a hard budget constraint is not only a means of saving revenue for government, but also an important instrument for inducing 'productive' efficiency. Public-sector enterprises need to be reorganized along competitive lines. Empirical research on privatization in the U.K. and elsewhere shows that a competitive environment is more important for 'allocative' efficiency than ownership *per se*. The Korean conglomerates (the so-called 'Chaebol') provide a useful model for realizing economies of large-scale production without reducing competitive pressure and market discipline. Monopolistic and monolithic enterprises should be broken into a few separate companies, and

become parts of multi-product conglomerates in the public sector. These conglomerates should have complete operational freedom, including the freedom to sell or merge companies. The distribution and price controls on public-sector enterprises should be abolished (Chapter 5).

5. *Competition* : Productive and allocative inefficiencies are not confined to the public sector, but are a feature of the entire economy. Cross-country research as well as industry-level studies show that a competitive environment is crucial for promoting efficiency in resource use and resource allocation in the economy. In the past, the industrial licensing system and macro-economic policies (including fiscal policy) have prevented competitive inducements to efficiency. This has to be reversed. The capacity-based industrial licensing system should be abolished. Fiscal, financial and tariff policies should be used to provide the necessary signals for resource allocation (Chapter 3). In view of external financing difficulties, import liberalization, which raises the import-to-GDP ratio, is not a feasible option in the near future. However, the rates of effective protection for inefficient domestic manufacturing can be reduced by moving towards more uniform tariffs across industries (in respect of both inputs and outputs). There is also a need for simplification, transparency and uniformity in import policy. The tariff system should cease to be cost-based, and no financial subsidies or credit concessions should be provided to support inefficient and non-competitive production.

6. *Controls* : The system of physical and discretionary controls, inherited from World War II, has outlived its utility. These methods have proved much less efficient than what was once assumed in directing economic activity to desired channels and optimizing the use of resources. In view of administrative constraints and information gaps, such controls have failed to cope with the rapidly changing technological and international environment. They have also given rise to corruption and economically wasteful activities, such as rent-seeking. Direct physical controls on production and international trade should be

replaced by non-discretionary fiscal, credit and financial controls. This will improve the quality of state intervention and make it more effective. This has been the experience of several other highly interventionist, but economically successful, countries—such as Japan and Korea. Several government committees have recommended a shift to non-discretionary methods of state intervention, but the actual progress has been negligible. An important priority now is to make a bold departure.

7. *Decentralization* : This is both a political and an economic necessity. Politically, with the emergence of strong regional parties and with several different parties in power at the centre and states, decentralization of state power has become necessary. Decentralization will also have the incidental advantage of reducing the power of dominant coalitions at the centre by creating several competing power bases. From an economic point of view, over-centralization is an important cause of inefficiency and the diversion of resources from production to administration (Kornai, 1959). Action at two levels is necessary: planning and financing of activities which are the responsibility of state governments (such as investments in rural development, education and social services) should be transferred from the centre to the states, and the states in turn should transfer the responsibility for local area planning to local institutions. Past experience does not show that centralized or higher-level planning in these areas necessarily leads to better and more efficient planning. A decentralization of the planning process has been discussed extensively in the context of the formulation of the Eighth Plan (Ghosh, 1991). There also seems to be a political consensus in favour of it. The decision-making process in respect of the public sector, including financial institutions, should also be decentralized from government secretariats to enterprises. Effective decentralization is feasible if, as suggested earlier, a hard budget constraint is imposed on public-sector enterprises, and if these enterprises are less dependent on the government budget.

8. *Literacy* : The importance of literacy, both as an end in itself and as a means of raising the growth-rate of output, has long been recognized in the economic literature. India's overall record in this area leaves much to be desired. Nearly half the country's population continues to be illiterate; the proportion is significantly higher in several states, and for women as a group. One outstanding example of a successful implementation of the literacy programme is Kerala, where the literacy ratio reached 91 per cent, according to the preliminary results of the 1991 census. Kerala's example shows that full literacy is an achievable goal even in a poor country, and that techniques to reach this goal are available (e.g. through mass literacy campaigns). There is also evidence to show that high literacy rates—especially high female literacy rates—are associated with low rates of population growth, which is an important development objective for India. In Kerala, higher literacy rates have resulted in a lower than average rate of population growth (1.31 per cent per annum as against the average of 2.11 per cent for India). Higher literacy rates have also been associated with better performance in terms of a number of other health and social indicators, such as infant mortality rates. On the other hand, in various states (such as Madhya Pradesh, Rajasthan and U.P.) abysmally low literacy rates have been associated with higher-than-average population growth rates and poor performance in terms of health indicators. Full literacy should be the national development goal of the 1990s (just as self-sufficiency in food was the dominant objective of national planning after the disastrous droughts of 1965-7).

9. *Food and poverty* : It should be explicitly recognized that a programme of fiscal and balance-of-payments correction will impose social costs. Experience also shows that, unless compensatory policies are put in place, a reduction in domestic absorption generally affects the poor more than the better-off sections of society. In an expenditure-reduction programme, governments find it easier to

cut investment than cut consumption. A cut in investment affects employment and the demand for goods and services. As employees in the organized sector enjoy the protection of labour laws and other social-security measures, the burden of adjustment falls heavily on workers in the unorganized sectors. Similarly, expenditure cuts are generally more severe on social sectors than on administration or industrial sectors. It is easier to cut expenditure on, say, new schools or new hospitals which have not yet been started, than on lumpy investments in industrial plants, which are in the process of implementation. The interests and power of organized lobbies are also greater in respect of the latter sort of projects. In several countries of Latin America and Africa, per capita expenditure on social sectors in the 1980s declined at a higher rate than overall expenditure. The past experience of stabilization programmes in Latin America and Africa also show that programmes which fail to protect the poor, and which do not spread the costs of adjustment equitably among different sections of society, invariably run into trouble because of the social and political tensions that they generate. It is important that the strategy to reduce fiscal deficits in India does not neglect this aspect. Food subsidies should continue to be maintained. A part of the revenue gain from reduction of other subsidies and higher recovery of costs should be used to expand rural employment programmes. Rural public works programmes have been successfully used to increase food availability during droughts. A similar approach is necessary during a period of fiscal adjustment.

10. *Administration* : As pointed out in Chapter 1, both in India and elsewhere, in the post-independence period, widespread intervention by the state was necessary to alter colonial patterns of production and trade. The results were beneficial as growth rates accelerated, and progress was achieved in reducing the incidence of poverty. However, over time, in response to various pressures and needs, the state has expanded in all directions. The over-extension of the state has now become a problem, and has outstripped available managerial and administrative capacities. The

economic costs of delays and the overlapping of functions have been enormous, and these have been recognized by India's Plans since the early seventies. The vast expansion of the state has also given rise to the emergence of various types of lobbies and coalitions which have eroded the capacity of the state to intervene autonomously in the interests of society as a whole. The quality of public services has declined as their fiscal costs have increased. It is clear now that an important priority of the nineties is to reduce the size of the state, and to make the administrative apparatus more functional. The latter objective cannot be realized unless the area of state activity is reduced at all levels, and confined to what is socially necessary and beneficial. Several of the suggestions made earlier in respect of decentralization of planning, the management of the public sector, and the choice of policy instruments are likely to contribute to this objective.

This is necessarily a selective list of priorities. There are other important objectives and priorities. But it is likely that if India succeeds, in the early nineties, in implementing the programmes suggested herein, all else will become easier to accomplish. The way ahead is difficult, but it is also full of promise and opportunity. India's present difficulty must not be allowed to overshadow the considerable achievements of the past, nor to dim the vision of the future.

List of References

Acharya, S., and Associates (1985), *Aspects of Black Economy in India*, National Institute of Public Finance and Policy, New Delhi (reprinted in 1986).

Acharya, S. (1988), 'India's Fiscal Policy', in Lucas, R. and Papanek, G. (eds.), *The Indian Economy: Recent Development and Future Prospects*, Westview Special Studies on South and Southeast Asia.

Adiseshiah, M.S. (1988), 'Of Plans, Planning and Beyond', Fifth C.D. Deshmukh Memorial Lecture (14 January 1989), New Delhi, reprinted in *Financial Express*, 25 and 26 January 1988.

Agarwal, M. (1988), 'A Comparative Analysis of India's Export Performance, 1965-80', *Indian Economic Review*, vol. 23, no.2, pp. 231-61.

Aharoni, Y. (1986), *The Evolution and Management of State-Owned Enterprises*, Cambridge, Mass: Ballinger.

Ahluwalia, I.J. (1985), *Industrial Growth in India: Stagnation Since the Mid-Sixties*, Delhi: Oxford University Press.

Ahluwalia, M.S. (1986), 'Balance of Payments Adjustment in India, 1970-71 to 1983-84', *World Development*, vol.14, no.8.

Alavi, H. (1972), 'The State in Post-Colonial Societies—Pakistan and Bangladesh', *New Left Review*, no. 74, July-August, pp. 59-81.

Ando, A., and Modigliani F. (1963), 'The Life-Cycle Hypothesis of Saving: Aggregate Implications and Tests', *American Economic Review* (March 1963), pp. 55-84.

Anglade, C., and Fortin, C. (1987), 'The Role of State in Latin America's Strategic Options', *CEPAL Review*, no.31, April 1987. United Nations Economic Commission for Latin America and the Caribbean, Santiago, Chile.

Arrow, K.J. (1962), 'The Economic Implications of Learning by Doing', *Review of Economic Studies*, vol. 29 (June 1962), pp. 661-9.

Bagchi, A., and Sen, T. (1991), 'Budgetary Trends and Plan Financing At the States During Sixth and Seventh Plans: An Overview', paper presented at the seminar on state finances, National Institute of Public Finance and Policy, 19-20 April 1991, New Delhi (mimeo.).

Bairoch, P. (1975), *The Economic Development of the Third World since 1900*, Berkeley: University of California Press.

———. (1982) 'International Industrialization Levels from 1750 to 1980', *The Journal of European Economic History*, vol. 11, no.2.

Bajaj, J.L., and Agarwal, O.P. (1991), 'State Finances: Uttar Pradesh', paper presented at the seminar on state finances (19-20 April 1991), National Institute of Public Finance and Policy, New Delhi (mimeo).

Balassa (1978), 'Exports and Economic Growth: Further Evidence', *Journal of Development Economics*, vol.5.

Balassa (1990), 'Outward Orientation', in Chenery H., and Srinivasan, T.N. (ed.), *Handbook of Development Economics*, vol.2, Amsterdam: North Holland.

Bardhan, P.K. (1984), *The Political Economy of Development in India*. Delhi: Oxford University Press.

———. (1988), 'Alternative Approaches to Development Economics', in H. Chenery and T.N. Srinivasan (eds.), *Handbook of Development Economics*, vol.1, Amsterdam: North Holland.

———. (1990) 'Symposium on the State and Economic Development', *Journal of Economic Perspectives*. vol. 4, no.3.

Bartoli, G. (1989), 'Fiscal Expansion and External Current Account Imbalances', in Blejer, I., and Ke-young Chu (eds.), *Fiscal Policy, Stabilisation and Growth in Developing Countries*, Washington D.C.: International Monetary Fund.

Bauer, P.T., and Yamey, B.S. (1957), *The Economics of Underdeveloped Countries*, Cambridge: Cambridge University Press.

Bergsman, J. (1970), *Brazil: Industrialisation and Trade Policies*, London: Oxford University Press (for O.E.C.D.).

Bhagwati, J., and Desai, P. (1970), *India: Planning for Industrialisation*, London: Oxford University Press (for O.E.C.D.).

Bhagwati, J. (1974), *Illegal Transactions in International Trade*, Amsterdam: North Holland.

———. (1978), *Anatomy and Consequences of Exchange Control Regimes*, Cambridge, Mass: Ballinger.

———. (1982), 'Directly Unproductive Profit Seeking (DUP) Activities', *Journal of Political Economy*. vol. 90, pp. 988-1002.

———. (1986), *Investing Abroad*, Discussion Papers Series no. 319, Columbia University (mimeo).

———. (1987), 'Indian Economic Performance and Policy Design', Seventh Sir Purushottam Thakurdas Memorial Lecture, Bombay: Indian Institute of Bankers, reprinted in *Business Standard*, Calcutta, 24-26 December 1987.

———. (1988a), 'Poverty and Public Policy', *World Development*, vol. 16, no. 5.

———. (1988b), 'Export-Promoting Trade Strategy: Issues and Evidence', *The World Bank Research Observer*, vol. 3, no.1.

Bhatty I.Z., and Sarma M.T.R. (1977). 'Savings Behaviour in India and Implications for Policy', in Wadhva, C.D., *Some Problems of India's Economic Policy*, New Delhi: Tata McGraw-Hill.

Biswas, B., and Nandi, S. (1986), 'The Black Market Exchange Rate in a Developing Economy: The Case of India', *The Indian Economic Journal*, vol.33, no.3, pp. 23-33.

Bliss, C. (1990), 'Trade and Development', in Chenery, H., and Srinivasan, T.N. (ed.), *Handbook of Development Economics*, vol. 2. Amsterdam: North Holland.

Bruton, H. (1990), 'Import Substitution', in Chenery H., and Srinivasan, T.N. (ed.), *Handbook of Development Economics*, vol. 2, Amsterdam: North Holland.

Buchanan, J.M. (1991), 'Economics in the Post-Socialist Century', *The Economic Journal*, vol. 101, no. 404, pp. 15-21.

Buiter, W.H., and Patel, U.R. (1990), 'Debt, Deficits and Inflation: An Application to the Public Finances of India', Department of Economics, Yale University, New Haven (mimeo).

Cardoso, E.A., and Dornbusch, R. (1989), 'Foreign Private Capital Inflows', in Chenery, H., and Srinivasan, T.N., *Handbook of Development Economics*, vol. 2. Amsterdam: North Holland.

Chakravarty, S. (1974), 'Reflections on the Growth Process in the Indian Economy', Reprinted in C.D. Wadhva, (ed.), (1977), *Some Problems of India's Economic Policy*, New Delhi: Tata McGraw Hill.

———. (1987a), *Development Planning: The Indian Experience*. Oxford: Clarendon Press.

———. (1987b), 'Marxist economics and contemporary developing economies', *Cambridge Journal of Economics*, vol. 11, no. 3.

———. (1990), 'Inaugural Address', in Datta Roy Choudhury, U., and Bagchi, A. (eds.), *Domestic Savings in India: Trends and Issues*, National Institute of Public Finance and Policy, New Delhi: Vikas.

Chelliah, R.J. (1989), 'Strategy For the Nineties', Indian Merchants Chamber, Bombay (mimeo).

———. (1991), 'The Growth of Indian Public Debt: Dimensions of the Problems and Corrective Measures', New Delhi: National Institute of Public Finance (mimeo).

Chenery, H., Shishido S., and Watanabe, T. (1962), 'The Pattern of Japanese Growth, 1914-1954', *Econometrica*, January 1962.

Cline, W.R. (1984), *International Debt: Systemic Risk and Policy Response*, Washington D.C.: Institute for International Economics.

Colletta, N.J., and Sutton, M. (1988), 'Achieving and Sustaining Universal Primary Education: A Study of International Experiences relevant to India', Washington D.C.: World Bank (mimeo).

Cook, P. and Kirkpatrick, C., eds. (1988), *Privatisation in Less Developed Countries*, Brighton: Wheatsheaf Press.

Cooper, R.N. (1971), 'Devaluation and Aggregate Demand in Aid Receiving Countries', in Bhagwati, J. *et al*., eds. (1971), *Trade, Balance of Payments and Growth*, Amsterdam: North Holland.

Dandekar, V.M. (1988), 'Indian Economy since Independence', *Economic and Political Weekly*, 23 April 1988, vol.23.

Datta-Chaudhuri, M. (1990), 'Market Failure and Government Failure', *Journal of Economic Perspectives*, vol. 4, no. 3.

Datta Roy Choudhury, U. (1990), 'Savings Behaviour in Households: Trends and Pattern', in Datta Roy Choudhury, U., and Bagchi A. (eds.), *Domestic Savings in India: Trends and Issues*, New Delhi: Vikas.

Deaton, A. (1989), *Saving in Developing Countries: Theory and Review*, paper presented at the First Annual World Bank Conference on Development Economics, sponsored by the World Bank, Washington, D.C., 7-28 April 1989.

Debray, R. (1967), 'Problems of revolutionary strategy in Latin America', *New Left Review*, no. 45, September-October.

de Mattos, C.A. (1987), 'The State Decision-Making and Planning in Latin America', *CEPAL Review*, no. 31, April 1987, United Nations Economic Commission for Latin America and the Caribbean, Santiago, Chile.

Denison, E.F. (1962), 'Education, Economic Growth and Gaps in Information', *Journal of Political Economy*, vol. lxx, Supplement.

Denoon, D.B.H. (1986), *Devaluation under Pressure: India, Indonesia, and Ghana*, Cambridge: MIT Press.

Desai, A.V., *et al.* (1990), 'India's Export Performance and Policy', New Delhi: National Council of Applied Economic Research (mimeo).

Dhar, P.N. (1989), 'Constraints on Growth: Reflections on the Indian Experience', Delhi: Institute of Economic Growth (mimeo).

Diaz-Alejandro, C.F. (1970), *Essays on the Economic History of the Argentine Republic*, New Haven: Yale University Press.

———. (1975), 'Trade Policies and Economic Development', in Peter B. Kenen (ed.), *International Trade and Finance: Frontiers for Research*, Cambridge: Cambridge University Press.

Dornbusch, R., and Fischer, S. (1985), 'The World Debt Problem: Origins and Prospects', *Journal of Development Planning*, United Nations, no. 16.

Dornbusch, R., (1989), *The Road to Economic Recovery*, Background Paper for the Twentieth Century Fund Task Force on International Debt, New York: Priority Press Publications.

Dornbusch, R., and Reynoso, A. (1989), 'Financial Factors in Economic Development', *American Economic Review*, vol. 79, no. 2, pp 204-9.

Eaton, J. (1989), 'Foreign Public Capital Flows', in Chenery H. and Srinivasan, T.N., *Handbook of Development Economics*, vol. 2, Amsterdam: North Holland.

Feder, G. (1983), 'On Exports and Economic Growth', *Journal of Development Economics*, vol. 12.

Fields, G. (1984), 'Employment, Income Distribution and Economic Growth in Seven Small Open Economies', *Economic Journal*, March 1984, vol. 94.

Findlay, R. (1986), 'Trade, Development and the State', Economic Growth Center, Yale University (mimeo).

Fishlow, A. (1985), 'The State of Latin American Economics', in *Economic and Social Progress in Latin America*, Washington, D.C.: Inter-American Development Bank.

———. (1990), 'The Latin American State', *Journal of Economic Perspectives*, vol. 4, no. 3.

Fransman, M., and King K. (1984), *Technological Capability in the Third World*, New York: St Martin's Press.

Gaiha, R. (1989), 'Poverty, Agricultural Production and Prices in Rural India - a Reformulation', *Cambridge Journal of Economics*, vol. 13, no. 2.

Galbraith, J.K. (1991), 'Economics in the Century Ahead', *The Economic Journal*, January 1991, vol. 101, no. 404.

Galenson, W., and Leibenstein, H. (1955), 'Investment Criteria, Production and Economic Development', *Quarterly Journal of Economics*, vol. 69, pp. 343-70.

Gallagher, J., and Robinson, R. (1953), 'The Imperialism of Free Trade', *The Economic History Review*, vol. VI, no. 1 (second series).

Gerschenkron, A. (1962), *Economic Backwardness in Historical Perspective*, Cambridge: Harvard University Press.

Gersovitz, M. (1988), 'Savings and Development', in *Handbook of Development Economics*, ed. Chenery, H. and Srinivasan, T.N. (eds.), Amsterdam: North Holland.

Ghosh, A.K. (1989), 'Rural Poverty and Relative Prices in India', *Cambridge Journal of Economics*, vol. 13, no. 2.

———. (1991), 'Eighth Plan: Challenges and Possibilities-IX ', *Economic and Political Weekly*, vol. 26, pp. 807-14.

Government of India (1951), *First Five Year Plan, 1951-56*, New Delhi: Planning Commission.

———. (1956), *Second Five Year Plan, 1956-61*, New Delhi: Planning Commission.

———. (1961), *Third Five Year Plan, 1961-66*, New Delhi: Planning Commission.

———. (1964), *Report of the Industrial Development Procedures Committee* (T. Swaminathan, Chairman), New Delhi.

———. (1965), *Report of the Monopolies Enquiry Commission*, Delhi.

———. (1967), *Final Report on Industrial Planning and Licensing Policy*, (R.K. Hazari, Chairman), New Delhi.

———. (1969), *Report of the Industrial Licensing Policy Enquiry Committee*, (S. Dutt, Chairman), New Delhi.

———. (1970), *Fourth Five Year Plan, 1969-74*, New Delhi: Planning Commission.

———. (1976), *Fifth Five Year Plan, 1974-79*, New Delhi: Planning Commission.

———. (1978a), *Report of the High Powered Committee on Companies and MRTP Acts* (R. Sachar, Chairman), New Delhi.

———. (1978b), *Report of the Committee on Import-Export Policies and Procedures* (P.C. Alexander, Chairman), ministry of commerce, January 1978.

———. (1979), *Report of the Committee on Controls and Subsidies* (V. Dagli, Chairman), Delhi.

———. (1981), *Sixth Five Year Plan, 1980-85*, New Delhi: Planning Commission,.

———. (1984), *Report of the Committee on Trade Policies*, (Abid Hussain, Chairman), New Delhi: ministry of commerce.

———. (1985a), *Report of the Committee to Examine Principles of a Possible Shift from Physical to Financial Controls* (M. Narasimham, Chairman), New Delhi: ministry of finance.

———. (1985b), *Long Term Fiscal Policy*, New Delhi: ministry of finance.

———. (1985c), *Seventh Five Year Plan, 1985-90*, vol.1, New Delhi: Planning Commission.

———. (1986a), *Administered Price Policy: A Discussion Paper*, New Delhi: ministry of finance.

———. (1986b), *National Policy on Education*, New Delhi: Ministry of Human Resource Development.

———. (1990), *Budget Speeches of Union Finance Ministers, 1947-48 to 1990-91*, New Delhi: ministry of finance.

Grossman, G.M., and Helpman, E. (1989), *Comparative Advantage and Long-Run Growth*, NBER working paper no. 2809, Cambridge: National Bureau of Economic Research.

Guhan, S. (1991), 'State Finances in Tamil Nadu 1960-90: A Survey', paper presented at the seminar on state finances, (19-20 April 1991), New Delhi: National Institute of Public Finance and Policy (mimeo).

Gupta, S.P. (1989), *Planning and Development in India*, New Delhi: Allied Publishers.

Haberler, G. (1959), 'International Trade and Economic Development', reprinted in G. Meier, ed. (1975), *Leading Issues in Economic Development* (3rd edition), Delhi: Oxford University Press.

Hamilton, C. (1989), 'The Irrelevance of Economic Liberalization in the Third World', *World Development*, vol. 17, no.10, pp. 1523-30.

Hanson, A.H. (1963), 'The Crisis of Indian Planning', *Political Quarterly*, October-December 1963, reprinted in Hanson, A.H. (1969), *Planning and Politicians*, London: Routledge and Kegan Paul.

Haque, N., and Montiel, P. (1989), 'Consumption in Developing Countries: Tests for Finite Horizons and Liquidity Constraints', *Review of Economics and Statistics*, vol. 71.

Harriss, J. (1987), 'The State in Retreat? Why Has India Experienced such Half-Hearted Liberalization in the 1980s?', *IDS Bulletin*, Sussex, vol. 18, no. 4.

Haveman, R.H., and Wolfe, B. (1984), 'Schooling and Economic Well-being: The Role of Non-market Effects', *Journal of Human Resources*, 19, no. 3. pp. 377-407.

Helleiner, G.K. (1990), 'Trade Strategy in Medium-Term Adjustment', *World Development*, vol. 18, no. 6. pp. 879-97.

Heston, A., and Summers, R. (1980), 'Comparative Indian Economic Growth: 1870 to 1970', *American Economic Review*, vol. 70, no. 2.

Heston, A. (1983), 'National Income', in D. Kumar and M. Desai (eds.), *The Cambridge Economic History of India*, vol. II, Cambridge: Cambridge University Press.

Hirschman, A.O. (1968), 'The Political Economy of Import- Substituting Industrialisation in Latin America', *Quarterly Journal of Economics*, vol. 82, no.1.

———. (1980), 'The Welfare State in Trouble: Systemic Crisis or Growing Pains', *The American Economic Review*, vol. 70, no. 2.

———. (1982), *Shifting Involvements: Private Interest and Public Action*, Oxford: Martin Robertson.

———. (1987), 'The Political Economy of Latin American Development: Seven Exercises in Retrospection', *Latin American Research Review*, vol. 22, no. 3.

Houthakker, H.S. (1965), 'On Some Determinants of Saving in Developed and Underdeveloped Countries', in E.A.G. Robinson (ed.), *Problems of Economic Development*, London: Macmillan.

International Monetary Fund (1987), 'Theoretical Aspects of the Design of Fund-supported Adjustment Programs' occasional paper no. 55, Washington D.C.

International Monetary Fund and World Bank (1987), *Papers Presented at the Symposium on Growth Oriented Adjustment Programs*, 25-27 February 1987, Washington D.C.

International Monetary Fund, World Bank and others (1990), *The Economy of the U.S.S.R.: Summary and Recommendations*, Washington, D.C.

Iyer, R.R. (1991), *A Grammar of Public Enterprises: Exercises in Clarification*, New Delhi: Centre for Policy Research.

Jalan, B. (1975), *Essays in Development Policy*, New Delhi: Macmillan.

Jones, C., and Roemer, M. (1989), 'Editors' Introduction: Modeling and Measuring Parallel Markets in Developing Countries', *World Development*, vol. 17, no.12, pp. 1861-70.

Joseph, J.K. (1989), 'Growth Performance of Indian Electronics Under Liberalization', *Economic and Political Weekly*, vol. 24, no. 33.

Kanbur, R. (1988), 'The Principles of Targeting', Development Economics Research Center, University of Warwick, U.K. (mimeo).

Kay, J.A., and Thompson, D.J. (1986), 'Privatisation: A Policy in Search of a Rationale', *The Economic Journal*, vol.96, March 1986, pp. 18-32.

Kelkar, V., Kumar, R., and Nangia, R. (1990), 'India's Industrial Economy: Policies, Performance and Reforms', New Delhi (mimeo).

Kelkar, V., and Kumar, R. (1990), 'Industrial Growth in the Eighties: Emerging Policy Issues', *Economic and Political Weekly*, 27 Jan. 1990, vol.25.

Kennedy, P. (1989), *The Rise and Fall of the Great Powers*, New York: Vintage Books.

Khatkhate, D.R. (1988a), 'Assessing the Impact of Interest Rates in Less Developed Countries', *World Development*, vol. 16, no. 5, pp. 577-88.

———. (1988b), 'Assessing the Level of Interest Rates in Less Developed Countries', *Economic and Political Weekly*, 9 July 1988, pp. 1427-32.

———. (1991), 'Management of Economic Power in India', Washington D.C. (mimeo).

Kindleberger, C.P. (1980), 'Government Policies and Changing Shares in World Trade', *American Economic Review*, vol. 70, no. 2.

Kirkpatrick, C. (1989), 'Some Background Observations on Privatisation', in Ramanadham, V.V. (ed.), *Privatisation in Developing Countries*, London: Routledge.

Kochanek, Stanley A. (1985), 'The Politics of Regulation: Rajiv's New Mantras', *Journal of Commonwealth and Comparative Politics*, vol. xxii, November 1985.

Kohli, A. (1989), 'Politics of Economic Liberalization in India', *World Development*, vol. 17, no. 3.

Kornai, J. (1959), *Overcentralisation in Economic Administration: A Critical Analysis based on Experience in Hungarian Light Industry*, Oxford: Oxford University Press.

———. (1980), *Economics of Shortage*, Amsterdam: North-Holland.

———. (1990), *Vision and Reality, Market and State*, New York: Routledge.

Krueger, A.O. (1974), 'The Political Economy of the Rent-Seeking Society', *American Economic Review*, vol. 64, no. 3, pp. 291-303.

———. (1978), *Foreign Trade Regimes and Economic Development: Liberalisation Attempts and Consequences*, Cambridge, Mass: Ballinger.

———. (1982), *Trade and Employment in Developing Countries: Synthesis and Conclusions*, Chicago: University of Chicago Press.

———. (1990), 'Government Failures in Development', *Journal of Economic Perspective*, vol. 4, no. 3.

Krugman, Paul R. (1987), 'The Narrow Moving Band, the Dutch Disease and the Competitive Consequences of Mrs. Thatcher', *Journal of Economic Development*, vol. 27, pp. 41-5.

Kurien, C.T. (1987), 'Managing the Economy', presidential address, section 5 of the XIIth Indian Social Science Congress, Mysore, reprinted in *The Economic Times*, 12 and 13 August 1987.

———. (1989), 'Indian Economy in the 1980s and on to the 1990s', *Economic and Political Economy*, 15 April 1989.

Kuznets, S. (1955), 'Towards a Theory of Economic Growth', in Levachman, R. (ed.), *National Policy for Economic Welfare at Home and Abroad*, New York: Doubleday & Co.

Lal, D. (1990), 'International Capital Flows and Economic Development', in Scott, M., and Lal, D. (ed.), *Public Policy and Economic Development: Essays in honour of Ian Little*, Oxford: Clarendon Press.

Lall, S. (1990), *Building Industrial Competitiveness in Developing Countries*, Paris: O.E.C.D.

Lall, S., and Streeten, P. (1977), *Foriegn Investment, Transnationals and Developing Countries*, London: Macmillan.

Levy, V. (1981), 'On Estimating Efficiency Differentials between Public and Private Sectors in a Developing Economy—Iraq', *Journal of Comparative Economics*, vol. 5.

Lewis, W. A. (1954), 'Economic Development with Unlimited Supplies of Labor', reprinted in A.N. Agarwala and S.P. Singh,(eds.), *The Economics of Underdevelopment*, London: Oxford University Press.

———. (1962), 'Education and Economic Development', *International Social Science Journal* (Paris), vol. 14, pp. 685-99.

———. (1978), *Growth and Fluctuations*, London: George Allen and Unwin.

Little, I.M.D., and Clifford, J.M. (1965), *International Aid*, Chicago: Aldine Publishing Company.

Little, I.M.D., Scitovsky, T., and Scott, M. (1970), *Industry and Trade in Some Developing Countries: A Comparative Study*, London: Oxford University Press (for O.E.C.D.).

Lockwood W.W. (1954), *The Economic Development of Japan*, Princeton: Princeton University Press.

Love, J. (1980), 'Raul Prebisch and the Origins of the Doctrine of Unequal Exchange', *Latin American Research Review*, vol. 15, November 1980.

Madhur, S. (1990), 'Household Savings in Financial Assets' (mimeo), New Delhi: Planning Commission.

Mahalanobis, P.C. (1953), 'Some Observations on the Process of Growth of National Income', *Sankhya*, vol. 12, pp. 307-12.

———. (1955), *Draft Recommendations for the Formulation of the Second Five Year Plan, 1956-1961*, Planning Commission, 1955.

———. (1960), 'Operational Research Models Used for Planning in India', reprinted in P.K. Bose and M. Mukherjee, *Papers on Planning*, Calcutta.

McCarthy, F., Taylor, L., and Talati, C. (1987), 'Trade patterns in developing countries, 1964-82', *Journal of Development Economics*, vol. 27, nos 1-2, pp. 5-39.

Mckinnon, R.I. (1973), *Money and Capital in Economic Development*, Washington, D.C.: Brookings Institution.

Meier, G.M. (1990), 'Trade Policy and Development', in Scott, M. and Lal, D., eds. *Public Policy and Economic Development: Essays in Honour of Ian Little*, Oxford: Clarendon Press.

Michaely, M. (1977), 'Exports and Growth: An empirical investigation', *Journal of Development Economics*, vol. 4.

Misra, S. (1991), 'India's Textile Sector', New Delhi: Centre for Policy Research (mimeo).

Mitra, A. (1977), *Terms of Trade and Class Relations*, London: Frank Cass.

Modigliani, F. (1970), 'The Life Cycle Hypothesis of Saving and Inter-Country Differences in the Saving Ratio', in Eltis W.A., *et al.* (ed.), *Induction, Growth and Trade: Essays in Honour of Sir Roy Harrod*, London: Clarendon Press, 1970.

Mohan, R. and Aggarwal, V. (1990), 'Commands and Controls: Planning for Indian Industrial Development, 1951-1990", *Journal of Comparative Economics*, vol. 14, pp. 681-712.

Morris, S. (1991), 'The Holding Company, Performance Contracts and Task Orientation: Clearing the Ground', Institute of Public Enterprise, Hyderabad: Osmania University (mimeo).

Mukherjee, M. (1969), *The National Income of India, Trends and Structure.* Calcutta.

Mulji, S. (1990), 'Vision and Reality of Public Sector Management: The Indian Experience', in Scott, M. and Lal, D., eds. *Public Policy and Economic Development*, Oxford: Clarendon Press.

Mundle, S., and Govinda Rao, M. (1990), 'The Volume and Composition of Government Subsidies in India: 1987-88', New Delhi: National Institute of Public Finance and Policy (mimeo).

Munnell, A. (1988), 'Comments' on Andrews, William D., and David F. Bradford, 'Savings Incentives in a Hybrid Income Tax', in Aaron, H.J., *et al.* (eds.), *Uneasy Compromise: Problems of a Hybrid Income-Consumption Tax*, Washington: The Brookings Institution, pp. 269-300.

Nandy, A. (1989), 'The Political Culture of the Indian State', *Daedalus*, Journal of the American Academy of Arts and Sciences, vol. 118, no. 4.

Nayyar, D. (1976), *India's Exports and Export Policies in the 1960s*, Cambridge: Cambridge University Press.

———. (1978), 'Industrial Development in India', *Economic and Political Weekly* (Special Number), vol.13, pp. 1265-78.

Nunnenkamp, P. (1986), 'State enterprises in developing countries', *Intereconomics*, July/August, pp. 186-93.

Nurkse, R. (1953), *Problems of Capital Formation in Underdeveloped Countries*, Oxford: Basil Blackwell.

———. (1959), 'Pattern of Trade and Development', Wicksell Lectures, reprinted in S. Haberler and R.M. Stern, *Equilibrium and Growth in the World Economy*, Cambridge: Mass., 1961.

Olson, M. (1982), *The Rise and Decline of Nations*, New Haven: Yale University Press.

Otani, I., and Villanueva, D.(1989), 'Theoretical Aspects of Growth in Developing Countries: External Debt Dynamics and the Role of Human Capital', *Staff Papers*, Washington, D.C.: International Monetary Fund, vol. 36 (June 1989), pp. 307-42.

Pack, H. and Westphal, L.E. (1986), 'Industrial Strategy and Technological Change: Theory versus Reality', *Journal of Development Economics*, 22, pp. 87-128.

Panchamukhi, V.R. (1978), *Trade Policies of India: A Quantitative Analysis*, Delhi: Concept Publishing Co.

Parikh, K. and Suryanarayana, M.H. (1991), 'Fertiliser Subsidy: Alternatives and Implications', Bombay: Indira Gandhi Institute of Development Research (mimeo).

Patel, I.G. (1985), *On the Economics of Development: Towards a Consensus*, Stemp Memorial Lecture, University of London.

———. (1987), 'On Taking India into the Twenty-First Century', Kingsley Martin Memorial Lecture, November 1986, reprinted in *Modern Asian Studies*, vol. 21, no. 2.

Patnaik, P. (1987), 'A Perspective on the Recent Phase of Indian Economic Development', paper presented to the *Social Scientist* seminar on Four Decades of Development, November 1987.

Patton Culbertson, W. (1989), 'Empirical Regularities in Black Markets for Currency', *World Development*, vol.17, no.12, pp. 1907-19.

Peacock, A.T., and Wiseman, J. (1967), *The Growth of Public Expenditure in the United Kingdom*, London: Allen and Unwin.

Pearson Commission (1969), *Partners in Development*, New York: Praeger.

Pinstrup-Andersen, P. (1988), *Food Subsidies in Developing Countries: Costs, Benefits and Policy Options*, Baltimore: Johns Hopkins Press.

Polak, J.J. (1957), 'Monetary Analysis of Income Formation and Payments Problems', International Monetary Fund, Staff Papers, vol. 5, reprinted in IMF (1977), *The Monetary Approach to the Balance of Payments*, Washington, D.C.

Prebisch, R. (1950), *The Economic Development of Latin America*, United Nations.

Psacharopoulos, G. (1984), 'The Contribution of Education to Economic Growth: International Comparison', in John W. Kendrick, ed., *International Comparisons of Productivity and Causes of the Slowdown*, Cambridge: Ballinger.

———. (1988), 'Education and Development: A Review', *World Bank Research Observer*, The World Bank (Washington), vol. 3, no. 1, January 1988, pp. 99-116.

Raj, K.N. (1984), 'Some Observations on Economic Growth in India over the period 1952/53 to 1982/83', *Economic and Political Weekly*, vol. 19, 13 October 1984.

———. (1986), *New Economic Policy*, Delhi: Oxford University Press.

Ramanadham, V.V. (1989), *Privatisation in Developing Countries*, London: Routledge.

Rangarajan, C., *et al.* (1989), 'Dynamics of Interaction Between Government Deficit and Domestic Debt in India', *Reserve Bank of India Occasional Papers*, vol. 10, no. 3.

———. (1990), *The Balance of Payments Scenario*, Seventh G.L. Mehta Memorial Lecture, Bombay: Indian Institute of Technology.

Rao, K.C.S., and Madhavi Latha, K. (1990), 'Productivity and Operating Efficiency in Public Enterprises: A Study', *Prajnan*, vol. xix, no. 1.

Rao, V.K.R.V. (1983), *India's National Income, 1950-80: An Analysisof Economic Growth and Change*, Delhi: Sage Publications.

Reddy, Y.V. (1989), 'Privatisation in India', in Ramanadham, V.V., ed., *Privatisation in Developing Countries*, London: Routledge.

Reserve Bank of India (1982), *Capital Formation and Saving in India, 1950-51 to 1979-90*, Report of the Working Group on Savings Appointed by Government of India (K.N. Raj, Chairman), Bombay.

———. (1990), *Report on Currency and Finance 1989-90*, Bombay.

Rodrik, D. (1990), 'How Should Structural Programmes be Designed', *World Development*, vol. 18, no. 7, pp. 933-47.

Romer, P.M. (1986), 'Increasing Returns and Long-Run Growth', *Journal of Political Economy*, vol.94, pp. 1002-37.

———. (1987), 'Crazy Explanations for the Productivity Slowdown', in Fischer, S., ed., *NBER Macroeconomics Annual*, Cambridge, Massachusetts: MIT Press.

Rosenstein-Rodan, P.N. (1943), 'Problems of Industrialisation in Eastern and South-Eastern Europe', *Economic Journal*, vol. 53, pp.202-11.

Rossi, N. (1988), 'Government Spending, the Real Interest Rate, and the Behaviour of Liquidity-Constrained Consumers in Developing Countries', *Staff Papers*, International Monetary Fund, vol. 35, (March 1988), pp. 104-40.

Roy, T., and Sen, K. (1991), 'Changes in Saving Rate and its Implications for Growth', *Economic and Political Weekly*, vol.26, no.20 (20 April 1991), pp. 1055-8.

Rubin, B.R. (1985), 'Economic Liberalization and the Indian State', *Third World Quarterly*, vol. 7, no. 4.

Rudolph, L., and Rudolph S. (1987), *In Pursuit of Lakshmi: The Political Economy of the Indian State*, Bombay: Orient Longman.

Sachs, J.D. (1987), 'Trade and Exchange Rate Policies in Growth-Oriented Adjustment Programs', Paper presented at the symposium on Growth-Oriented Adjustment Programs, World Bank, Washington, D.C., 25-27 February 1987 (mimeo.)

———. ed. (1989), *Developing Country Debt and the World Economy*, Chicago: The University of Chicago Press.

Sarkar, H., and Panda, M. (1990), 'Short term Forecasting and Policy Analysis through a Structural Macro-economic Model for India', paper presented at the UNDP-ESCAP seminar on Inter- Country Model System, Bangkok, January 1990.

Sau, R. (1988), 'The Green Revolution and Industrial Growth in India: A Tale of Two Paradoxes and Half', *Economic and Political Weekly*, 16 April 1988, vol. 23.

Saul, J. (1979), 'The State and Revolution in Eastern Africa', Heinemann and Monthly Review Press, reprinted in David Held, *et al.*, ed. (1983), *States and Society*, Oxford: Martin Robertson.

Schick, A. (1990), 'Why the Deficit Persists as a Budget Problem: Role of Political Institutions', in Premchand, A., ed., *Government Financial Management: Issue and Country Studies* Washington, D.C.: International Monetary Fund.

Schultz, T. (1963), *The Economic Value of Education*, New York: Columbia University Press.

———. (1988), 'Education Investments and Returns', in Chenery, H., and Srinivasan, T.N. (1988), *Handbook of Development Economics*, vol.1. Amsterdam: North Holland.

Scitovsky, T. (1954), 'Two Concepts of External Economies', *Journal of Political Economy*, vol. 62.

Scott, M., and Lal, D. (1990), *Public Policy and Economic Development*, Oxford: Clarendon Press.

Sen, A. (1983), 'Development: Which Way Now?', *The Economic Journal*, vol. 93.

———. (1989), 'Indian Development: Lessons and Non-Lessons', *Daedalus*, Journal of the American Academy of Arts and Sciences, vol. 118, no. 4.

Seshan, A. (1987), *The Burden of Domestic Debt in India*, Reserve Bank of India Occasional Papers, vol. 8, no. 1.

Shapiro, H., and Taylor, L. (1990), 'The State and Industrial Strategy', *World Development*, vol. 18, no. 6, pp. 861-78.

Shetty, S.L. (1990), 'Overall Aspects of Savings: Measurement of Savings in Real Terms', in Datta Roy Choudhury, U., and Bagchi, A., *Domestic Savings in India: Trends and Issues*, New Delhi: Vikas.

Singer, H. (1950), 'The distribution of gains between investing and borrowing countries', *American Economic Review*, Papers and Proceedings, vol. 40, pp. 473-85.

Singh, M. (1964), *India's Export Trends and the Prospects for Self-Sustained Growth*, Oxford: Clarendon Press.

———. (1986), *The Quest for Equity in Development*, R.R. Kale Memorial Lecture, Poona.

Smith, R. (1989), 'Factors Affecting Saving, Policy Tools, and Tax Reform', *IMF Working Paper*, no. 89/47, International Monetary Fund, 23 May 1989.

Solow, R.M. (1956), 'A Contribution to the Theory of Economic Growth', *Quarterly Journal of Economics*, vol. 32, pp. 65-94.

Srinivasan, T.N. (1985), 'Neo-classical Political Economy, the State and Economic Development', *Asian Development Review*, pp. 38-58.

Stern, N. (1991), 'The Determinants of Growth', in *The Economic Journal*, vol. 101, no. 404, pp. 122-33.

Stiglitz, J.E. (1991), 'Another Century of Economic Science', *The Economic Journal*, vol. 101, no. 404.

Streeten, P.(1981), *Development Perspectives*, London: Macmillan.

———. (1986), 'Suffering from Success', in Foxley, McPherson and O' Donnell, eds., *Development, Democracy and the Art of Trespassing*, Notre Dame: University of Notre Dame Press.

Summers, L.H., and Carroll, C. (1989), 'The Growth-Saving Nexus', paper presented at the NBER Conference on Saving, Maui.

Sundrum, R.M. (1987), *Growth and Income Distribution in India: Policy Performance Since Independence*, Delhi: Sage Publications.

———. (1990), *Economic Growth in Theory and Practice*, London: Macmillan.

Swarup, D. (1990), 'India: Developments in Government Accounting and Financial Management', in Premchand, A., ed., *Government and Financial Management: Issues and Country Studies*, Washington, D.C.: International Monetary Fund.

Taylor, L. (1988), *Varieties of Stabilisation Experience: Towards Sensible Macroeconomics in the Third World*, WIDER Studies in Development Economics, Oxford: Clarendon Press.

Thirsk, W.R. (1990), 'Recent Experience with Tax Reform in Developing Countries', *Ricerche Economiche*, vol. 44, no. 2-3.

Toye, (1988), 'Political Economy and the Analysis of Indian Development', *Modern Asian Studies*, vol. 22, no.1.

Uzawa, H. (1965), 'Optimum Technical Change in an Aggregative Model of Economic Growth', *International Economic Review*, 6, pp. 18-31.

Venti, S.F., and Wise, D.A. (1987), 'IRAs and Savings', in Feldstein, M., ed., *The Effects of Taxation on Capital Accumulation*, Chicago: University of Chicago Press, pp. 7-48.

Vickers, J., and Yarrow, G. (1988), *Privatisation: An Economic Analysis*, Cambridge: M.I.T. Press.

Westphal, L.E. (1990), 'Industrial Policy in an Export-Propelled Economy: Lessons from South Korea's Experience', *Journal of Economic Perspectives*, vol. 4, no. 3.

Wolf, M. (1982), *India's Exports*, Oxford: Oxford University Press (for World Bank, Washington).

World Bank (1987a), *Korea: Managing the Industrial Transition*, vol. I, Washington, D.C.

———. (1987b), *World Development Report*, Washington, D.C.

———. (1988), *Targeted Programs for the Poor during Structural Adjustment*, A Summary of the Symposium on Poverty and Adjustment, Washington, D.C.

———. (1990), *World Development Report*, Washington, D.C.

Index

Acharya, S. 191, 207
Adiseshiah, M.S. 35
Administration
  India 8, 9, 10, 17
Advance Licenses 114, 158
Africa, vii, 62, 75, 126, 145, 148, 176, 192, 216, 217, 225
Agarwal, M. 178
Aggarwal, Y.P. 59
Aggarwal, V. 70, 88, 92, 94
Agriculture 10, 23, 25, 26, 33, 34, 35, 58, 65, 84, 120, 125, 147, 179
  export 10
  income growth 24
  neglect of 23
  production 3, 218
Aharoni, Y. 93
Ahluwalia, I.J. 34, 53
Ahluwalia, M.S. 46, 151
Aid 3, 30, 45, 98, 103, 104, 122, 143, 144, 159
  utilization 159
Aid India Consortium 3, 45
Alavi, H. 4
Allocative efficiency 75, 76, 122, 191, 221
Ando, A. 168
Anglade, C. 92
Argentina 126, 128, 133, 146, 154, 217
Arrow, K.J. 35, 50
Asia 38, 47, 72, 87, 145, 148, 176, 192

Bagchi, A. 179
Bairoch, P. 35
Bajaj, J.L. viii, 178
Balance of payments
  and fiscal deficits 132, 133
  consequence of 104
  crisis problem 2, 17, 25, 46, 97, 105, 107, 108, 179, 216, 218
  India's performance, 14
  nature of 6, 17, 102
  policy for 16
  political economy 106-107
  review 1956-57 to 1989-90 97-107
  viability 14, 97
Balassa, B. 119, 121, 153, 154
Bardhan, P.K. viii, 6, 35, 64, 90
Bartoli, G. 157
Bauer, P.T. 151
Benthamite social welfare function 5
Bergsman, J. 111
Bhagwati, J. 7, 34, 35, 52, 83, 86, 94, 107, 119, 122, 123, 145, 153, 154, 158
Bhatty, I.Z. 205
Biswas, B. 158
Black money, 191 also see 'Parallel economy'
Bliss, C. 154
Brazil 36, 54-57, 73, 104, 111, 128, 133, 146, 152, 155, 158
Bruno, M. 120, 122
Bruton, H. 120, 121
Buchanan, J.M. 18
Budget constraint
  soft, hard 18, 79, 181, 196-198, 207, 221
Budget/Budgetary deficit 6, 181
  Also see 'Fiscal deficit'

Budget speeches 6, 105
Buiter, W.H. 178
Bureaucratic-military apparatus 4

Capital-Output ratio 9, 25, 34, 68, 150, 169, 173
India's 34
Cardoso, E.A. 144
Carroll, C.H. 50
Cash Compensatory Support (CCS) 113
Chakravarty, S. 26, 33, 92, 93, 204, 206
Chelliah, R.J. 33, 178, 182
Chenery, H. 122, 144, 154
Chief Controller of Imports and Exports (CCI&E) 115
China vii, 24, 25, 26, 30, 36, 54-57, 62, 173
Clifford, J.M. 159
Cline, W.R. 144
Coalitions, distributional (heterogeneous, powerful) 6, 208
Collective choice 5
Colletta, N.J. 48
Colonial pattern of trade 28
Colonial state 4
Commercial loans 98, 149 also see 'External debt, India'
Competition 10, 18, 19, 72, 73, 75, 83, 85, 86, 88, 106, 221
Concessional assistance 101
Controls 2, 11, 15, 17, 19, 21, 23, 25, 33, 45, 65, 77, 78, 79, 81, 83, 84, 86, 91, 92, 125, 127, 128, 159, 171, 172, 191, 200, 222, 223
Cook, P. 93
Cooper, R.N. 127
Current account deficit 2, 15
financing of 15
Czechoslovakia 129

Dandekar, V.M. 24, 33, 68, 92
Datta Chaudhari, M. 27, 90, 92
Datta Roy Choudhary, U. 174, 203
de Mattos, C.A. 92
Deaton, A. 203
Debray, R. 4
Debt service payments, ratio 101, 148
factors affecting 148
in heavily indebted countries 147, 148
Debt-export ratio 147, 148 also see 'Debt service payments, ratio'
Decentralization 203, 223, 225
Default 3
Denison, E.F. 39
Denoon, D.B.H. 158
Desai, A.V. 116
Desai, P. 83, 94, 153
Development Strategy 11, 13, 21, 23, 26, 30, 35, 43
Dhar, P.N. 33, 74
Diaz Alejandro, C.F. 155
Directly unproductive profit-seeking (DUP) activities 86
Dornbusch, R. 144, 146, 147, 152, 218
Duty drawback system 139

Eastern Europe 4, 130, 173
Eaton, J. 144
Education, contribution to growth 38-39
Effective Exchange rate (EER) 155
Effective rates of protection 10, 139, 153, 222
Electronic industry 112, 113
Essential Commodities Act 204
Exchange Controls 84, 115, 142
Exchange rate policy 142
Expenditure, Government

'policy based' approach, 187-189, 220
components of 182
constitutional limit on 189, 220
policies 186, 188
political problem 206
programmes 106
reasons for growth in 184, 185
trend in 184
Export import policy 135, 136
Export promoting trade policy
definition of 83
Export, India's performance 16, 25, 107, 108, 110
Export-oriented units 114, 116
Exports
and growth 120
and import policy, 136, 138
incentives 110, 113, 114, 136, 138
of high growth countries 37
pessimism 23, 116, 117
textiles 109, 110
Extended Fund Facility (EFF) 100
External assistance 3, 197 See also 'Concessional assistance'
External debt 2, 76, 98, 101. 127, 132, 144, 219, 220
growth of 119
India 101
interest on 141
policy for 141, 219
structure of 132

Feder, G. 119
Fields, G. 154
Fifth Five Year Plan 131, 156
Financial and Credit controls 84
Findlay, R. 154
First Five Year Plan 22, 45
Fiscal crisis 4, 79, 104, 177, 179, 201 also see 'Fiscal deficit'
Fiscal deficits 1, 3, 7, 17, 98, 99, 102, 104, 105 also see 'Fiscal crisis'
and balance of payment 132
simulation exercise 135
Fiscal incentives for savings 175, 176
Fischer, S. 147
Fishlow, A. 16, 76, 87, 90, 128
Food 25, 29, 30, 65, 94, 185, 188, 195, 204, 218, 224, 225
subsidy 185, 188, 225
Foreign Exchange Regulation Act (FERA) 84, 92, 115
Foreign Exchange Reserves 1, 3, 99, 151
Foreign investment 17, 82, 84, 91, 143, 144, 145, 159
direct 143, 144
Fortin, C. 92
Fourastie, J. 20
Fourth Five Year Plan 60
Fransman, M. 121
Free trade imperialism 118
Free Trade Zones 114
Fukuyama, F. 95

Gaiha, R. 35
Galbraith, J.K. 49, 53, 130
Galenson, W. 33
Gallagher, J. 153
Germany 4, 63, 90, 119, 207
Gerschenkron, A. 27
Gersovitz, M. 169, 203
Ghosh, A.K. 35, 223
Gonzalez, F. 62, 91
Government
role of 13, 62, 64, 65, 77, 90 (Also see State, role of)
Govinda Rao, M. 184, 186
Gradualist approach vs. 'shock treatment', 129, 135
Grossman, G.M. 50
Growth
determinants of 13

export-adequate 17, 128
export-led 17, 123, 128
in developing countries 62
India's growth performance 23-24, 43-44, 50-51
relationship with exports 119
Guhan, S. 177, 178
Gulf war 1, 141, 157
Gupta, S.P. 92

Haberler, G. 154
Hamilton, C. 155
Hanson, A.H. 12
Haque, N. 203
Harriss, J. 33, 106, 152
Haveman, R.H. 39
Helleiner, G.K. 124, 128, 154
Helpman, E. 50
Heston, A. 34
Heterodox stabilisation 128, 155
High Growth Countries
experience 36
literacy in 38
savings in 36
Hirschman, A.O. 20, 61, 64, 154
Holding Company 78, 80 also see 'multi-product conglomerates'
Household savings
theory of 168
Houthakker, H.S. 51
Human development index 25
Hungary vii, 129

Import and export controls 92
Import export Policy 132
Import liberalization 16, 21, 99, 102, 103, 106, 123-127, 135, 155, 219
Import substitution 19, 23, 28, 69, 88
Individual Retirement Accounts (IRA) 175
Indonesia 24, 38, 54-57, 192
Industrial licencing 82, 83, 88, 89, 100, 170, 172
Industrial Policy Resolution (1956) 194
Industry (manufacturing)
growth of 2, 42, 102, 218
Infant mortality rate, India 25
Interest rate policies 173, 174, 175
International Development Association (IDA) 46, 47, 101
International Monetary Fund (IMF) 100, 105, 109, 179
Invisibles 99, 100, 101, 141, 162, 167
Inward-looking (inward-orientation) 83, 118, 120, 121, 123, 124, 219
Iyer, R.R. 93

Jalan, B. 11
Japan 31, 63, 72, 90, 119, 125, 126, 154, 157, 200, 223
Jones, C. 159
Joseph, J.K. 10, 112, 113

Kaldor, N. 50, 204
Kalecki, M. 204
Kanbur, R. 81
Kaunda, K. 62, 91
Kay, J.A. 75
Kelkar, V. 10, 69, 94, 106, 152, 153
Kennedy, P. 28, 35
Kerala 11, 224
Khatkhate, D.R. 174, 205
King, K. 121
Kirkpatrick, C. 93
Kochanek, S.A. 33, 106
Kohli, A. 33, 106
Korea 24-26, 31, 36, 38, 48, 54-57, 72, 73, 87, 90, 109, 123, 125, 126, 139, 150, 157, 174, 192, 200, 221, 223

Kornai, J. 184, 196, 197, 207, 223
Krueger, A.O. 86, 90, 154
Krugman, P.R. 50
Kumar, R. 10, 69, 153
Kurien, C.T. 33
Kuznets, S. 27

Lal, D. 144
Lall, S. 31, 73, 145, 200
Latin America (South America) 20, 48, 62, 75, 92, 104, 128, 140, 145, 148, 152, 173, 175, 176, 192, 205, 216, 217, 220, 225
Leibenstein, H. 33
Levy, V. 76, 93
Lewis, W.A. 28, 51, 52
Life cycle theory of savings 168, 169
Lipton, M. 7
Literacy
  importance of 53
  in high growth countries 38
  in India 47, 224
  performance 11
Little, I.M.D. 9, 129
Lockwood, W.W. 154
Long term fiscal policy (LTFP) 10, 181, 182, 192
Love, J. 153

Macro-economic policies 10, 11, 12, 17, 18, 52, 69, 71, 97, 102, 103
Madhur, S. viii, 174
Mahalanobis, P.C. 33, 153, 207
Malaysia 24, 38, 54-57, 73, 145
Marshall, A. 38, 51
McCarthy, F. 126
Mckinnon, R.I. 173
Meier, G.M. 118, 154
Michaely, M. 119
Middle East 4, 46, 109, 141
Misra, S. 109, 153
Mitra, A. 34
Modigliani, F. 168
Mohan, R. 70, 88, 92, 94
Monopolies and Restrictive Trade Practices Act (MRTP) 82
Montiel, P. 203
Morris, S. 7, 202
Mukherjee, M. 34
Mulji, S. 94
Multi-Product conglomerates 18, 201 also see 'Holding Company'
Mundle, S. 184, 186
Munnell, A. 175

Nandi, S. 158
Nandy, A. 91
National Bureau of Economic Research 120, 206
National Council of Applied Economic Research (NCAER) 134
National Development Council 66
National Institute of Public Finance and Policy (NIPFP) 191, 192
National Saving Certificates (NSC) 175
Nayyar, D. 34, 107
Nehru, J. 94
Neo-classical Literature 19, 20, 86
New Economic Policy 21, 67
New education policy (national policy) 48, 53
Nunnenkamp, P. 76, 93
Nurkse, R. 23, 27, 51, 117

Olson, M. 5, 6, 64
Organization for Economic Cooperation and Development (OECD) 10, 120, 155

Otani, I. 40
Outward orientation 16, 119, 122
Over-centralization 9, 184, 223
Also see 'Decentralisation'

Pakistan 30, 87, 98, 108, 109
Panchamukhi, V.R. 107, 153
Panda, M. 157
Parallel economy 4, 69 also see 'Black money'
Paranjape, H. 88
Parikh, K. 207
Patel, I.G. 33, 90, 178
Patnaik, P. 33
Peacock, A.T. 206
Pearson Commission 63
Perez, A. 62, 91
Performance budget 182
Physical vs. financial control 2, 171, 172, 222 also see 'Controls'
Pinstrup-Andersen, P. 94
Planning 4, 9, 12, 13, 18, 21, 23-26, 31, 33, 34, 48, 53, 59, 62, 66-71, 85, 86, 88, 92, 97, 117, 150, 159, 170, 171, 201, 202, 223, 224, 225
and macro-economic policies 69
command type 9, 31
crisis in 12
in India 67
Soviet model 21
techniques 12
Polak model 133, 157
Polak, J.J. 133
Political economy vii, 12, 64, 91, 106, 220
India's 12, 64, 106
Post-colonial society 4
Poverty 4, 5, 26, 27, 34, 35, 50, 65, 66, 81, 94, 170
Prebisch, R. 28, 117
Price and distribution controls 83
Privatisation 73-77, 221
Productive efficiency 221
Psacharopoulos, G. 39
Public Accounts Committee (PAC) 190
Public debt 17, 219, 220
Public Savings 12, 14, 31, 44, 53, 168
consequences of decline in 178
in India 177
target and achievement 182
Public Sector
and exports 132
assets of 77
control of 91
enterprises 18, 202
financial policy 84
goals 201
management of 15, 18, 201, 221
personnel policy 78
privatization of 74
profits of 93
reorganisation of 200, 202

Raghavan, S.N. 51
Raj, K.N. 33, 34, 42, 88, 205
Ramanadham, V.V. 74, 93
Rangarajan, C. 17, 107, 151, 164, 178
Rao, V.K.R.V. 33
Reddy, Y.V. 93
Remittances 84, 99, 100, 109, 115
factors affecting 150
incentives for 150
Rent-seeking 7, 86, 87, 89, 125, 222
Replenishment licences (REP) 110, 113, 134, 137, 140
premium on 134
Revenue deficit 18, 177, 178, 186, 190, 193, 215, 220 also see 'Budget deficit'
Reynoso, A. 205

Robinson, J. 50
Robinson, R. 153
Rodrik, D. 124, 126, 127, 133
Roemer, M. 159
Romer, P.M. 50
Rosenstein-Rodan, P.N. 27, 117
Rossi, N. 174
Roy, T. 43
Rubin, B.R. 7, 33, 106
Rudolph, L. 33
Rudolph, S. 33

Sachs, J.D. 124-126, 133, 157
Sarkar, H. 157
Sarma, M.T.R. 205
Sau, R. 33
Saul, J. 4
Savings
  and fiscal incentives 175, 176
  and interest rates 173, 174
  in high growth countries 36
  in India 14, 170, 203
  role in growth 14
  theory of 17, 168, 169 See also 'public savings'
Savings and growth relationship
  causal link 37, 51
Schick, A. 206
Schultz, T. 39
Scientific consensus 19
Scitovsky, T. 9, 10, 27, 129, 154, 155
Scott, M. 9, 10, 129, 154, 155
Second Five Year Plan 3, 5, 8, 22, 85, 97, 171, 203
Sen, A. 29, 50, 53
Sen, K. 43
Sen, T. 179
Seshan, A. 178
Seventh Five Year Plan 9, 105, 180
Shapiro, H. 124, 127
Sharma, O.P. 158
Shock treatment (radical approach; big bang) 128, 129
  in Eastern Europe 129, 156
  in U.S.S.R. 129, 156
  relevance to India 131
Singapore 38, 54-57, 73, 90, 145
Singer, H. 28
Singh, M. 25, 33, 107
Sixth Five Year Plan 105, 172, 195
Smith, R. 175
Solow, R.M. 50
Srinivasan, T.N. 7, 90
State,
  role of 11, 12, 13, 65 also see 'Government, role of'
Stern, N. 40
Stewart, F. 121
Stiglitz, J.E. 87
Streeten, P. 52, 63, 64, 145
Strout, A.M. 122, 144
Subsidies
  export 137, 186
  fertilizer 185, 188
  food 185, 188, 225
  on domestic raw materials 114
  volume and composition 186
Summers, L.H. 50, 90
Summers, R. 34
Sundrum, R.M. 24, 33, 37, 40, 51, 92, 122, 154
Suryanarayana, M.H. 207
Sutton, M. 48
Swarup, D. 206

Taiwan 24, 31, 36, 54-57, 73, 90, 123, 125, 126, 157
Talati, C. 126
Tamil Nadu
  state finances 177, 178
Targetting of subsidies 81
Tax policy (tax reform) 192
Taylor, L. 124, 126, 127, 154, 155, 157
Thailand 24, 38, 54-57, 73, 109, 145
Third Five Year Plan 8, 171, 204

Thirsk, W.R. 192
Thompson, D.J. 75
Toye, J. 7, 33

U.S.S.R. vii, 4, 129, 217
Unofficial exchange rate 158
Uttar Pradesh 178, 224
Uzawa, H. 50, 145

Venti, S.F. 175
Vickers, J. 75
Villanueva, D. 40

Westphal, L.E. 90, 92
Wise, D.A. 175
Wiseman, J. 206
Wolf, M. 83, 107, 151, 152
Wolfe, B. 39
World Bank (IBRD) 61, 75, 92, 93, 101, 108, 110, 111
World Institute for Development Economics Research (WIDER) 124

Yamey, B.S. 51
Yarrow, G. 75

Zero based budgeting 183